D1608048

CHILDLIKE ACHILLES
ONTOGENY AND PHYLOGENY IN THE *ILIAD*

W. THOMAS MacCARY

CHILDLIKE ACHILLES
ONTOGENY AND
PHYLOGENY IN THE
ILIAD

ILLUSTRATED BY
ABIGAIL CAMP

NEW YORK   COLUMBIA UNIVERSITY PRESS   1982

Library of Congress Cataloging in Publication Data

MacCary, W. Thomas.
Childlike Achilles.

Includes bibliographical references and
index   1. Homer.   Iliad.   2. Homer—Characters—
Achilles.   3. Homer—Criticism and inter-
pretation.   I. Title.
PA4037.M27   883'.01   82-4458
ISBN 0-231-05504-8   AACR2

Columbia University Press
New York   Guildford, Surrey

Copyright © 1982 Columbia University Press
All rights reserved
Printed in the United States of America

Clothbound editions of Columbia University Press books are Smyth-
sewn and printed on permanent and durable acid-free paper.

THIS BOOK IS DEDICATED TO:

JOHN McKESSON CAMP II

AND

MARGARET MUNROE THROWER MacCARY

CONTENTS

PREFACE

My purpose in this study is to provide a critical model adequate for reading the *Iliad*. Although the kernel of my thesis is psychoanalytic—the poem evokes memory traces of early childhood experience—I have not been content simply to observe the poem from that perspective. Rather I have determined to situate the relevant precepts of Freudian and post-Freudian psychology (basically the theory of narcissism and "mirroring") within the Western philosophical tradition, with its attempts to describe the process through which the individual locates himself in his time and culture. In speaking then of Achilles' relation with the other Greek heroes at Troy, I can speak simultaneously of the ontogeny of the ego in Freudian terms and the phylogeny of Western man in Hegelian terms. This approach also facilitates references to previous work on the character of Achilles and the whole problem of a Homeric world view, since the two scholars who have most informed our understanding of this problem, Snell and Fränkel, refer explicitly to Hegel. Hence, there is an inordinately long "bibliographical essay" serving as the introduction.

In this first section it might seem that I am using the *Iliad* as a case study to prove general critical theories, but in fact this attempt to locate my own criticism of the *Iliad* against previous contributions is essential to what follows. First it was necessary to come to terms with Snell's and Fränkel's Hegelian reading of Homer and to measure their effectiveness against the humanist and structuralist readings of Whitman and Redfield. In doing so, constant reference to the *Iliad* was appropriate, for only by showing their readings to be inadequate could I establish the place for my own reading. Furthermore, this dialectically derived critical model then gives some coherence to the series of philological studies that make up the second part of the study. My intention is always to produce a self-conscious reading in which criticism and scholarship correct each other.

In the main body of the study, I follow the standard philological approach to the text, relating key passages to each other, and then to my critical model, according to the use of certain words and formulaic phrases. Here I am particularly indebted to those I call "the second generation of Parryan analysts"—Nagler, Nagy, and Peabody—for their own critical model of the working of traditional formulaic poetry. They have warned us to seek no longer the original expression of a formula complex, but rather to appreciate a potential for meaning in the entire system. This philological sophistication seems comparable to the dialectical criticism of Snell and Fränkel in that both disciplines seek not absolute truths in a forgotten past, but meaning as a function of relations gradually revealed and then self-consciously appreciated. We are never to forget that we are readers of a poem orally composed, and witnesses to events fixed in an alien culture. We can no more place ourselves actively in that tradition of oral poetry than we can become Greek warriors before Troy.

We must therefore be conscious of ourselves reading, and pay as much attention to our own familiar circumstances as to the superficially unfamiliar circumstances of the poem. The *tertium comparationis* that makes our literary response possible must be that experience actually ours which we can recall under the influence of the poet's recitation of Achilles' experience. The critical question is, then, "How and to what extent are we all Achilles?" and this must supplant the scholarly questions: "How did Achilles come to be the focus of the poem? To what extent is he historically determined?" It is to be expected that answers to the former question will provide better understanding of the latter questions, if only to expose the impossibility of providing a definitive answer.

Nagy differs from Nagler and Peabody in his insistence on original rather than relative and derivative meaning for particular Homeric words and phrases. His technique is followed here, but instead of saying that the poet (or his tradition) reveals the original truth in certain complexes of words, I accept Gadamer's cautionary advice and say only that the poet has created meaning against his tradition: neither poet nor critic has any direct access to truth lying *behind* the text. This might be called a phenomenological perspective on etymology; I claim no absolute *etymos logos*.[1] The most salutary effect on Homeric studies to be expected from the work of Nagler, Nagy, and Peabody—joined by Redfield and Austin, who incorporate these methods into their own structuralist perspectives—is the union and mutual correction of criticism and scholarship. No longer can we naively believe in our ability to recapture the historical reality of an *Ur-Iliad* or to put ourselves in the place of an early audience to the poem's recitation. Nagy's claim for the "etymological" significance of *therapōn* can be questioned by linguistic scholars and his claim for a deep thematic concern for mediating *mētis* and *biē* can be questioned by post-structuralist critics. The discussion continues and we approach the center of the poem, but there is no infallible scholarship or criticism to assure us of reaching it and adequately defining our experience.

The rough schema of my argument is as follows: we must not be forced by the romanticism of conventional and structuralist critics to a revision of Snell's observation on the "primitive" pre-philosophical nature of the Homeric world view; rather, we must extend Snell's application of the Hegelian principle of philosophical development beyond its strictly historical limits to the area of individual development: ontogeny recapitulates phylogeny, or, not only has there been progressive change in the history of mankind, but this change is recorded and reexperienced in the development of each human being. It was no outrageous thing for Snell to read Homer with Hegel, since Hegel's philosophical system has its roots deep in Homeric epic and many crucial passages of *The Phenomenology of Mind* echo Homeric language and situation. Freudian and Hegelian ontologies might seem contradictory, since one is based on the power of the unconscious (an archaic structure) and the other predicates a self-consciousness to human experience (a teleological system), but both are dialectical and conservative: nothing is lost from the system, but change occurs through progressive stages of manifestation and recognition.

The principle that ontogeny recapitulates phylogeny is no longer, in its fully developed Haeckelian form, acceptable as biologically sound.[2] Recent clinical evidence does support, however, its psychological validity. Our response to the *Iliad* can be explained as a recollection of the infantile struggle to define the self in terms of the mother's image, projected to the child, of himself, a struggle that is erotic in Freudian terms and a response to sense impression in Hegelian terms. We find in the *Iliad* a concentration on this narcissistic struggle and seek thereby to explain the paradox that in a poem about a war fought for a woman the focus of attention is on the relationship between the hero and his dear male companion. We therefore postulate an "Achilles complex" experienced by everyone to some extent. Various investigations in the text of the *Iliad* confirm the "originary" force of this conceptual experience. The myth of Achilles presents a family without the father, and an unusually strong tie between mother and son. Women are neither feared nor desired in the *Iliad*; the heroes generally, and Achilles in particular, look to male companions for emotional security, though not for physical love. Patroklos and Hektor are both doubles of Achilles, the first libidinally, the other aggressively, invested. Other heroes are best seen as foils for the better definition of these two basic relationships of Achilles. The poem's expressed attitude of the uselessness of old age and the glory of death in youth is further confirmation of the narcissistic nature of its material; the linguistic aspect of this thematic structure is, of course, that young men act and old men talk. Achilles is notoriously better at the former than the latter and seems to prefer death in action to continued existence in language.

The *Iliad* is unique in the power of its evocation of archaic mental structures and unique in its antiquity and tremendous influence, but other heroic epics share the same peculiar features. We need a dialectical and analogical appreciation of how literary genres develop and appeal to memory traces of different stages in human development, both ontogenetic and phylogenetic. I mean by this that epic is a recapitulation of pre-oedipal experience, lyric the culmination of *le stade du miroir* and tragedy the high drama of oedipal conflict. Beyond this, with Frye, we pass over into the ironic worlds of comedy and philosophy, arriving finally at the nostalgia of romance, which is mature man's attempt to console himself for his lost youth. The distance between epic and romance might seem slight, especially if one anaesthetizes literary response with such labels as tone, mode, and affect, but the huge and horrifying reality of epic is its recapitulation of the narcissistic dilemma and this must be compared to the anaclitic acquiescence of the spirit to the eternal mother which characterizes romance. The *Iliad* shocks and appalls us not because the jealousy of the heroes for their own honor and their hatred for the enemy on the battlefield are so intense—we have not all been to war—but because we relive in these struggles the intensity of our own struggles to define ourselves by the images of ourselves supplied us in our early years.

We shall find throughout the Hegelian and Freudian treatises, from which we take the figure for our critical model, the mirror, that device by which man defines himself. A concern of conventional critics is the relation between Achilles and his peers in the Greek camp before Troy. We shall see that these others continue to return to him the image of completeness and perfection which his mother Thetis originally projected to him, but that the central drama of the *Iliad*, developing from the confrontation with Agamemnon through the ransoming of Hektor's body, is a contradiction of that image, a denial of his continued existence as complete or perfect. The classical traditions of Western philosophy and psychoanalysis are essentially concerned with man's struggle, beginning in infancy (his own and that of his race) to develop a sense of self, and in both traditions this is seen as a dynamic, mutually influential relationship with the world, first seen as an extension of the self, then as an Other (mother), and finally as a series of assimilations between self and Other, where the self constantly breaks away (alienation) only to reenter with an ever more heightened sense of derivation and therefore contentment.

Hegel shows us a constantly progressing, historically determined dialectic of increasing self-consciousness where the subject repeatedly breaks away from his world, reconstitutes the world in himself, and then remerges with the world, a tension between his own specificity and the abstraction of collective human experience. Freud and his followers show that this pattern of separation and reincorporation is fundamental to the formation of the ego. I shall therefore attempt to analyze the *Iliad*, with these critical models, as Achilles' struggle to conceive himself in the mirror which his world presents to him, his own psychic phenomenology.

ACKNOWLEDGMENTS

I composed this piece at the American School of Classical Studies in Athens, between January and June 1980, supported, in part, by a Lawrence H. Chamberlain Fellowship and a grant from the Council for Research in the Humanities, both of Columbia University. The original text received much careful consideration from Madeline Aria, Milton Kapit, Jeff Mitscherling, Peter Rose, Richard Sacks, Laura Slatkin, Randolph Thrower, and two anonymous readers appointed by Columbia University Press. I profited by all their criticism and tried to incorporate as many of their suggestions for improvement as my own original conception would allow. I have been fortunate in the attention given the project by William Bernhardt, Angelia Graf, Joan McQuary, John Moore, and Ken Venezio, all of the Columbia University Press.

I am under obligation of a different order to Richard Caldwell, who has, for fifteen years, encouraged and guided my study of psychoanalysis. His friendship has been one of the few constants in the bewildering variety of my academic career.

I have dedicated the book to my wife and a dear friend, both of whom supported the project unquestioningly, strange though it often seemed to them.

I have quoted throughout from the Greek text of David B. Moore and Thomas W. Allen for Oxford University Press. Richmond Lattimore has allowed me to quote at length from his incomparable translation of the *Iliad*, and the University of Chicago Press has generously waived the requisite payment. (All line references are to the Greek text.)

The illustrations are taken from the "Achilles amphora" in Berlin (cover), the "Sosias cup" in the Vatican (title page), and the "Mykonos pithos" on Mykonos (chapter headings).

I apologize for the inconsistencies in my transliteration of Greek names. I have followed Lattimore's precision where I could, but had to make exceptions of Achilles, Aeneas, Ajax, and Meleager.

CHILDLIKE ACHILLES
ONTOGENY AND PHYLOGENY IN THE *ILIAD*

I
THEME: THEORETICAL STATEMENT

I.1
ON RE-READING SNELL'S HOMER

 One of the great and, I hope, illuminating, paradoxes of my approach to the *Iliad* is that while as method I reject historical specificity in the appreciation of a literary text, nevertheless I insist upon the relative historicism implicit in Snell's Hegelian distinction between the Homeric worldview and our own. As we shall see, there is in *Phänomenologie des Geistes* a constant recapitulation of previous phases, so that Hegel's "Homeric moments" are spread out over the entire six-part evolution of the manifestation of Absolute Spirit, and not confined only to the section on self-consciousness, which seems to be based chronologically on the Greeks, or to the antipenultimate section on art. I think, then, that we must first determine to what extent Snell, following Hegel, actually conceives of a historical development in human thought, and how such a development is determined by, both originally and to our perception, the nature of language and self-consciousness.

Clearly the format of *Die Entdeckung des Geistes*, as does its title, invokes Hegel: if we consider that Marx made a materialist conception of history out of Hegel's idealist conception of history (which he claimed he had "placed upon its head; or rather, turned off its head, on which it was standing and placed upon its feet"),[1] then we can consider Snell to have made of the history of Greek literature an actual inscription of Hegel: he sees the evolution of the literary genres to have been determined by the development of philosophical thinking.[2]

His evidence is linguistic, his approach philological; he says essentially
that because Homeric characters use several different terms for mental
and emotional processes—"*psychē* is the breath, the air which maintains the life of man; the *thymos* is the organ of internal (e)motion,
and the *nous* is the mind in its capacity as an absorber of images"[3]—
they seem not to have an integrated image of themselves as individuals.
He supports this conclusion by pointing to an analogous emphasis on
parts of the body rather than on the body entire and refers the reader
to geometric vase painting for examples of figures whose torsos are
articulated to a marked degree. (Even here the question of absolute
historicity arises: is this feature of the Homeric poems due to the
peculiar conservatism of the oral tradition which might have preserved
Mycenean conceptions of mental functioning, or, as Snell implies, is
this an eighth-century phenomenon, i.e., contemporary with the pu-
tative date of the "composition" of the *Iliad*, on the eve of the Ionian
beginnings of Greek philosophy?) I shall let a recent critic of Snell's
view state one of the more obvious objections:

Homer's picture of the world, as Snell sees it, is vivid but chaotic, the Homeric
mind as passive receptor of external impressions, incapable of imposing any
structure on those impressions. That view is inevitable if Homer is graded
according to his understanding of the Platonic conception of body and soul.[4]

Austin is not ignorant of Snell's dependence upon Hegel for his
schema. He should know then that the schema implies not only a
perceptual difference between Homer and Plato, but an equally great
perceptual difference between Plato and Hegel himself. The magni-
tude of the issues involved can be grasped only in the full realization
of Hegel's self-proclaimed achievement: he thought that he was re-
creating philosophy in response to Kant's claim that things known
from experience are not worth knowing since they are only *phaino-
mena* (appearance) and not even *noumena* (man's unprovable notions
of reality). Hegel thought that his dialectical system (so different from
Plato's because it moves through the negation of the negation to the
fully revealed notion, from which nothing of the seemingly self-con-
tradictory moments has been lost) could reveal to philosophical man
Absolute Spirit as it reveals itself in man's relation to the world. With
Snell, then, not only are we not all Homeric men, but neither are we

Homer (in his ironic remove from his characters) nor even Plato, but rather the products of the complete evolution of Western philosophy in Hegel.

I think what Austin really objects to is Homer's being used as philosophy and found wanting. It is the concept of the primitive in all its manifestations that he cannot accept, whether it be historical primitivism, generic or cultural. We must keep in mind, though, that insofar as Hegel's system is historical, it involves a more subtle distinction between primitive and advanced, or pre-philosophical and philosophical. Austin's fear that Homer is disgraced by Snell is unfounded. While it is true that Homer is the start and Plato the climax of Snell's study, there is no suggestion whatsoever that Snell would accept Plato's dismissal of Homer for being mendacious and morally irresponsible (and by implication aesthetically unpleasing and intellectually inferior). Rather, Homer is to Snell what Homer, Plato, and all subsequent commentators on the human condition are to Hegel: seemingly contradictory moments in the grand self-revelation to man of his own nature (or, more precisely, the manifestation in the relation between man and his world of Absolute Spirit). Austin's own most favorable reviews have come from conventional critics who claim for poetry a privileged status in human experience, and in their spirited defense of poetry these critics often trivialize its virtues.[5] No one, certainly not Snell, is arguing that Homer is worst for being first. Snell does not face this issue of poetry as a privileged text, but he certainly makes clear his trepidation, his almost religious awe, in approaching this monument and questioning its mysteries. Though he can answer only with another mystery, he shows himself to be firmly within the Hegelian dialectic when he suggests that the stage of mental functioning which the Homeric text represents is not a stage lost to our experience, i.e., we have not altogether gone past it even now in our reading of Homer and of Hegel and of Snell:

We must be convinced that despite these complications [philosophical and philological] the strange thoughts are intelligible to us, and that there is a vital meaning in what we have delimited, although we may not be able to define its precise significance in our own words. We need not be unduly skeptical, particularly when the foreign material is Greek. For here we come face to face with our own intellectual past; . . . Perhaps we shall be able to establish contact with Greek thought, not only through the medium of historical recollection, but also because the ancient legacy is stored within us, and we may recognize in it the threads of our own involved patterns of thinking.[6]

This sounds a bit like Jung's "collective unconscious," or at least the literary canon established upon it by T. S. Eliot. I think, however, that Snell's thinking is more rigorous. He believes, as does Hegel, that many modes of thinking are available to man at any one time: obviously we cannot all be philosophers in the tradition of Hegel. Our positive response to Homer proves that our minds can still work as he presents the minds of his characters working, that we can suspend the analytic propensities which have become part of our heritage. Perhaps we should try to define the Homeric mode first, and then consider the inescapable implication that though we can think like Homer, Homer could not think like us—or, more precisely (and precision is important to the question of the privileged poetic text)—we can think like Homer's characters, but Homer's characters cannot think like us.

A crucial passage in the *Iliad* is Athene's appearance to Achilles to prevent him from killing Agamemnon.[7]

. . . . . Πηλεΐωνι δ' ἄχος γένετ', ἐν δέ οἱ ἦτορ
στήθεσσιν λασίοισι διάνδιχα μερμήριξεν,
ἢ ὅ γε φάσγανον ὀξὺ ἐρυσσάμενος παρὰ μηροῦ
τοὺς μὲν ἀναστήσειεν, ὁ δ' Ἀτρεΐδην ἐναρίζοι,
ἦε χόλον παύσειεν ἐρητύσειέ τε θυμόν.
ἦος ὁ ταῦθ' ὥρμαινε κατὰ φρένα καὶ κατὰ θυμόν,
ἕλκετο δ' ἐκ κολεοῖο μέγα ξίφος, ἦλθε δ' Ἀθήνη
οὐρανόθεν· πρὸ γὰρ ἧκε θεὰ λευκώλενος Ἥρη,
ἄμφω ὁμῶς θυμῷ φιλέουσά τε κηδομένη τε·
στῆ δ' ὄπιθεν, ξανθῆς δὲ κόμης ἕλε Πηλεΐωνα
οἴῳ φαινομένη· τῶν δ' ἄλλων οὔ τις ὁρᾶτο·
θάμβησεν δ' Ἀχιλεύς, μετὰ δ' ἐτράπετ', αὐτίκα δ' ἔγνω
Παλλάδ' Ἀθηναίην· δεινὼ δέ οἱ ὄσσε φάανθεν·
καί μιν φωνήσας ἔπεα πτερόεντα προσηύδα·   (1.188–201)

. . . . . And the anger came on Peleus' son, and within
his shaggy breast the heart was divided two ways, pondering
whether to draw from beside his thigh the sharp sword, driving
away all these who stood between and kill the son of Atreus,
or else to check the spleen within and keep down his anger.
Now as he weighed in mind and spirit these two courses
and was drawing from its scabbard the great sword, Athene descended

from the sky. For Hera the goddess of the white arms sent her,
who loved both men equally in her heart and cared for them.
The goddess standing behind Peleus' son caught him by the fair hair,
appearing to him only, for no man of the others saw her.
Achilleus in amazement turned about, and straightway
knew Pallas Athene and the terrible eyes shining.
He uttered winged words and addressed her.

Athene appears here in at least three simultaneous modes: the realistic, the imagistic, and the symbolic.[8] She is real in that Achilles
sees her and feels her close to him: she first grabs him by the hair of
the head and then he sees her. As image she is the externalized process
of his own thinking, or, rather, his experience of her is that kind of
visual (primary process) experience that often takes the place, in dream
and poetry, of mental functioning. She is symbol of wisdom and ra-
tional restraint: as Athene she is not only external but alien, the product of a second mental (secondary) process which replaces the first,
"Should I kill Agamemnon?" Needless to say, the fact that she grabs
him by the hair of the head suggests some restraint exercised by *nous*
over the *thymos* of his shaggy breast. It is in this intimate and arresting
posture that all these functions come together and impress us as forcefully as they do Achilles.

On the basis of this one scene, though it has resonance with many
others, especially Hera's address to Athene and Poseidon (at 20.115-
31), where she simply describes how gods appear (*phainesthai*) to men
(on which see below, II.12), it is possible to suggest a model for the
interpretation of the relations between gods and men in the *Iliad* which
differs slightly from the exhaustive studies of Nilsson and Lesky.[9] It
seems that these and other critics have always approached the problem
from the perspective of the actual existence of the gods, or at least of
the heroes' belief in the gods' existence, i.e., as some sort of study of
the history or philosophy of religion. This does little to explain our
response to the text. The essential question in that dimension is how
completely do we respond to Athene's appearance and physical pressure, and our response depends, of course, on the degree of identity
we feel with Achilles: have we accepted, one hundred and eighty lines
into the poem, his view of the world as animated by spirits who move
physically in and out of his mind and close to and far from his body?

I hope that having put the question this way, the unanimous response must be, "We identify totally with Achilles; we believe in Athene." Why is this so?

One thinks immediately of Auerbach in this regard, that he has answered this question in his essay on "Odysseus' Scar," and, indeed, that the whole of *Mimesis* is a kind of extension of and elaboration on Snell's Hegelian literary history, but devised, of course, in a binary rather than a unitary path of development, i.e., there is the Greek "tradition" of concrete reality immediately appreciable (all foreground) and there is the Judaeo-Christian "tradition" of prefiguration wherein all that appears is a remanifestation of all that has gone before and a prophecy of important things to come (background). The Greek moment defies interpretation—its truth is on its face—but the Judaeo-Christian tradition demands interpretation because nothing is only as it seems.[10]

If repetition and progression (prefiguration and background) are not part of the purely Greek experience, do we err (with Snell) in attempting a Hegelian reading of Homer? I do not think so, not only for the reason he himself gives—that Homer is a part of our tradition, so what might seem mysterious in him to us is on reflection familiar—but also because we know ourselves through the Greeks and they know themselves through Homer and, above all, because Homer himself is part of a tradition. Although we do not have the rest of Greek oral epic poetry, we feel the *Iliad* as a moment in a continuing pattern rather than as a purely self-relevant creation. Furthermore, Homeric epic is not all foreground in the sense that it deals only with surface reality, and the Homeric mind is not all fragmented in the sense that it cannot integrate its own experience. I am not sure there is any absolute difference between Achilles' response to Athene's appearance and the response of the perfect reader. If we do not feel physically her tug on the hair of our heads, then we are experientially deficient. Where the great difference comes is between Achilles' response (and the perfect reader's response) on the one hand, and the critically appreciated response on the other: for both Achilles and the perfect reader the appearance of Athene is physically felt and therefore is real and concrete and all those other impressions that archaic Greek poetry is celebrated (rightly) for achieving; but in the critically examined response there is a new dimension and this is the transcendence of the moment, or the dialectical approach to the notion fully revealed, without contradiction. The critically appreciated response is different from the Achillean response, because it has been examined and distanced and hypostatized. We know that we are readers reading and Achilles does not know that he is a thinker thinking. The fairest distinction, then, between the perfect reader and Achilles is that the former (unconsciously) suspends his available critical faculty, whereas this faculty is hypothetically not available to Achilles. (We must speak hypothetically, our assumption being that Homer has exercised Achilles' mind to its limits and not simply used the "poetic device" of simplifying Achilles' mental processes.)

In this respect, then, again, we must remind Austin that there is as much difference between Hegel and Plato as there is between Plato and Homer: Hegel's dialectic is capable of moving from moment to moment, to a final realization-recognition of the full, all-inclusive notion, whereas Platonic dialectic is "static" and exclusive, a gradual elimination of individual moments which frequently ends in *aporia*, and never succeeds in negating preliminary negations. Plato's reading of Homer is notoriously deficient. Auerbach's is slightly distorting because he is intent on drawing a contrast between Homeric and biblical description. It is possible to argue that Hegel and Snell have distorted our reading of Homer by interposing a conceptual distance between us and Achilles which does not exist between Achilles and Athene, but this argument would be hypocritical in the extreme, because we can never, except through the suspension of disbelief, which is the proper response to poetry and defines its privileged status, truly believe in Athene.[11] Hegel, then, with his progressive idealism, has provided the necessary epistemological basis for our critical reading, and Snell has simply insisted on its actualization in the language and thought of Homer.

Our hypothesis thus far is that whereas in both Homeric and Platonic thought there is opposition and exclusion, there is inclusion through negation in the transcendent movement of Hegelian dialectic, an integration of subject and object in a superior self-conscious subject: we realize with Hegel that we are not only both *nous* and *thymos*, but also Athene. The difference between Homer and Plato we have yet to define, but Snell has pointed the way by showing that there is a lack of integration in the Homeric self-conception that makes Platonic ideas inconceivable, i.e., there is consolidation in neither subject nor object. Austin speaks of Snell's picture of the Homeric world as characterized by lack of "structure," a key term for his later attempt to replace Snell's Hegelian critical model with a Saussurian or Lévi-Straussian structuralist model. He seems to think that Snell has denied to Homeric man the ability to think in oppositions, and goes on to show that, of course, he can, since he sees the sun rise and set and mentally arranges his whole world according to that paradigm.[12]

With reference back to the passage describing Athene's appearance to Achilles, we note that there can never have been any question in any reader's mind as to Achilles' ability to weigh alternatives. (A very real question would be whether he can handle independent alternatives, mutually contradictory alternatives, and transformational alternatives, with equal facility, but we shall not raise the question here.)[13] What is at issue is whether he is conscious of his conscious choice, and the answer must be negative. If one is dissatisfied with Snell's picture of the Greek attempt to establish a center, a hard core of consciousness, perhaps a more appealing picture would be the externalization or alienation of consciousness. Homer does not depict Achilles' choice as being made by an agency of the self which can examine the self in conflict.[14] Two Platonic contrasts spring to mind— in fact, one probably Socratic, the other Platonic: Socrates' *daimōn* warns him not to do something, having taken up its position on the philosopher's shoulder, so as to whisper in his ear; much more sophisticated, of course, is the philosophical progress of the soul of the *erastēs* in the *Symposium*: intellectual activity is conceived on the model of erotic excitement, the sensation of the soul leaving the body.

We can claim then for the Platonic world view and, of course, therefore, for Platonic dialectic, at least a nascent notion of the power of negation in the assimilation of subject and object—the *erōmenos* disappears—and thus a potential for the transcendence of seeming oppositions which we claim for Hegelian dialectic. But again, Snell is precise and suggestive in reminding us that Greek scientific thought remained static, that "Even Aristotle does not yet understand motion in its dynamic nature." In his assimilation of literary genres and philosophical modes to aspects of the verb, he likens Plato's *hairesis* to the aorist.[15] The Greeks, with not even Plato excepted, could not conceive of an external self, whose existence is historically determined, with the ability to transform objects of contemplation and thereby reconcile their falsely seeming opposition. Nor, I think, would Snell credit even the sophists with his own observation—again, within the Hegelian framework—of the "semantic potential" of language, so at odds with the structuralists' view of language as made up of differences which repeat, but do not change. Can the negation be negated is all we need to ask of Plato, Lévi-Strauss, and Austin, on the one hand (No!); Hegel and Snell, on the other (Yes, of course!). Our whole theoretical program here is to establish the difference between the philosophical (or critical) operation (dialectic) and its subject (Nature, the nature of being, or the literary text). That Platonic metaphysics—the progress toward the forms—is a model for the childhood development of the cognitive process can have escaped no one. But who is watching the process? Is there a witness to the encounter of the *erastēs* and the *erōmenos*? Is there a truly transcendent self-consciousness that can experience the *erastēs'* experience of the *erōmenos*? This becomes crucial when we consider, as Plato suggests and Freud insists, that the *erōmenos* is the narcissistic object (or the ideal ego) of the *erastēs*, i.e., that the Platonic model for philosophical speculation is intrapsychic.

I think two remarks of Fränkel, whom I regard as having refined rather than contradicted Snell's thesis, will clear this matter up. First, on the related issues of philosophical development and the conjunction between language and meaning, Fränkel makes a candid admission:

I do not adhere to the doctrine that we have no right to ascribe to a thinker a notion for the unequivocal expression of which he possessed and used no specific tool. Quite to the contrary: It is perfectly normal for this or that concept to have existed in a person's mind in a less definitive form, long before someone else couched it in dry and set philosophical phraseology.[16]

The method he opposes is that of traditional philological research: take a word and follow its changes in signification over a period of time, through a series of texts. One thinks of the various studies of *dikē*, for instance, or *sophrosynē*. What Fränkel wants to see is the tendency toward meaning, Hesiod prefiguring Heraclitean dualities, and even Parmenides with a Platonic idea. He has, of course, been disputed on these points, and forcefully, by Cherniss and his followers.[17] I wonder, though, whether such disputes can take place on a mutually acceptable semantic ground. Again, we seem to be faced with the inherent contradictions between historical scholarship (by which I mean the study of texts in their historical context) and philosophical or dialectical criticism (by which I mean an attempt to see intellectual history from a perspective which can integrate and define various trends and movements: the thing in its coming-into-being).[18] Obviously we need constant pressure from those who think they can read historically to prevent all philosophy from reducing itself into a series of conflicts between metaphysics and phenomenology (or ontology and epistemology): Plato and Aristotle, Kant and Hegel, Heidegger and Husserl. At the same time we need the great speculative thinkers who can assume a position of such superiority that the full range of Western thought comes into focus and we see it as a gradual revelation, not of truth, but of meaning as a function of different perceptions of truth, which is only then, at their writing, finally apparent.

I am not yet ready to deal fully with structuralism's possible use in explicating the text of Homer, but I must here at any rate point up a contradiction, if not in Lévi-Strauss' own method of myth analysis, at least in the application of that method to Greek literature. At the conclusion of his study *Du miel aux cendres*, Lévi-Strauss considers the relation between mythic thought and philosophical thought, suggesting that the transition from the former to the latter is neither universal nor inevitable:

If this tendency towards abstraction can be attributed to mythic thought itself, instead of being, as some readers may argue, wholly imputable to the theorizing of the mythologist, it will be agreed that we have reached a point where mythic thought transcends itself and, going beyond images retaining some relationship with concrete experience, operates in a world of concepts which have been released from any such obligation, and combine with each other in free association; by this I mean that they combine not with reference to any external reality but according to the affinities or incompatibilities existing between them in the architecture of the mind. We know, as it happens, just such a dramatic change took place along the frontiers of Greek thought when mythology gave way to philosophy and the latter emerged as the necessary pre-condition of scientific thought.

But, in the case with which we are now concerned, we cannot speak of progress.[19]

We certainly appreciate that Plato does not use myth as Homer does. Lévi-Strauss' description of concepts combining according to the "architecture of the mind" is a brilliant depiction of the Cave, or Er, or any number of other passages where Plato gives his thought a physical model, aware that not all of his audience have progressed so far along the divided line as to be able to "see" without such aids. Lévi-Strauss' sensitivity to the criticism that what he finds in a particular body of myth might be the stuff of his analysis rather than of the myths themselves is subtly expressed here. When he speaks of a point of transcendence, he uses a Hegelian model in that nothing of the content of mythic thought is lost, but rather that content is carried to a higher level where its concerns are clearer. What we miss, however, is the Hegelian concept of self-consciousness: what really separates the mythopoeic thinker from the philosopher is the latter's consciousness of himself thinking. We should speak intentionally, then, of Plato's "self-conscious" use of myth (as opposed to Homer's "naive" use of myth).

Jameson has already made this point generally, in referring to the same passage of Lévi-Strauss: "Mythological thought is therefore a kind of philosophizing which is not yet aware of itself; or, conversely, we may see in the very birth of philosophy itself, in ancient Greece, 'a moment in which mythical thought transcends itself . . . '"[20] We see Achilles coming into self-consciousness in the course of the poem; he is in advance of the other heroes in this progress. This is a function of his attitude toward them and the gods. His difference is that he is determined by and on his difference. This is true heroism. He refuses to be drawn back into modes of thinking which collapse all men into undifferentiated patterns of behavior and belief. Thinking and speaking are in turn functions of each other, and we must consider Achilles' use of, and attitude toward, language, raising the question of the special case of formulaically composed poetry. We even realize that self-consciousness is the key to good criticism: knowing our difference from our heroes and our poets is the absolute prerequisite for reading.

In order to perform our function we must believe that there are constants in human experience which do find expression in literary texts and that this expression is often metaphorical and metonymic, which particularly requires interpretation. We note, however, that even as we interpret the *Iliad*, we never turn a concrete thing into an abstract quality; rather we say that one concrete thing (or experience) recapitulates another, and therein lies its meaning. Achilles can weigh alternatives and so reach a decision, but because he cannot, like us, step outside himself and contemplate himself making that decision, then he must *imagine* Athene making it for him. His goddess and our modern philosophy might be weighed on some absolute scale of human achievement which would then incline in her favor, but we cannot turn back. No more could Achilles conceive of himself as an external self than we can conceive of ourselves being aided by Athene, except in the moment of suspended disbelief which the poem makes possible. If I seem to be contradicting the previous reading of this passage which I protested to accept, it is because I say "outside" when they say "inside"; but Fränkel resolves this paradox:

Wenn so der Mensch wie ein Kraftfeld ist, dessen Linien in Raum und Zeit hinausziehn ohne Grenze und Schranke, so können ebenso ungehindert auch andre Kräfte in ihn hineinwirken, ohne dass es Sinn hätte zu fragen, wo das Eigne anfängt und das Fremde afhört. Auch aufnehmend und leidend sind diese Menschen bedingungslos der Welt geöffnet—so weit geöffnet, dass die für unser Bewusstsein grundlegende Antithese zwischen dem Ich und dem Nichtich für das homerische Bewusstsein noch nicht besteht.

If man is, as it were, a field of energy, whose lines extend into space and time without limit or restraint, then external forces, for their part, operate in him without hindrance, and it is meaningless to ask where his own force begins and that from outside ends. In what they receive and suffer also, these men are wholly open to the outside world, so wide that our own basic antithesis between self and not-self does not yet exist in Homeric consciousness.[21]

Clearly Fränkel in this way states positively what Snell's critics accuse him of saying negatively, and I think we shall come to appreciate that Fränkel's formulation of the "decenteredness" of the Homeric mind fits more comfortably into a Heideggerian context while Snell remains unrepentantly Hegelian. Nevertheless, Fränkel's language calls up an image of dispersal rather than consolidation of matter, with the strong suggestion that *das Ich,* almost by definition, "implies" a nucleus, but has not yet found one. Snell is even more insistent:

Geistige und seelische Wirkungen sind Einflüsse der von aussen wirkenden Kräfte, und der Mensch steht vielerlei Mächten offen, die auf ihn eindringen, die ihn durchdringen können.

Mental and spiritual acts are due to the impact of external factors, and man is the open target of a great many forces which impinge on him and penetrate his very core.[22]

(Note that Snell's text does not imply the "core" which the translator has read into it.)[23]

I hope that the two principal problems raised in this section—that of the external soul or self and that of existence as a function of awareness—will be solved in the last section of the essay, where I invoke Freudian and post-Freudian psychoanalytic theory to account for these phenomena. By denying Achilles the ability to project himself outside himself—consciousness and conscience are imposed upon him from without in the "person" of Athene—we do not deny him the speculation of *le stade du miroir,* but only the movement of the Hegelian dialectic toward the notion of the self. Achilles is in one sense not yet one, but still trying to define his unity by "speculating" his image (notably, of course, in Patroklos and Hektor), and the field, the ground of this speculation is Thetis and her maternal *semblables,* Athene and Hera. If we seem here to be too insistent on the question of the one and the many, it is in anticipation of the paradox that Lacan has defined in Hegelian terms: there must be several selves before there can be one. In the meantime we note that fragmentation exists in the world as object as a function of the fragmentation of the subject: because Achilles cannot conceive of himself as an integrated being, he cannot see Being itself meaningfully organized.

I.2

HEGEL'S HOMER

 It will prove instructive now, having suggested some of the consequences that Snell's Hegelianism had for his reading of Homer (and the rest of Greek literature), to consider briefly the place of Homer in Hegel's own work. (I concentrate on the *Phenomenology*, though the *Aesthetics* has the fullest treatment of epic as such.) In tracing the gradual revelation of Absolute Spirit through the history of Western philosophy, Hegel begins with the dynamic relation between subject and object in sense-perception:

A concrete actual certainty of sense is not merely this pure immediacy, but an example, an instance, of that immediacy. Amongst the innumerable distinctions that have come to light, we find in all cases the fundamental difference—viz. that in sense-experience pure being at once breaks up into the two "thises," as we have called them, one this as I, and one as object. When *we* reflect on this distinction, it is seen that neither the one nor the other is merely immediate, merely *is* in sense certainty but is at the same time *mediated*: I have the certainty through the other, viz. through the actual fact; and this, again, exists in that certainty through an other, viz. through the I.[1]

The mutual dependence of subject and object is a constant Hegelian theme that becomes more and more elaborated as the successive stages of consciousness are traversed. We already see here, though, the beginning of his "phenomenology" and its grounding in dialectic. It could be argued that the negation of the negation is not yet present, but its presence is implied in the concept of sense-certainty: mutual mediation of subject and object constitutes a process which transcends the two. This premonition is ratified in the sequel, the stage of self-consciousness:

> I distinguish myself from myself; and therein I am immediately aware that this factor distinguished from me is not distinguished. I, the self-same being, thrust myself away from myself; but this which is distinguished, which is set up as unlike me, is immediately on its being distinguished no distinction for me. (p. 211)

It seems that the subject-object relationship has been internalized, that a second self has become the object. At the same time, however, the dynamics of self-consciousness almost imply a third agent, the self as aware of the lack of distinction between the self as object and the self as contemplated subject, or quasi-object. And here Hegel's language becomes figurative, as if the complexity of his perception demanded some concrete expression which could be both example and definition:

> And self-consciousness is thus only assured of itself through sublating this other, which is presented to self-consciousness as an independent life; self-consciousness is *Desire*. Convinced of the nothingness of this other, it definitely affirms this nothingness to be for itself the truth of this other, negates the independent object, and thereby acquires the certainty of its own self, as *true* certainty, a certainty which it has become aware of in objective form. . . (p. 225)

When Hegel says that self-consciousness is desire, especially in a context of opposition and negation, we know that we are witnessing his struggle to describe the individual's struggle to define himself in the face of his world, and that one stage of this definition takes the form of a willing-into-nothingness (absorption) of all objects, and this is a brilliant definition of desire, a clear contrast with Freud's attempt one century later to place the beginning of desire at the transition of the child from the stage of autoerotism to that of primary narcissism, i.e., when he recognizes the absence of the mother and attempts to replace her with an image of himself.[2] For Hegel desire is the willing into nothingness of the object; for Freud desire is the willing into being of the subject out of nothingness.

In moving dialectically toward the notion of mind through the different moments of self-consciousness, Hegel is gradually revealing Mind or Spirit (*Geist*) in all substance: the individual can only become aware of himself in the face of Nature gradually becoming aware of itself. This is the text, I believe, on which Snell's concept of "semantic potential" is based. Snell says of linguistic elements what Hegel says of all reality, that they contain meaning inherently (*an sich*), which requires developed self-consciousness to free it into explicit being (*für sich*). Always there is the emphasis on the process towards the manifestation of Absolute Spirit, and it is of course in his metaphysical belief in this force that we must recognize the great gap separating Hegel's "phenomenology" from Husserl's. At the same time, however, Hegel's constant attention is upon the subject as perceiver and gradual revealer of Absolute Spirit, and herein lies his great advance over Platonic and Aristotelian metaphysics. It is the dynamics of the dialectic that impress us, the fact that Hegel, in anticipation of twentieth-century phenomenologists and existentialists, can see meaning as a tension not only between subject and object, but between the subject and that subject's perception of the object, i.e., between a constantly evolving sense of self (dialectically derived) in tension with a constantly evolving sense of the object as both determined by the subject and by its own "self-animating" spirit.

Consciousness has *qua* self-consciousness, henceforth a twofold object—the one immediate, the object of sense-certainty and of perception, which, however, is here found to be marked by the character of negation; the second, viz. itself, which is the true essence, and is found in the first instance only in the opposition of the first object to it. Self-consciousness presents itself here as the process in which this opposition is removed, and oneness or identity with itself established. (p. 220)

Even when insisting upon the apprehension of "spiritual daylight" Hegel's attention is still internal to the subject:

A self-consciousness has before it a self-consciousness. Only so and only then is it self-consciousness in actual fact; for here first of all it comes to have the unity of itself in its otherness. Ego which is the object of its notion, is in point of fact not "*object.*" The object of desire, however, is only independent, for it is the universal, ineradicable substance, the fluent self-identical essential reality. When a self-consciousness is the object, the object is as much ego as object. (pp. 226–27)

It is in this insistence on the self-reflective mode of human experience, especially as defined in terms of desire and its satisfaction by incorporation, that I find Hegel so much a philosopher of the self and consider his *Phenomenology* a text to be set between Plato's *Symposium* (and *Phaidros*) and Freud's "On Narcissism," to constitute the major contributions to the analysis of the erotic basis of ontology. (Needless to say, I mean to add a fourth text, a pre-philosophical text, to that triumvirate, the *Iliad* itself.)

Let us now only briefly contemplate the parallel arguments that Plato, Hegel, and Freud develop. Plato finds the energy for philosophical speculation in an erotic moment, the contemplation of the *erōmenos* by the *erastēs*:

So as he continues in this converse and society, and comes close to his lover in the gymnasium and elsewhere, that flowing stream which Zeus, as the lover of Ganymede, called the "flood of passion," pours in upon the lover. And part of it is absorbed within him, but when he can contain no more the rest flows away outside him, and as a breath of wind or an echo, rebounding from a smooth hard surface, goes back to its place of origin, even so the stream of beauty turns back and re-enters the eyes of the fair beloved . . . So he loves, yet knows not what he loves; he does not understand, he cannot tell what has come upon him; like one that has caught a disease of the eye from another, he cannot account for it, not realizing that his lover is as it were a mirror in which he beholds himself.[3]

We are not so much concerned here with the source of that energy, the fact that Plato's theory of ideas and hence his whole metaphysical system is based upon a model of unconsummated desire: the *erastēs* in refusing to give physical expression to his desire for the *erōmenos* is pressed on by the intensity of his passion to a contemplation of beauty beyond the beauty manifested in the *erōmenos* himself, to the idea of beauty itself, and therefore truth. We are here more concerned with the fact that the *erastēs* finds in the *erōmenos* a mirror for his own beauty, that the eyes of the *erōmenos* are a mirror for the reflection of himself, so that the erotic pattern is superficially homosexual but essentially narcissistic. We shall come to question the exact status of the *erōmenos* at a later point, but now let us realize only that for Plato desire by definition is for the mirror image of oneself and that desire can only be transformed into philosophy by sublimation; furthermore, the nature of the desire is such that it is not so much a longing for what the *erastēs* lacks as for the possession, first physical, then "conceptual," of the beauty which is and is not the *erastēs'* own, i.e., the *erastēs* recognizes his own beauty in the *erōmenos*, but he realizes that just as his *erōmenos* is only a reflection of his (the *erastēs'*) beauty, so he is only a reflection of that absolute beauty which he must henceforth seek out.

In Hegel the pattern is similar, but more self-conscious. We are not nearly so aware of the erotic energy behind the whole operation of perception, since the object is never identified as lover or beloved, but the process itself is defined in terms of desire: "self-consciousness is the state of Desire in general"; "self-consciousness is Desire"; "this immediacy of the object is itself, however, thoroughgoing mediation; it has its being only by cancelling the independent object, in other words it is Desire. The satisfaction of desire is indeed the reflection of self-consciousness into itself—is the certainty which has passed into objective truth."[4] All this can, of course, be reduced to the Apollonian-Socratic motto *gnōthi seauton* ("know yourself"), insofar as the beauty or truth that is sought is, and is not, found within the self. We are interested, however, in the mechanisms of mediation that are necessary for this final revelation. Whereas the Platonic model is libidinal, the Hegelian is aggressive: "self-consciousness . . . negates the independent object and thereby acquires the certainty of its own self."

Freud tells us that the (male) child has originally two objects of desire, himself and the woman who tends him, and that according to his "choice" between these two objects might be determined the later orientation of his desire, homosexual or heterosexual; that, indeed, if his choice is of the mother, this choice is "anaclitic," i.e., dependent or secondary to his actual needs, which she just happens to fill at that crucial time in his life.[5] Desire, then, in the models of Plato, Hegel, and Freud, is self-directed, self-reflective, indeed, a "philosophy of the self." What Hegel and Freud achieve beyond the Platonic conception is the transcendence of the self as subject, and the recognition that the self can "incorporate" its object. In Hegel this is done, originally, through the process of negating the object, thrusting it into the "other world," and then restoring it as proof of self-consciousness. In Freud it is done by introducing the notion of the "ideal ego," a controversial concept in the formative stage of Freud's thinking between the second and third topographies, where it seems finally to be combined with the "ego ideal" to constitute the superego. In Freud's consideration of the ideal ego in the paper "On Narcissism," however, we have a basis for the later clinical and theoretical work of the French, English, and American analysts who have concentrated their attention on early childhood development and found in the period after the first six months of life a tension between the child as he begins to recognize his difference from the mother, and the image of the child which his mother projects to him.

Although Freud says that the ideal ego is the maturing child's reconstitution of his "infantile ego" in all its nostalgic perfection, post-Freudian theorists like Kernberg (see below, I.6) do not speak of the ego as if it were always already there, but rather describe it as a developing function of object relations, i.e., as mediation of self and other before these boundaries are clear. In short, if we can appropriate Freud's term and use it in the context of post-Freudian theory, the ideal ego preexists the ego, and it is only in the tension between the ego as it begins to become conscious of itself as distinct from the ideal ego that the self as such is established.[6] This, obviously, all takes place in a context of desire: the child wants to become what is his mother's image of him (and this image is of course a function of her own desire to complete herself in any number of ways for any number of reasons), while at the same time yearning nostalgically for the lack of tension which was his experience in the undifferentiated world of his symbiosis with the mother, when he felt his mother to be an extension of himself. If he is to develop independent of his mother—the first compromise which his desire must make with reality—then he must accept as the object of his desire (to fill the gap he now feels where once she undifferentiatedly was) either her image of him as the pattern by which to define himself (and all other objects of desire) or herself (likewise the pattern for future objects of desire, and more generally a feeling of dependence—*anaclisis*—on the world outside himself and different from himself). This latter choice represents, paradoxically, a compromised regression to the primal stage of undifferentiatedness. There is also here a prefiguration of the later oedipal drama, but whereas there the pattern of conflicts is triangular (with the father, mother, and son), here the conflict is, I think we may say, intrapsychic and potentially entropic: if the child is *to be*, he must define himself in relation to some object. The objects available to him are his mother herself and his mother's image of himself. If he refuses both these objects, then psychically he deteriorates, regressing to the state of nonbeing from which desire was to lead him forth to fulfill his potential to be.

My own notion of the nature of the drama of the *Iliad* might be sketched at this point, although there is more yet to be seen of Homer in Hegel, particularly on the nature of violence and negation of the other. Hegel and Freud have already helped us to see, potentially, Achilles' relation to Patroklos as his choice of himself as object, and Thetis as the all-powerful mother to whom he constantly turns for reassurance of his own existence. That the father Peleus is aged, weak, and absent should warn us that this is not an oedipal drama, but a pre-oedipal drama, where the father plays less of a part, and indeed the lack of oedipal conflict in the *Iliad* will be seen as the expected corollary, if not the cause, of the general underestimation of women in the poem. If the mother is constantly available to the son, he will choose her image of himself as object rather than the mother herself. Hegel, with his emphasis on aggression, also accounts for Achilles' relations with Hektor, which we shall now try to express, first in Hegelian, then in Freudian, terms.

In one of the most famous sections of the *Phenomenology*, known as "Lordship and Bondage," Hegel considers the dynamic relations between self-conscious subjects. It is a difficult section within a difficult work, primarily because Hegel's thought is developing on several planes simultaneously. In speaking of these confrontations of consciousness, he continues to concern himself with man as an active, creative spectator in his world, but he is also speaking about being as such, how one thing is distinguished from another through negation. Behind all this epistemology and ontology there is a controlling metaphor which I think is Homeric: warriors who define their existence in conflict with other warriors so that they must either kill or be killed. We shall come to recognize this as the absolute essential ethos of the *Iliad* and to appreciate its resonance with our own early experience. Hegel's presentation is the first and most important step in that direction:

The relation of both self-consciousnesses is in this way [a twofold action aimed at the destruction of the other's life and at the risk of its own life] so constituted that they prove themselves and each other through a life-and-death struggle. They must enter into this struggle, for they must bring their certainty of themselves, the certainty of being for themselves, to the level of objective truth, and make this a fact both in the case of the other and in their own case as well. And it is solely by risking life that freedom is obtained; only thus is it tried and proved that the essential nature of self-consciousness is not bare existence, is not the merely immediate form in which it at first makes its appearance, is not its mere absorption in the expanse of life. Rather it is thereby guaranteed that there is nothing present but what might be taken as a vanishing moment—that self-consciousness is merely pure self-existence, being-for-self. The individual who has not staked his life, may, no doubt, be recognized as a Person; but he has not attained the truth of this recognition as an independent self-consciousness. (pp. 232–33)

On the logical level this is how we define things, in terms of their opposites, through negation. On the level of interpersonal relations, this is how we deal with other people, reducing them to qualities which we then expropriate, thereby denying them full existence. This is the vulgar sense of "sexual object," when the person desired is dehumanized, as in "He used her; she was nothing but his sexual object." In the technical terms of post-Freudian psychology "real objects" are distinguished from "part objects" and "self-objects." What brings the whole concept full circle is the notion of fetishism, as first applied to erotic life by Krafft-Ebbing and to social and economic life by Marx. If the fetish is an aspect of the self hypostatized, i.e., thrust into the unreal world of symbolism and "congealed" there, like the exchange value of commodities or a god, then all libidinally or aggressively invested objects are to some extent fetishes in that they represent externalized needs: one desires what one was, either in the person who stirs memory traces of the infantile experience of a complete and perfect self or in the person who, like the mother, can complete and perfect the self. Aristophanes' speech in Plato's *Symposium*, cited by Freud in "On Narcissism," is the perfect "mythic" statement of this truth.

The martial metaphor in Hegel takes us to another level, however, and we realize that once again we are dealing with the relation between the individual and the society from which he springs: Hegel says he can be self-conscious only if he is conscious of his determining field, how, that is, he has come to be himself. We are then forced to see the other self-consciousness as a phantom, the world's view of the true self-consciousness, a *Doppelgänger* or alter ego thrown up out there to madden the individual until he confronts this phantom and establishes dialectically his relation to and derivation from it.

In reading this back against the *Iliad* we immediately see Achilles as the individual, determined on establishing himself as such, and yet, through his complex relations with Patroklos, forced to meet the phantom double Hektor in a life-and-death struggle. Humanistic readings of the *Iliad* have raised the question of man's superiority to the gods, the fact that man, given a limit to his life, lives more intensely than can a god, whose "fate" is endless, changeless leisure, i.e., a lack of definition, an absence of struggle, a true existential void.[7] Similarly, any one interested in comparing the *Iliad* with other heroic epics must consider the insistence of the genre on the sharpest possible distinction between life and death: when heroes face off against each other, make their abusive speeches, and then do battle, it is almost inevitable that one will fall and die, and one will emerge victorious and unscathed. What Hegel tells us, and Freud will explicate, is that the battle is for self-definition and the "enemy" is an aggressively invested image of the self. Patroklos and Hektor are both then doubles of Achilles to whom he is bound by the erotic and aggressive ties of ontic doubt. We shall find even further confirmation of this interpretation of the action of the *Iliad* in the work of the literary theorist René Girard, who has examined both the triangular or mimetic basis of desire—the desired object is only desirable to the extent that it is disputed by a rival: the "normal" oedipal complex—and the antagonistic and mimetic basis of sacrificial violence—ritual murder is an attempt to introduce differentiation into the chaos of identity: the fact that we are all Oedipus causes us to expel one Oedipus.[8]

Also in Hegel is an appreciation of the peculiar nature of Homeric heroic society: men generally, at a certain stage in their "historical" development, depend so completely upon their society for definition that we look back upon such men as having lived in a golden age. In determining that these men enjoy an age of reason Hegel briefly suggests his own conviction that ontogeny recapitulates phylogeny; only, perhaps, in his system the phenomenon would be better expressed as "ontology retraces its steps through each evolutionary stage of its self-revelation":

Just as reason, when exercised in observation, repeated in the medium of the category the movement of "consciousness" as such, namely, sense-certainty, perception, and understanding, the course of reason here, too, will again traverse the double movement of "self-consciousness," and from independence pass over into its freedom. (pp. 374–75)

He goes on to distinguish reason which is aware of itself merely as an individual and reason which demands and brings forth its reality in an other. This latter process takes place in the realm of the Social Order, the Ethical World (*Sittlichkeit*), which is defined as the absolute spiritual unity of the essential substance (*Wesen*) of individuals in their independent reality. It is here that we find our Homeric heroes:

In a free nation, therefore, reason is in truth realized. It is a present living spirit, where the individual not only finds his destiny (*Bestimmung*), i.e., his universal and particular nature (*Wesen*), expressed and given to him in the fashion of a thing, but himself is this essential being, and has also attained his destiny. The wisest men of antiquity for that reason declared that wisdom and virtue consist in living in accordance with the customs of one's own nation. (p. 378)

Hegel's specific reference is clearly to Socrates and Plato, but as he describes the emergence of the individual from this collective identity we cannot help thinking of Achilles saying no to Agamemnon's ambassadors:

. . . the individual, as he immediately finds his existence in the actual objective social order, in the life of his nation, has a solid imperturbable confidence; the universal mind has not for him resolved itself into its abstract moments, and thus, too, he does not think of himself as existing in singleness and independence. When, however, he has once arrived at this knowledge, as indeed he must, this immediate unity with mind, this undifferentiated existence in the substance of mind, his naive confidence is lost. (p. 379)

Here we need consider briefly the various views of Achilles' relation to the heroic society of the Greek camp before Troy in preparation for a later attempt to integrate these primarily social and political views into our analysis of the character of Achilles as determined by erotic and aggressive object investments.

We might start with E. R. Dodds' application of the distinction between shame-culture and guilt-culture to the Homeric world and the Archaic Age respectively. One should remember that Dodds' attempt to define the peculiarities of the mental processes in Homer— men are subject to "psychic intervention"—is almost contemporary with that of Snell, but strangely independent.[9] It is a major contribution, of course, but suffers from the very rationalist perspective which it claims is not the only legacy of Greek civilization. Set securely within the Anglo-American tradition of static common sense, it has none of the dialectical excitement of Snell's work. We are asked to see successive stages of the Greek irrational unfold without ever asking ourselves from what perspective we see this or even what is the nature of human thought and perception. Though a study with many brilliant insights, it lacks a philosophical framework, and there is a tendency for different and often contradictory concepts to be invoked at different stages of the argument. This one concept, though, of the difference between shame-culture and guilt-culture, has stuck in the tradition of Homeric criticism and is highly instructive:

Homeric man's highest good is not the enjoyment of a quiet conscience, but the enjoyment of *timē*, public esteem: "Why should I fight," asks Achilles, "if the good fighter receives no more *timē* than the bad? (9.315ff.) And the strongest moral force which Homeric man knows is not the fear of god, but respect for public opinion, *aidōs* . . . The situation to which the notion of *atē* is a response arose not merely from the impulsiveness of Homeric man, but from the tension between individual impulse and the pressure of social conformity characteristic of a shame-culture. In such a society, anything which exposes a man to the contempt or ridicule of his fellows, which causes him to "lose face," is felt as unbearable.[10]

Bowra, in his synthetic study of different traditions of heroic poetry (roughly contemporary with Snell's and Dodd's work on Homer) considers this vulnerability to public opinion a hallmark of the genre: "Often enough, honor must be satisfied by bloodshed, since the hero feels that he has been too deeply insulted for forgiveness or appeasement to be possible, and can hardly continue to exist unless he destroys those who have wounded him in the centre of his being."[11]

Of course, Fränkel would stipulate that there is no center to his being, and that this is the cause of his extreme vulnerability: *das Ich ist nicht abgekapselt*. What manner of men are these who fear not the gods or any retribution for offensive deeds they might commit, but only the lack of respect among their fellows? Dodds is certainly right to speak of them as almost pre-religious. Paradoxically, the man who fears a retributive god has developed a strong sense of his own worth. He believes that, to some extent, he has free will, and therefore is accountable to his god for his actions. Homeric man, and the heroic type generally, has no such long-range perspective, but rather looks to the moment and his immediate social circle for definition of his worth. He is also likely to have a close male companion to whom he constantly appeals for comfort and support.

The dynamics of this situation, which must be taken as a contrast to most other situations we meet with in literature, can be explained in several different ways: socially, politically, theologically, philosophically, and psychologically. Let us begin where several recent critics have, with the social structure of the Greek camp before Troy. We need not ask all the bothersome questions about who is really in charge and why; we need only understand that there is a code by which these men live and that this allows them to seek their individual glory in the context of this pan-Hellenic operation. One might say that this attitude is more clearly expressed by some heroes than by others, that Diomedes, for instance, is engaged in a more selfish pursuit than Odysseus, who seems to keep things together when collective goals are lost sight of. We shall examine these differences later, when we consider the major heroes in their relations with Achilles. Here let us simply observe of the Trojan campaign that the whole is not greater than the sum of its parts.

In two studies of the language of Achilles, written twenty years apart, the conclusion is drawn that Achilles struggles linguistically as he does socially to overcome the restrictions imposed upon him by this strange, incohesive group of which he is, and is not, a part.[12] How is it that those who are more concerned with the individual than the society see the individual as uncentered in himself (*nicht abgekapselt*) and those who are more concerned with the society than the individual see the society as unintegrated, and, of course, those who are concerned with Achilles' place in his heroic society see him as somehow transcending their social code and discourse? Does all this mean that a centrifugal society produces a centrifugal personality in the individual who will then fly from its non-center? And, presumably, from his own? Rousseau had the strange notion that freedom for the individual was best defined as the ability to follow the general will of the society rather than depend upon other individuals.[13] Hegel follows this suit to some extent, but sees a natural development that will force men from the safety of such assimilation. Since all of Hegel's stages are defined by their successors, we should hear what he says of the "free nation" and think of Achilles:

From this happy state, however, of having attained its destiny, and of living in it, the self-consciousness, which in the first instance is only immediately and in principle spirit, has broken away; or perhaps it has not yet attained it; for both can be said with equal truth . . . Isolated by himself he is himself now the central essential reality—no longer universal mind . . . When the individual gets fixity in the form of singleness . . . the individual has thereby set himself over against the laws and customs. These latter are looked on as merely a thought without absolutely essential significance, an abstract theory without reality; while he *qua* this particular ego is in his own view the living truth. (pp. 378–79)

This typical reversibility of the Hegelian sequence prevents our trying to determine, by comparing the two texts, whether Achilles progresses beyond or has not yet arrived at the stage of integration which the other heroes enjoy. But if we compare this Hegelian text with the previously cited texts on the life-and-death struggle of one self-consciousness with another self-consciousness, we do have at least a philosophical and perhaps psychological model for the strange paradox of Homeric society. It is not only with the society's enemies that its members struggle, but with each other: their violence is derived from a lack of clearly conceived individual identity, as opposed to social identity. They therefore desperately need each other and their enemies to define themselves; both fellow-warriors and enemy-warriors are their Hegelian others who serve the purpose of mirrors to assure the subject of his continued existence. There can be no question of a common cause among individuals so lacking in self-perspective. Their gods are, of course, almost the same, and serve the same purpose, as other men. Only with a consolidated ego, an integrated self-image, is the projection of omnipotence into a divinity possible. Even with the requisite technical skills, it is unimaginable that Homeric man could fashion a Poseidon of Artemiseion or Pheidias' Apollo; but, of course, that is the same sort of provision that one would make in trying to conceive of Homer "writing" the *Oresteia*; i.e., even if he had the same poetic skills as Aeschylus. Man's ability to create plastic art is like his linguistic and literary ability: the conception demands and produces the tools for its expression. Gods are projections of man's self-images, and only in those peculiar times and places when events sequential in a Hegelian sense conspire to convince men of their evolved and complete perfection do men then mirror themselves in complete and perfect deities.

The strange nostalgia for a completely integrated society, which so dominates the thinking of such seemingly disparate commentators on the *Iliad* as Redfield and Havelock,[14] should here be mentioned. Redfield, as we shall see in the next section, takes his critical model from Lévi-Strauss, so we should not be surprised to find him validating the social order of the *Iliad* in the persona of Hektor. We only ask of him whether Hektor is really presented that sympathetically, and why, if the social order of the *Iliad* is all that cohesive, do men turn so jealously upon their fellows? Why are the heroes so determined to find rivals that they are as happy to be opposed to another of their own kind as to one of the enemy? Is Achilles really exceptional in his refusal of "the specialty of rule" or is he rather representative of the mutual hostility that ranges up and down the Greek hierarchy? Lévi-Strauss stresses that exchange is the structuring essence of societies: the exchange of goods, words, and women. Achilles refuses gifts, is not a good speaker, and recognizes that the women for whom he contends—both in Agamemnon's interest and against Agamemnon, both Helen and Briseis—are not worth the lives lost, certainly not his and Patroklos'. None of these exchangeables, then, has intrinsic value, but rather they are validated by the social habit of exchanging anything in order to confirm society's existence. The linguistic model then becomes inevitable: if men value the same goods, then socially they are speaking the same "language."

By another route Havelock has arrived at a similar reading of the

Iliad. Through his study of oral traditions of epic verse-making, he concludes that the *Iliad* is a handbook of heroic behavior, and carries forward all sorts of traditional knowledge, ranging from how to rig a ship to how to face one's own death in battle. It must be said about both of these readings that they contradict the poem's own focus, which is on Achilles' refusal to live within the heroic code. Furthermore, the *Iliad* presents Achilles as paradigmatic rather than perverse: all heroes feel about themselves pretty much as he does. In short, the *Iliad* tells us very forcefully that social institutions are no consolation for individual deprivation. Man in society is wretched and alone and has not even the image of a blissful past when society furnished him with all he required, but rather has only an image of himself as compromised by the demands of society. Patroklos' naked body tells Achilles what he is and what he has lost, "the armor of an alienating identity," in Lacan's phrase, "which will mark with its rigid structure the subject's entire mental development." It is resistance to social authority that consolidates the ego, usually by compromise, but the hero of the *Iliad* refuses to compromise and seeks death instead.

The nostalgia of the critics for an integrated society is not even ratified in the *Iliad* for a time before the Trojan War. Then, too, it was heroic competition for cities, cattle, a boar's tusks, or whatever. The point seems to be that those things we recognize as valueless from a hero's individual perspective—an excuse for fighting, not a reason—become the structuring principle for societies. Reading heoric poetry for a social message, then, is a contradiction; women and cattle and words are not important, but men's definition of themselves in terms of each other is overwhelmingly important. Perhaps we can understand the nostalgia of those socializing readers of the *Iliad* if we understand the nostalgia of Lévi-Strauss:

Lévi-Strauss' theoretical ploy (the institution of the homology and the binary code) permits him to remain faithful to the over-riding structuralist intention of avoiding the assumption of a pre-discursive, centered subject. But it is clear that his need to find transcendent "conditions" and "mutually convertible" systems expresses just the sort of nostalgia for an innocent center, and for the engineer's privileged claim to unproblematic access to a structure beyond structurality, that . . . Derrida finds pervasive in his texts.[15]

Derrida himself invokes Nietzsche:

Difference must be conceived without nostalgia; that is, it must be conceived outside the myth of the purely maternal or paternal language belonging to the lost fatherland of thought. On the contrary, we must affirm it—in the sense that Nietzsche brings affirmation into play—with a certain laughter and with a certain dance.[16]

Though these parental figures are potentially embarrassing to a Freudian perspective, the point is no worse taken: our critical methods determine our readings and vice versa. If we want validation for social structure and social experience we shall find it even in a heroic poem, i.e., a poem conceived from the perspective of a "pre-discursive, centered subject" who refuses all social demands upon him because society gratifies none of his desires. His centering in himself and in his society is fragile; that the hero is socially and individually *nicht abgekapselt* is the whole point of epic.

When Hegel actually comes to discuss epic as part of the section on art, which immediately precedes the section on religion that brings the *Phenomenology* to a close with the final self-revelation of Absolute Spirit, we have a straightforward reference to the *Iliad* and Achilles' place in it, as if only at his work's climax could he reveal its source and inspiration:

This Necessity, however, is the unity of the notion, a unity dominating and controlling the contradictory moments, a unity in which the inconsistency and fortuitousness of their action is coherently regulated, and the sportive character of their acts receives its serious value in these acts themselves. The content of the world of imagination carries on its process in the middle element detached by itself, gathering round the individuality of some hero, who, however, feels the strength and splendour of his life broken, and mourns the early death he sees ahead of him. (pp. 735–36)

This appreciation of the hero as mediation between god and man (the universal and the specific) as an analogy to the poet as mediation between the universal patterns of human experience and their concrete examples is possible only in the context of the overall dialectical movement of the argument, which demands that there be participation of truth in reality, but also that there be a controlling perception of this participation, which, I have tried consistently to show, is the essence of Hegel's system and is what makes him necessary to the critical effort. At this point in his argument Hegel is close to claiming the self-revelation of Absolute Spirit, the almost autonomous resolution of the contradictory moments in the notion itself, but even so he appeals to a controlling self-consciousness, and his model is Achilles. Hegel's whole system is based on the dynamics of mirror imagery, the life-and-death struggle between two self-consciousnesses to reach definition. In all metaphysical systems we feel some lessening of tension, some betrayal of the system itself when we reach its culmination in an all-determining first principle. In Plato's system there is the gap between the use of reason and the revelation of the Forms (*Republic*, 511 b–c, 555 c); in Aristotle's system the introduction of the Unmoved Mover seems rather an abbreviation of the argument than its logical conclusion (*Metaphysics* 1071 b 20–1072 a 20); in Hegel's system the final revelation of Absolute Spirit (when God becomes Man in Christ and this transfiguration is completely appreciated in philosophy) seems to turn the tables on us, to make us witnesses to an epiphany, whereas all along we had felt like antagonists in a drama under our own direction (*Phenomenology*, Sec. VIII). For Hegel's metaphysics to be useful as a critical model for the *Iliad* it must be allowed to deconstruct itself, so that we end not with the community of Christian philosophy, but with the isolated philosopher determined to see himself in all the transactions of nature. Only so can the poet and the critic identify with Achilles in his battle with the river.[17]

We start then with a hero de-centered in himself but in control of his poem; the poet sees the world through him and makes him the model of all the other men, the focus of all the gods. The critic must not falsify the poem's perspective by claiming for Achilles a self-consciousness he does not achieve, or forcing him to validate a social structure which contradicts his nature, or displacing him in his own poem to create sympathy for another character. The critic needs a model which can measure the wrath in terms of self-definition, and yet still not posit a false center, a nostalgic formation of social or human permanence—either man in culture transcending man in nature, or, almost vice versa, the individual able to appeal to a cosmic form of honor and nobility that transcends the social contract—which would force us into reading the *Iliad* as anything less than an uncompromising statement of the desperate disappointment every individual faces at every stage of his development. Not only does his reality refuse to gratify his demand for any proof of meaningful existence, but that very reality is recognized as the mirror which first returned to him the image it now denies. Like Achilles, we desire only the consolation of seeing ourselves in what is not ourselves, but even though it is there that we first conceived ourselves the mirror is always already broken.

This is surprisingly revealed to us in a footnote to Marx's *Capital*. As he defines the difference between the use-value and the exchange-value of commodities he finds an analogy for the latter in the relations between men:

> In a sort of way, it is with man as with commodities. Since he comes into the world neither with a looking glass in his hand, nor as a Fichtian philosopher, to whom "I am I" is sufficient, man first sees and recognizes himself in other men. Peter only establishes his own identity as a man by first comparing himself with Paul as being of like kind. And thereby Paul, just as he stands in his Pauline personality, becomes to Peter the type of the genus homo.[18]

Marx's point in the main text is that exchange-value is completely unreal, a purely symbolic relative value that is so created and hypostatized by the economic system that it obscures use-value, which is real: just as man is alienated from himself in the selling of his labor, so his products are alienated from themselves as they become commodities. Marx does not see any possibility for a negation of this negation: there is no way that men can reappropriate themselves or their useful products until the lost positive of a primitive social system without private property is restored. The nostalgic tradition runs from Rousseau through Marx to Lévi-Strauss. The *Iliad*, however, and then Hegel and Freud, and now Derrida and Foucault correct this false yearning, for they reveal that without struggle there is no definition. Our individuality exists only as a function of our suspension of disbelief in the values our society has formed for us and the models it has erected for our emulation. There is constant self-reflection but no essence, just as there is constant exchange but no real value. Achilles realizes this and tries to tell the horror of it, but we refuse to listen if we are humanists, and if we are nostalgic socialists we say that individuality is a perverse concept determined by the capitalist system. As critics of the *Iliad*, however, we should admit that the struggle is always already there, as a dynamic principle, and it is only variously materialized as individual identity, sexual antagonism, pursuit of plunder, battle, athletic games, and verbal disputes.

I.3
STRUCTURALIST AND HUMANIST
ATTEMPTS TO READ HOMER

In Hegel we clearly see Achilles and Hektor as two self-consciousnesses confronting each other, each determining his existence by his denial of existence to the other. Snell and Fränkel tell us how Homeric heroes lack cohesion, and Dodds tells us that they depend upon the opinion of other heroes to provide them with an identity. Our question in this philosophical tradition of Homeric criticism is always, "How does the hero see himself in relation to other heroes?" Strangely, in what might be called the humanistic tradition of Homeric criticism, which can be represented for our purposes by Whitman and Havelock among the conventional critics, Redfield and Austin among the structuralist critics, we hear the question, "How does the heroic society determine the hero?" This seemingly subtle difference is in fact sufficient to disalign completely the two schools. Without becoming too much concerned with the histories of German and French philosophy and their influence on the reading of Homer, we must attempt briefly to locate our own perspective. A secondary consideration is to illustrate how completely a reading of Homer will be determined by critical preconditions, and to argue therefore that these must be self-conscious.

In Redfield's study—which reveals its structuralist orientation in its main title, *Nature and Culture in the Iliad*, and its attempt to see beyond Achilles to the social center of the poem in its subtitle *The Tragedy of Hektor*—there is a candid account of what is being sought, and therefore found:

Achilles is a character strikingly lacking in both forethought and afterthoughts, and his judgements of others are as transitory as they are absolute . . . In the *Iliad* (I contend) the greatness of a man lies not in his capacity to construct an inner synthesis of his experience but in his effect on others, whether that effect is voluntary or involuntary, whether for good or for evil.[1]

I presume that Redfield refers here tacitly to Snell, Fränkel, and Dodds. He says, then, that if they are judging Achilles by philosophical standards and finding him wanting, they are not reading the *Iliad* entirely as they should, because there is also Hektor, who, though he might not appear any more self-conscious than Achilles, nevertheless has a socializing effect upon his family and friends: they all see in him what they would validate in themselves. One wonders, though, about priorities. Is a sense of self prior to a sense of social responsibilities? Is the sense that the *Iliad* must be defended against those who would find it primitive prior to the elevation of Hektor at Achilles' expense? To the first question I mean, of course, to provide a Freudian answer. If phylogeny can be said to recapitulate ontogeny, then we can argue that the man in the first stages of civilization, like the child in the first years of life, exerts all his energy to understanding how he functions as an individual, and only later can become aware of moral forces operating upon him through the family and larger social units. To the second question I propose a Hegelian answer. Hegel sees the individual man always predicted and determined by his experience of his nationality, his sense of being the same with his fellows, but as soon as this prediction and determination are consciously appreciated, then there is alienation and negation. Of course this negation is ultimately negated, when man reenters society self-consciously, but we must not forget that Hegel's paradigm for alienation is the Homeric hero, who dies young.

If ever there was an obvious correction offered by a systematic philosopher to a popular philosophical position, it is the correction of self-consciousness which Hegel made to Rousseau's notion of the general will. Perhaps a Homeric criticism informed by Hegel can correct the Homeric criticism so clearly descended from Rousseau through Lévi-Strauss. In his first and second discourses—"On the Sciences and the Arts" and "On the Origin of Inequality"—Rousseau develops those theses commonly associated with his name: a celebration of man in nature and a discouragement of intellectual and creative activity among the general public. These positions are demonstrably Platonic, though Rousseau's use of outrageous paradox sometimes obscures this. In the *Social Contract* we find developed that concept which was so influential in nineteenth-century political theory and which has, in fact, been cited as the single most formative influence on twentieth-century totalitarianism: the general will.

Hence, in order that the social pact shall not be an empty formula, it is tacitly implied in that commitment—which alone can give force to all others—that whoever refuses to obey the general will shall be constrained to do so by the whole body, which means nothing more than that he shall be forced to be free; for this is the condition which, by giving each citizen to the nation, secures him against all personal dependence.[2]

Rousseau's social contract is a compromise formation, an attempt to restore some of the virtues of man in nature to man in his fallen state. What precipitated this fall was the acquiescence of the many to the possession of property by the few, with its consequent vices of covetousness and ambition. By yielding to the power of the general will, the individual in Rousseau's civilized state at least saves himself from the degradation of dependence upon other individuals, which is the origin of inequality among men. Something has, of course, been lost as well as something gained, or restored: the individual gains his freedom by thinking according to the general will and refusing to express himself in opposition to it, for to think against the general will is to think wrongly. There is obviously nothing of the dynamics of democratic pluralism here, but rather the monolithic mind of the totalitarian state.

Rousseau's nostalgia for an undifferentiated citizen body, a collectivity of peoples without individuals, is contradicted by the competitive, contemplative, complicated modern world of capitalism and psychoanalysis, characterized by a paradoxical dependence between the self-alienation of materialism and the bourgeois insistence on individualism. Nowhere do we find in Rousseau any indication of Hegel's systematic, dialectical expansion of the relation between the subject and his objective world. The essence of that dialectic is, of course, self-consciousness, and this, by definition, prevents the contentment of the return which Rousseau seeks. One of Rousseau's most influential contemporary followers exactly reproduces the contrast between simple, undifferentiated, pre-capitalist societies and the modern world in his contrast between authentic and inauthentic societies. Lévi-Strauss defines his discipline:

. . . if we carefully consider the points on which anthropological investigations have been brought to bear, we note that in its increasingly intensive study of modern societies, anthropology has endeavored to identify levels of authenticity within them. . . . In the future, it will no doubt be recognized that anthropology's most important contribution to social science is to have introduced, if unknowingly, this fundamental distinction between two types of social existence: a way of life recognized at the outset as traditional and archaic and characteristic of "authentic" societies and a more modern form of existence, from which the first-named type is not absent, but where groups that are not completely, or are imperfectly, "authentic" are organized within a much larger and specifically "unauthentic" system.[3]

What Lévi-Strauss validates and seeks nostalgically is some correction in the collective experience of a traditional culture of that alienation which characterizes pluralistic societies. Redfield turns this observation back upon itself, and, whereas Lévi-Strauss and Rousseau find authenticity in those cultures which extend into societal order the structures of nature, Redfield finds in Homeric society some compensation for and correction of the isolating, death-directed individualism of nature:

Only within the order of culture do men have proper names and individual identities; as creatures of nature they are perfectly ephemeral. Nature cares nothing for the life of the species . . . Achilles is driven back on the bare truth: that he himself is alive and strong. He can (in this sense) assert himself, but it remains a bare assertion: once he is excluded from the fabric of culture, Achilles can find no meaning in his life, no uses for his strength. He has become a mere creature in nature.[4]

This appreciation of Achilles' position is basic to any reading of the *Iliad*. In withdrawing from the arenas of battle with one's enemies and

debates with one's friends, where heroic existence is tested and defined, Achilles ceases to exist as a hero. At the same time he begins
to question the bases of the concept of heroic existence, so that when
he reenters those arenas, he does so with a new self-consciousness.
Already then, the bipolar opposition of nature and culture, the individual and society, is inadequate to a description of the action of the
Iliad. Even if we deny to man the possibility of knowing anything but
that which is subject to spatial and temporal distortion, we nevertheless
allow him a suspension of his own disbelief in his ability to know, and
this allowance is not part of the heritage of Rousseau and Lévi-Strauss,
who both contradict their roles as philosophers of culture by questioning the moral value (Rousseau) and even the possibility (Lévi-
Strauss) of philosophy as such:

[Lévi-Strauss' structural anthropology] is Kantianism without a transcendental
subject . . . More a Kantian unconscious than a Freudian one; a categorical,
unifying unconscious . . . a categorical system without reference to a thinking
subject . . . homologous to nature; it might even be nature.[5]

It is certainly a strange denial of both metaphysical and phenomenological perspectives on being: qualities exist only in contradiction
and that contradiction cannot be defined except in terms of other
contradictions. Culture then consists in the structure of all the relations of all the contradictions in nature, and the individual can only
be absorbed by that structure, never master it. The obvious "original"
figure is language. Redfield says that Achilles can assert himself only
outside of culture, but can find no meaning to his life there. We shall
attempt to show that what Achilles finds in his self-conscious opposition to his society is, by definition, the meaning of his life. Even if
we deny to him a revelation of absolute truth, we must allow him to
have found meaning in the experience of his difference from the other
heroes, and in his insistence that if to live means to assimilate to their
pattern, then he must die. One way in which the poem makes clear
to us Achilles' attitude toward his relations with his fellows is his use
of language, and we shall consider some perceptions of this phenomenon, especially those of Redfield, in the next section. Meanwhile, we
might look at two other attempts to state the problem of the relations
between the hero and his society as presented by the poet.

If culture humanizes nature by giving the individual worth and dignity he would not otherwise enjoy, then, in the heroic society, which validates the individual's effort, the poet is extremely important, for he records the exploits of individuals, and thus, just as Redfield tells us culture should treat nature, immortalizes the individuals nature would condemn to nameless deaths. This is not a peculiarlarly structuralist perspective. We find it in critics following models radically different, but equally nostalgic:

Homer is about as close as poetry can ever come to a report on the normal juxtaposed over against the abnormal. To describe his manner as elevated is to use a poor metaphor. His power derives from his function, and his function does not carry him vertically upward above the spirits of men but extends him horizontally outward to the confines of the society for which he sings. He profoundly accepts this society, not by personal choice but because of his functional role as its recorder and preserver. He is therefore dispassionate, he can have no personal axe to grind, no vision wholly private to himself.[6]

Havelock goes on to claim for Homeric poetry an authority based on its implied identity between truth and expression, and thereby to explain Plato's condemnation of it:

But he is an oral poet composing according to certain psychological laws which were unique, which have literally ceased to exist, at least in Europe and in the West.

. . . Plato seems to have been convinced that poetry and the poet had exercised a control not merely over Greek verbal idiom but over the Greek state of mind and consciousness.[7]

The poet who sings unquestioningly the traditional values of his society by singing its tradition of orally composed epic certainly would have authority, indeed "authentic authority." To feel such undifferentiatedness is, though, not the usual reading of the *Iliad*. For the most part, modern readers of the poem have felt occasional idiosyncratic slants in the narrative (if only in the use of similes) and individual judgments. That the Homeric poems were, however, read as "the mind of the past" in the archaic and classical periods is indisputable. We must ask, then, by analogy, if the poet was so comfortable in his oral tradition of epic poetry, was the hero equally comfortable in his traditional code of behavior in war and council? We shall soon consider Parry's argument that Achilles found the formulaic system of epic poetry inadequate for the expression of his own position in heroic society and Redfield's response that it was his fellows' following of the code which Achilles found inadequate.

Let us now, however, formulate the adequacy of any perception of collective experience to the individual's expression of his own experience. Such a formulation is, of course, bound to be a model of specific or concrete, as metonymical or metaphorical revelation of the whole, ideal or abstract. We can distinguish, though, between the situation in Homeric epic, and in, for instance, Pindaric *epinikian*. Pindar tells us how each individual victor embodies every criterion of heroic excellence: athletic, social, genealogical, ethical, political. The poet, then, speaks for the tradition, and elevates the individual to it. There are, of course, those disconcerting warnings in Pindar, both in the episodes of the myths narrated and in the use of proverbs, to the effect that overstepping the divinely imposed limits upon the human condition is almost the definition of the heroic experience. We hear of Ixion and Tantalos and the arrow that misses its mark. In the *Iliad*, however, the individual hero's experience is validated against the limitations imposed by the tradition. Homer sings the tradition, but he also sings Achilles. Would any modern reader deny that the focus of the poem is Achilles' transcendence of the heroic code, so much so that one could even say that the code is used by the poet only to give ground for Achilles' overstepping it? How is this tension made possible and why do we respond to it as we do?

Arguments for Homeric neutrality cannot hold up against our identification with Achilles—not with Diomedes or Odysseus or Nestor, or even Hektor, those centripetal, secondary characters—and his experience is that all the traditional equipment (language, martial prowess, noble birth, friends, and mistress) is inadequate to sustain him. Indeed, language is a self-alienating structure that forces him to consider himself in other people's terms; his superiority as a warrior is contradicted in his subordination to the service of an inferior warlord; the polarity in his nature between divine aspirations and human limitations is determined by his derivation from a goddess-mother and a mortal father; his dear male companion is sacrificed to the twofold battle over relatively insignificant women, his own and his warlord's brother's.

If we pursue this interpretive thread we might end up where Whitman did, with an extremely attractive, consistent, and compelling humanistic reading of the *Iliad*: Achilles enjoys progress toward self-knowledge as a function of his disillusion with the heroic code, and finally, in the distancing consequent upon his acceptance of death, he experiences for the first time an emotional closeness with others.

But the miracle remains that he [Homer], and apparently he first, imagined the transcendence of the older schema by a figure who would typify, not material triumph, but the triumph of the spirit amid self-destruction, and that he could dramatize this paradox as the search for the integrity of the self against a panoramic background involving all the forces of the world, human and divine.[8]

Whitman's conception of the significance of Achilles' experience is of a transcendence, but it is metaphysical, a communication with the deathless, changeless form of heroic *arete*: Achilles believes that nobility is "an organic and inevitable part of the universe, independent of social contract." Achilles' love for Patroklos, like his hate for Hektor, "is likely to have cosmic implications."[9] I doubt that many readers feel comfortable with such denominations. To suggest that there is cosmic significance for any human event is to indulge in the pathetic fallacy, which might be allowed poets but must be forbidden critics. Our reading of the *Iliad* should be off-center: the poet is off the center of his tradition, linguistically and ethically, since he manipulates the verbal formulae and does not validate all aspects of the heroic code; the hero is off the center of the heroic code, finding it an inadequate frame in which to depict his life; the modern reader is certainly off the center of the poem, since the heroic code and the epic tradition are alien to him, but the hero is strangely familiar.

I am convinced that for various but similar reasons all previous attempts to read the *Iliad* have been inadequate because they hypostatize something inessential to the experience of the poem: social unanimity, human suffering, linguistic community, virtuous abstracts. Though all serious critics have realized that the *Iliad* is essentially concerned with the relations between self and others, their critical models have not illustrated its true orientation. With a Freudian model corrected by Hegel (i.e., a Lacanian model), I hope to be able to show that what we appreciate in the *Iliad* is our own individual inability to define ourselves in any terms but those provided us by our society, *and that herein true alienation lies.* We feel alienated from an image of ourselves that was not even originally of our own creation. It is doubly false since it is neither real (no image is), nor our own (but society's). Patroklos is not Achilles, but even that approximation of his reality is denied him by social mechanisms he cannot control. As the *Iliad* itself is an attempt to fix this evanescent image of its hero, so the critical appreciation of the poem must be a struggle to fix perspective. We must be conscious of ourselves reading and we must constantly negate the consequent negations: we are not Greek, we are not warriors, we have never been to Troy. The dynamics of our response will then require jumping the gap, like a short-circuiting spark, between universal expectations and specific experience. With Achilles we shall come finally to see ourselves in a flash, a contradiction of the difference between self and others, the concrete and the abstract, the subject and the object. Authentic being for the individual—hero, poet, critic—can only be momentary, a function of the difference between two nonexistent, only mutually constitutive, forcefields.

In recapitulating my objections to these previous attempts to read the *Iliad*, I would qualify them as defective in both affect and concept: neither do they locate the emotional center of the poem by explaining adequately our identification with Achilles, nor do they present in their critical models the complexities of the poem's world view. This kind of criticism is not dialectical: criticism should be both self-conscious and progressive.[10] With relative ease, we can dismiss Redfield's suggestion that the poem demands empathy with Hektor as individual. Hektor is, relative to Achilles, unconscious of heroic reality, as Whitman has shown.

Hector has no clear knowledge of the future. He is doing his best for his city; he is realistic enough to know that he may lose all, and brave enough to struggle on in any case, but he has no foreknowledge . . . He sees the present task; and not out of any transcendent vision of himself or of anything else.[11]

It is a close reading of Hektor's farewell to Andromache in Book VI which elicits Whitman's remarks: so blind is Hektor to the violence in which he is involved as both cause and effect, that he wishes for his son involvement in the same cycle.

"and some day let them say of him: 'He is better by far than his father,'
as he comes in from the fighting; and let him kill his enemy
and bring home the blooded spoils, and delight the heart of his
    mother."

(6.479–81)

The referent for this violence is the woman, insignificant in and of
herself, but capable of giving focus to men's battles: it is for her they
fight, both as prize and as incitement. We should shudder to see
Andromache as Brecht's Mother Courage, as responsible for her son's
death in her husband's wish, as if, in fact, she herself were to cast him
then from the battlements where she is standing. At the same time,
we are shown that men fight from an internal self-referential imperative. Hektor left Paris, whom both he and Helen had incited to battle,
to seek out Andromache, but when he does not find her inside his
house where she belongs (unless she is praying in the temple for the
city's safety) he is about to return to battle without further search:

. . . So
as he had come to the gates on his way through the great city,
the Skaian gates, whereby he would issue into the plain, there
at last his own generous wife came running to meet him,
Andromache, the daughter of high-hearted Eëtion.

(6.391–95)

The high point, then, of a sentimental reading of the *Iliad* is a
chance encounter: the ambivalence of Hektor over fighting and dying
is a marked contrast to Achilles' attitude. Hektor sees himself as others
do, fighting for family and city, while Achilles fights only for himself.
But even so, Hektor is more intent on his confrontation with other
men than he is on a reunion with his family. The violence continues
and is more frightening for being socially justified. Hektor's world view
is simply (because it is simple) not the world view of the *Iliad*. To read
the *Iliad* through the eyes of Hektor is like reading *Hamlet* through
the eyes of Horatio: there are more things between heaven and earth
than can be dreamed of in the philosophies of these secondary characters.

To what extent, even, can it be said that the poem presents a clear
dichotomy between peace and war? Certainly we must question
whether any sort of bipolar opposition is at work, a semantic mechanism whereby we are forced to see in facing columns, peace and war,
city and war camp, beseiged and beseigers, creative and destructive

forces, etc. The shield itself, which lends itself to that kind of analysis, is a perfect model of resistance to such simplification. In Hephaistos' depiction of the city at peace we see, after the wedding, a dispute involving the shedding of kindred blood (18.456–518), which, by definition cannot be arbitrated.[12] The violence will continue, with no bloodprice possible of payment, just as in the *Oresteia*, but here "the justice of Zeus" is a concept not yet even implied. There is violent confrontation between citizens in the city at peace, just as there is between enemies in the city at war; there is violent confrontation between Achilles and Agamemnon in council, just as there is between Achilles and Hektor on the battlefield; there is even fearful jealousy between Achilles and his beloved Patroklos: "do not take my glory (do not die for me)" (16.80–96).

If we were to argue that the definition of this violence is the theme of themes in the poem, how could we reduce it to a critical (philosophical) model? Would it be Heraclitean in its opposition of forces, peace defining war and war defining peace? This seems more appropriate than claiming for Homer a preconception of a Platonic form for peace, and denying therefore the existence of a negative form, war. Surely, what the poem presents is a negation of the negation that war presents to peace, and it is "mimetic violence." If we speak epistemologically and teleologically, the poem leads us dialectically to a definition of violence: war is violence and peace is the potential for violence, so violence is the definition the poem provides us for the human condition. If we speak ontologically and archaeologically, the poem leads us from the social manifestations of violence in the council and on the battlefield to an attempt by men to define themselves in terms of each other, originally in terms of that dialectically constituted image of themselves projected to them in their first experience of the world as Other.

We believe with Whitman that the *Iliad* is a poem of Achilles' "search for self," but we do not believe that there is comfort for hero, poet, or critic in the existence of any spiritual absolutes removed from the abuse of actual experience. Not only does the poem fail to present us with a pattern for the positive operation of these spiritual qualities, but it rather presents their contradiction. They are the first element in the triadic movement of its dialectic: like peace, they are negated by war, which is then negated by the recognition that violence is originary, as the self-defining conflict between self and other. Recognition is the key, we see finally. The poem does not collapse into bipolar opposi- tions, but forces us, in company with hero and poet, to a superior perspective from which we see violence as the spark jumping the gap between peace and war, and the authentic being of the individual as the spark jumping the gap between hero and heroic society. In neither case is our primary concern—violence, the individual, the *mēnis* of Achilles—more than this momentary flash caused by the conjunction of two falsely hypostatized entities. To find consolation, there, all too closely approximates blind hope.

In assimilating hero, poet, and critic, we argue for a strong reading of the *Iliad* on every level: its world view, at each stage of the literary process, is rendered more self-conscious. This is in marked contrast to the tendency in both structuralist and conventional criticism toward implosion: the critic unconsciously rewrites the poem. This method- ology is precisely prescribed by Lévi-Strauss:

The situation with myths is very much the situation we find with language. Any speaker who consciously applies phonological and grammatical laws in his speech—and we are pre-supposing, of course, that he has the requisite knowledge and virtuosity—would not be able to pursue the line of his argu- ment very long. In the same way, the exercise and practice of mythic thought demands that its properties remain hidden; if they are not, one would find himself in the position of the mythologist who cannot believe in myths because he spends his time expounding them. Mythic analysis does not and cannot have as its object to show how men think . . . We are not, therefore, claiming to show how men think the myths, but rather how the myths think themselves out in men and without men's knowledge.[13]

This unconsciousness which Lévi-Strauss finds necessary to writing about mythology—"Myths can only be explained by other myths"— is requisite at every level of the literary process as described by struc- turalist critics. Austin claims that Homeric similes function more straightforwardly than post-Homeric similes, because a certain order in the world is taken for granted. Thus, when Achilles is likened to the star Sirius, the power of the figure derives from the sure identi- fication between that heavenly phenomenon and the heat of summer. Achilles burns as does Sirius, and we need not be convinced first that

Sirius burns, which would be necessary in later poetry where poetry must reestablish its reality against the proofs of science. The patterns of human action, then, assimilate to the unquestioned patterns of nature.[14] One can see how readily Austin could find support for this premise in the operation of formula systems, which describe identically the functions of men, gods, and animals. Two corollaries of this axiom must, however, be recognized. A metaphysics of absence, a nostalgia for the lost primitive, is in operation here. Truth and meaning are identified and located in an undifferentiated past, when all men were poets (Rousseau) and myth-makers (Lévi-Strauss) and critics. Similarly, under the influence of this structuralism, the critic becomes the poet, just as the poem has become nature; hence, the shameless rewriting of Homer we find in Austin.[15] He has been absorbed by the material of poetry and begun to speak it like a native.

In one final figure to distinguish structuralist and conventional readings of the *Iliad* from the dialectical, self-conscious reading I am attempting, I suggest that the difference is the same as that between narcissistic and anaclitic choice of object in infantile experience, which is, of course, the originary figure for the whole study. Freud tells us that originally the child has two objects of desire, himself and the woman who nurses him, and thus there is a stage of primary narcissism for everyone. The choice of the mother is anaclitic because it "leans up against" the choice of the self: she is chosen because she fulfills the child's needs, not because she is desirable in and of herself. Narcissistic orientation in criticism is surely to seek in literature the mirror of the self, whereas anaclitic orientation is to seek absorption of the self in nature as reflected there. The one is conscious and philosophical and dialectical; the other intuitive, religious, and static. It could be argued that anaclitic criticism is peculiarly suited to certain genres and certain periods, like Romantic poetry. It must be allowed, however, that for a poem like the *Iliad*, which seeks definition of the self in violence with others, which focuses on the withdrawal of the individual from his society and his obsession with a close companion who will die in his armor, in his place, then a different kind of criticism is required, and thus we must continue to define its terms.

I.4

ON RE-READING PARRY'S HOMER

Simplistic codification is inevitable when the original, economic theory of a great thinker becomes the methodology of his less visionary disciples. This has been the fate of both Snell and Parry, the two men whose ideas have been most influential in Homeric studies in this century. I think I have shown that the richness of the classical German philosophical tradition implicit in Snell has gone unappreciated by his Anglo-American audience. Snell's attempt to recover the lost immediacy of experience expressed in the Homeric poems and available there for our self-conscious response is just as profound as, but more honest than, the primitivizing *recherche* of the structuralist and conventional critics who would make us all undifferentiated poets and Homeric characters.

The situation with Parry is slightly different: his own model was simplistic, and therefore successive generations of formula-analysts have struggled with a too narrow conceptual instrument to operate on the Homeric poems. Austin is right to try to turn the tide, to save the Homeric poems from the Philistines, especially the English, who, when they accept Parry, use him as an excuse to patronize the poetry rather than to allow poetry and critical model to adjust constantly and mutually to each other. Who, after all, is diminished in our eyes when we are told that a particular Homeric phrase is "otiose and inelegant," the poet or the critic? When, however, Austin shows empirically the

inadequacy of Parry's basic economic law of Homeric composition—
that there will be only one phrase to express a given thought in a given
metrical position—he is not asking us to throw out the whole thing,
but rather to realize that there is variety, and therefore "choice."
Almost simultaneous with Austin's objections to rigid "Parryism" and
his own meticulous proof of its shortcomings, there were revisions in
the conceptual framework of formula-analysis by Nagler and Peabody,
and now we have enthusiastic reviews of Nagler by Austin and of
Peabody by Nagler, so we know that formula-analysis has reached a
new stage.[1] I do not think it fulsome to praise them collectively for
having accomplished almost as much as Parry did originally. Implicit
in all their work—though I never find it clearly expressed—is the
recognition that Parry was wrong to claim that thought and expression
can be separated in Homer, any more than it could be in any other
poet: *podas ōkus Achilleus* simply does not mean simply "Achilles."

Nagler defines his project:

It is important to realize that one is committed to the existence of unknowns
even if one assumes that the poet memorizes and reproduces a fixed formula.
What form does the formula take when not being consciously remembered?
What is the "organic unity" that some scholars detect in certain fixed combi-
nations of words themselves? . . . And as for the softer Parryists, by the time
one has "conjugated," "expanded," "separated," and "displaced" the hapless
formula, economy of description alone would seem to indicate that one may
just as well "put it out of its misery". . . and frankly accept the concept of an
undetermined *sphota* on a higher ontological or psychological plane than any
given phrase.[2]

I do not choose to discuss the concept of *sphota*, which Nagler has
imported to Homeric studies from the classical tradition of Indian
philosophy of language, beyond the observation that he had ready at
hand, in the phenomenological study of language which stretches in
the Western tradition at least from Hobbes to Derrida, the conceptual
apparatus to make the same points. (Of course, comparisons between
the Homeric poems and Sanskrit poetry have become conventional,
so this borrowing is not so exotic as it might seem.)

. . . any one Gestalt or *sphota* beggars definition, for it is itself undifferentiated
with respect to any describable phonological feature. The given word, phrase,
or sentence is only a kind of hypostasis of this entity—an allomorph, as I have

been using the term—as a particular geometric shape is a hypostasis of its Platonic Form.[3]

In speaking of "hard Parryists" and "soft Parryists" Nagler suggests a physical analogy and we might perhaps extend it to include his own contribution: he has become, as we must all, a "trace-Parryist." Formulae do not exist in and of themselves, even as a family tree or a computer program. There is an absence at their "core" which they yearn to supplement, so that the structure they manifest in the poems, with all its permutations and extensions, is a structure of desire: how to express this thought, which is not even a thought, because we cannot think without words, and the Ur-formula is pre-verbal. Recalling Fränkel's description of Homeric man—*das Ich ist nicht abgekapselt*—one might say of the formula that it is a force field in which different phonemes attract and repel each other in the formation of themes.

It should be noted that the epithets which previous analysts have used to suggest the adaptive qualities of the "actual" formula all recall the psychic mechanisms first described by Freud in explaining dreams, and then extended to other areas of mental activity, like wit, error, and the formation of neurotic symptoms (not to mention art): "conjugated," "expanded," "separated," and "displaced" are like the four basic functions of dream-work, by which the latent content of the infantile sexual experience, stored as memory in the unconscious, makes itself acceptable to the censorship of the pre-conscious system and emerges into conscious life: representation, condensation, decomposition, displacement.

This frame of reference brings us by another route to the essential problem. Just as we ask what is the content of the unconscious and how does it manifest itself, so we ask what is the basic idea of the formula-system and how does it manifest itself? In both cases we must say that there is no original content in the sense of a discoverable truth. In the case of the unconscious, Freud began to question the experiential origin of what went on there as soon as he gave up his theory of infantile seduction, i.e., before *The Interpretation of Dreams* (1900). Lacan has gone so far as to claim that the structure of the unconscious is like the structure of language, suggesting that, again, "original" meaning is a contradiction in terms, since meaning in language is a function of difference and absence, not of exact correlation and application. Thinking and speaking are not processes which involve any historical or physical material. Both are structures of desire, which implies lack. When we analyze systems of Homeric formulae we might feel some self-delusory satisfaction in being able to convince ourselves that we have found the first, generative bud of the system, the original and pure expression from which all others represent variation and decadence. But we can never in the text determine that this is it, this is what it really means, no more than we can say, in trying to decide the earliest version of a myth, "This is what it is all about and the later versions are all corrupt."

I hope that the parallel between conventional formula-analysis and conventional criticism of the *Iliad* is now clear: both seek nostalgically an authentic, absolute, original reality that does not and never did exist. Derrida develops the trope of "original writing" for this very reason. Like the machine in Kafka's "Penal Colony," reality inscribes us with its messages but our sensory (psychic) systems must deal with this pain in its own indirect (hallucinatory) manner. All we can hope to recover is not the truth of the machine's message, but how we as readers have created meaning out of the sensation of inscription.

In Peabody's work we find a serious attempt to come to terms with the relation between sound and meaning in oral poetry. Though I am unable to understand his claim to distinguish "phonemic repetition" from "thematic repetition," especially in light of his own analysis of sound- and thought-patterns in *Works and Days*, I nevertheless find his conceptual framework extraordinarily attractive:

The thought of an oral tradition—the significant structures of its informational data—lies in the linguistic texture of its songs. A singer effects, not a transfer of his own intention, but a conventional realization of traditional thought for his listeners, including himself. This thought does not originate with any one individual; rather, it has been organized and has accumulated during millenia of cultural experience. This thought is realized and phenomenalized, however, by individuals at particular moments in time . . .
    The fundamental data of an oral tradition—the substance of its traditional thought—are the phonic structures that constitute the cores of formulas.[4]

Nowhere is the organic relationship between sound and meaning more apparent than in the nightingale fable (202–11) and the *didōmi* passage

(354–59) of *Works and Days*. We see meaning being manipulated by sound here, as if the poet were twisting his tongue rather than his brain for thought. No conventional etymological connection can be made between *aēdōn* and *aoidos*, but clearly Hesiod has fabricated something that is an *etymos logos*.[5]

What does *didōmi* mean? Somehow the concept doubles back upon itself—like Freud's primary words which are totally ambivalent and thus reflect the absence of negation in the unconscious—since one gives in the expectation of receiving, and only "good' giving fulfills this expectation; cf. the good and bad *aidōs* (319–26). Such fullness of meaning becomes apparent only through incantation: one calls upon the word in all its forms to render up its secrets.[6] We shall consider below some passages in the *Iliad* where the same sort of incantation is evident. Whatever the relative chronology of the Hesiodic and Homeric poems, the greater frequency of such passages in Hesiod suggests that he is working at an earlier stage in what might be called the conceptual evolution of poetry, closer to the beginnings of poetry in the rituals of magic and religion. With such texts before us we are forced to invent a new definition for poetry: to make (*poiein*) poetry (only the Greek redundant idiom is accurate) is to ask of language its secrets, but since language is the means as well as the material of poetry, all that can be accomplished is a constant inversion and re-inversion, or, as Pucci has shown, a movement from bipolar opposition to chiasmos. A reveals B, and B reveals A, A and B being opposites that are conceivable only in terms of each other, and for that very reason they are represented by the same phonemic pattern.[7]

This is poetry in its primal state, a serious effort to find reality in language; all other poetry is a nostalgic attempt to restore this immediacy. The "anxiety of influence" has already set in by the time Archilochos begins to write lyric, and constantly measures himself against Homer and his epic.[8] It is not then and thereafter a question of the poet struggling with language but of one poet struggling with another poet's language. And so this new tradition continues, always with a new poet and a new language used against the old, an oedipal conflict over truth as the absent mother. Then, too, in poetry of the post-original phase, language is used against itself in an almost conscious effort at its own cancellation. One wants meaning immediately experienced and language is seen as a mediation which, if called attention to, can be effaced. The result in post-original poetry is, of course, the opposite of that intended: language becomes hypostatized and the meaning of the writing of poetry is the only subject which poetry can adequately deal with.

Nagy has presented us with precisely the observation we need to free ourselves from this preoccupation with the seeming unconsciousness and ambivalence of language (the structuralist preoccupation) and of the oral epic tradition. He tells us to think in terms of tradition, rather than of the poem, when we try to analyze Homeric formulae and elements of plot: they were consistently evolving and we have in the extant poems only isolated moments of their manifestation.[9] At the same time he distinguishes between epic and cult ritual so as to suggest a liberating analogy: "the plot of Epic represents the ritual antagonism in a format where the God actually contrives the hero's death. What Epic will not represent, however, is the symbiosis of God and Hero in cult."[10]

This point is made in his large argument for the tendency of heroes to assimilate to the gods who then kill them. We are, of course, reminded of Girard's sacrificial crisis: we kill our double to protect our identity.[11] Epic is careful not to allow god and hero to become confused. The hero must die, and death is to this extent the basic "theme" of all epic, just as Girard considers death the only reasonable conclusion to any serious novel, since only death can end the desire stimulated by the rivalry of similars for the other.[12] We simply insist here, as we did above in our discussion of structuralism, that in epic, as in all poetry (unlike myth and ritual), there is a superior perspective, an organizing intelligence, which, though it dooms the hero to fail, nevertheless insists on his uniqueness. The hero is *therapōn* ("minion, companion, double") to the god and the hero must die when the assimilation threatens to become identity, just as Patroklos as *therapōn* to Achilles must die when he threatens to usurp his master's glory. The dynamics of the epic genre are figured in the struggle of the hero to define himself absolutely, to break the bonds of ambivalence and bipolar opposition in which all human thought about itself is caught. We shall come to see that the struggle is narcissistic, that strangely the god needs the hero as much as the hero needs the henchman, which is how the *erastēs* needs the *erōmenos*, i.e., as a reflection of his own beauty.

In the meantime, let us reassure ourselves that epic is a process. We feel its mode to be objectivity because the controlling hand of the traditional poet is so light on the reins. But we still know that control is there: no truly undifferentiated communal effort could make manifest the heroic dilemma. The individual poet struggles with the language of the tradition so that it becomes a language of his own creation. These individual moments in the notion of a "formulaic" series have an adversary relationship with all the other moments, so that they, too, are struggling to be unique. Poetry is more fluid, less fixed in form, in the oral epic tradition—the paradox is here evident, since one is inclined to say less "formulated," which, of course, is what it *is*, more than anything else—than later in written lyric and tragedy. Nevertheless, we have every reason to suppose that the poets' struggle for excellence—to be the best "Homeric" poet—was just as intense as it was among the poets Parry and Lord recorded in Yugoslavia. So, too, the epic hero's struggle is more intense to define himself because his conception of himself is based entirely upon the mirrors of himself provided by his friends and enemies. Russo and Simon have rightly pointed out, using Fränkel's phrase *das Ich ist nicht abgekapselt*, that there is no fixed core to the epic tradition just as there is no fixed center to the epic hero.[13] Both are constantly in a state of coming-into-being. We shall see this soon as the pre-literary and pre-philosophical statement of the narcissistically determined pre-oedipal experience: the father's presence as similar and rival is not sufficiently felt to validate the mother as object of desire in the son's eyes, so that instead of investing the mother libidinally and the father aggressively, the son invests images of himself (derived originally from the mother) both libidinally and aggressively. Hence the *Iliad* focuses not on Achilles' relations with Agamemnon and Peleus, or Thetis and Briseis, but upon his love for Patroklos and his hatred of Hektor, the two mirrors who assure him of his own continued (complete and perfect) existence.

I.5

ACHILLES' PLACE IN THE *ILIAD*, DEFINED LINGUISTICALLY AND PSYCHOANALYTICALLY

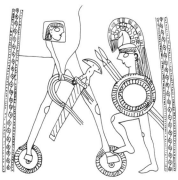 Adam Parry has done much to establish, clarify and, to some extent, revise, his father's theory. Friedrich and Redfield have been inspired by a suggestive article of the younger Parry's to attempt an analysis of the language of Achilles. In an extraordinary footnote at the beginning of their published results they state the problem of the hero and the poet (and in Achilles' case, as Redfield previously pointed out, the hero as poet) in the epic tradition, invoking Rousseau and his pre-Romantic preoccupation with presence and the desire for an end to desire:

The success of Parry's article has perhaps resulted from the fact that he ascribed to this archaic epic a very modern attitude—modern in the sense that it can hardly be traced back beyond J. J. Rousseau. For Rousseau, as for many of his heirs, culture meant society; society meant structure, and structure meant constraint and the suppression of the individual. In *The Origin of Inequality*, Rousseau concluded that human freedom and happiness would be possible only in a world in which men had nothing to do with one another; he says that this would be a world without language. A variant of this position holds that experience, to be authentic, must be unverbalizable ('the idea once expressed, is a lie') and that an authentic hero must be inarticulate. Parry makes Achilles relatively inarticulate, a hero who can express himself only by "misusing" his language.[1]

We should trace the steps by which Parry reaches this hypothesis on the heroic misuse of language:[2]

The formulaic character of Homer's language means that everything in the world is regularly presented as all men (all men within the poem, that is) commonly perceive it. The style of Homer emphasizes constantly the accepted attitude toward each thing in the world, and this makes for a great unity of experience. (p. 3)

There is not need, as there is in Plato's day, for a man to "define his terms". . . . the formulaic expressions which all men use are felt to be in perfect accordance with reality, to be an adequate representation of it. (p. 4)

. . . since the economy of the formulaic style confines speech to accepted patterns which all men assume to be true, there need never be a fundamental distinction between speech and reality; or between thought and reality—for thought and speech are not distinguished; or between appearance and reality—for the language of society is the way society makes things seem. (pp. 4–5)

Only in the person of Achilles do we find so much as a hint that appearances may be misleading, and conception in the form of words, a false and ruinous thing. (p. 5)

Homer, in fact, has no language, no terms, in which to express this kind of basic disillusionment with society and the external world . . . Achilles has no language with which to express his disillusionment. Yet he expresses it, and in a remarkable way. He does it by misusing the language he disposes of. (p. 6)

Achilles' tragedy, his final isolation, is that he can in no sense, including that of language (unlike, say, Hamlet), leave the society which has become alien to him. (p. 7)

Friedrich and Redfield disagree about Achilles' use of language and about his place in or outside of society. They summarize the position taken by Claus[3]—essentially that Achilles does not reject the heroic code, but applies its principles to a situation where they prove inadequate—and attempt to replace Parry's Shakespearean analogy with another: "Achilles then . . . is less Hamlet than Coriolanus, he becomes alienated from his community in an attempt to remain true to the code the community has taught him . . ."[4]

I cannot help thinking that in this later effort Redfield, at least, is trying to make of Achilles the kind of figure he so celebrated in Hektor in his previous study: i.e., a man committed to social values and the maintenance of the community. Now Achilles is back at the center of his poem, but I insist that he is unrecognizable as Achilles. Homer's Achilles certainly is no Hamlet (though he is suicidal), but neither is he a Coriolanus (he is certainly not manipulated by women and forced into compromising positions by their political ambitions for him). He is not tragic because he cannot feel guilt. He cannot feel guilt because he has not accepted limitations on his desire. His desire is entirely for self-images, since he is unable to invest true objects, the absolute precondition for social life.

I shall later argue that tragedy almost by definition implies an abnormal resolution of the Oedipus complex, a turning away from the mother (and all women) because antagonism with the father has convinced the tragic hero that the desired female and all sublimated manifestations of desire for the female, such as political ambition, are adulterous and corrupt. Achilles, we shall see, never even reaches the point of desiring the female: he is still trying to convince himself of his own existence and hence choosing as erotically and aggressively invested self-objects male doubles of himself, Patroklos and Hektor.

So, too, the Homeric Achilles' problem with language is not that which Friedrich and Redfield attribute to Parry's Achilles, i.e., Rousseau's wish for total isolation, lack of differentiation, silence (restoration of symbiosis with the mother). (Note that in another essay, *The Origin of Language*, Rousseau insists that men began speaking to each other not out of *need*, but out of *desire*, so that the first language was poetry, the language of love; Rousseau is strangely innocent of the Platonic identification between need and desire.)

The Homeric Achilles, as Friedrich and Redfield themselves show, uses language to create himself in his own image; not to communicate with others, but to define himself to himself. Friedrich and Redfield, comparing Achilles' speeches with those of other heroes, conclude that he can only be said to misuse language when one thinks of the proper use of language as being conative (convincing others of what you believe) rather than expressive (convincing yourself that you are right). This sounds tantalizingly close to the conventional distinction between epic and lyric, and later we shall have occasion to consider Achilles as a lyric persona caught in epic, but here let us just acknowledge the validity of Friedrich's and Redfield's distinction. By speaking in strongly marked antitheses, by refusing to concede points to his interlocutor, or to anticipate objections, or to consider alternatives; by developing "idiosyncratic" images, and providing details of self-relevant background, and elevating "subliminal ideas to consciousness," Achilles shows himself a master of language. Why, then, do his fellows consider him deficient in speaking? Because, of course, he does not speak to or for them. He is an absolute rule unto himself and though they might use him as a model by which to judge themselves, he uses none but himself to judge himself. This we call narcissism: one seeks not the completion of the self in the other, but the assurance and definition of the self in the mirror image(s) of the self in the other.

For Achilles language is a verbal mirror and the peculiar way he uses it shows that he does truly resent the double fact that his existence can only be defined by his function in a society of others, and in the terms which that society's language imposes upon him. He becomes a poet, as Redfield has seen, but not to make himself a negative exemplar of the heroic code, as Redfield has suggested; rather to make language work against the alienated reality that language creates, to redeem physical reality by reinvesting the lived-in world with fresh realization of his own existence.

Here we need to invoke Fränkel's law about attributing to a certain poet or philosopher in a certain period concepts that he does not yet have precise and dogmatic terminology to express. Friedrich and Redfield are aware of the phenomenological and existential dilemmas presented to man living in language, i.e., in a structure alien to himself and inadequate to accommodate his desired realization of himself. They think that Parry also had this awareness and because they can trace it back only to Rousseau, they refuse to allow Parry to project it all the way back to Homer and his character Achilles. I doubt that Fränkel himself would ever have allowed an extension of his principle to cover three millennia. I think that the Hegelian system, however, would accommodate it: in his intellectual history there is a constant return of philosophical insight at ever higher levels of discourse. One can see this in operation now, with the rediscovery of Rousseau by the structuralists: he simply prefigured their nostalgia for a lost stage of nondifferentiation, where communication is unnecessary because all desires are met internally. From a Freudian perspective this means the symbiotic stage in infantile development when a child views the mother as an extension of himself. From a structuralist perspective this means culture homologous with nature. From a religious perspective, this means the apotheosis of the female principle, i.e. Marianism and its various prefigurations.

It is instructive to recognize in Rousseau's nostalgia for a silent, desireless past, a prefiguration of the Russian formalists' concern for literature's capacity to restore the immediacy of concrete experience, that paradox, considered briefly above, of art-language canceling out the damaging distance which common language creates between man and his world,[5] and, of course, again, that anxiety of influence which poets feel in the face of previous poetry, particularly the poets of the Romantic Period, whose precursor we recognize in Rousseau.[6] The same problems in literary criticism keep emerging and being solved by ever more sophisticated, self-conscious critics, just as the same philosophical problems keep emerging and being solved by ever more refined and self-conscious philosophers. This should not surprise us, since there are some important constants in human experience and these are the very phenomena which poets, critics, and philosophers concern themselves with.

It is, of course, psychoanalysis which has particularly concerned itself with this "ahistorical" aspect of human experience. There have, however, been several recent attempts at psychoanalytic readings of the *Iliad*, or at least psychoanalytic suggestions for reading the *Iliad*, which, though helpful as a start, are also misleading, and these must be qualified before we can see what psychoanalysis has yet to reveal to us about the meaning always inherent in the poem, and appreciated there unconsciously by the naive reader, but never critically assessed. For even within psychoanalysis itself—more there than elsewhere, in fact—the standard models available for critical application to literature are insufficient for the *Iliad*. Preoccupation with the Oedipus complex and its consequential guilt have prevented analytically inclined critics from appreciating the *Iliad*'s focus on pre-oedipal problems and their social, political, and religious sublimations. Freudian theory that is exclusively oedipal in orientation takes us just as far from Achilles as Rousseau, Saussure, and Lévi-Strauss. We never refuse relevance to a philosophical or psychological insight because its fashionable date follows the date of the text under consideration; we simply refuse to allow any notion, of whatever date, to distort our text.

Simon is right to point out that the Homeric figures present us with memories of our childhood experiences of ourselves, but he is too willing to follow conventional criticism in insisting on distance:

The heroes are just close enough to us and human enough to serve as models, but sufficiently remote and superhuman that we need not require ourselves to reach their level. Such poems tell us what it was like in the old days, when men who were close to the gods, or even children of the gods, walked the earth. The old days are comfortably set in the long ago . . . either ancient times or the timelessness of childhood dreams.[7]

So, too, though he invokes Lacan's concept of *le stade du miroir*, he applies it not to the relationship between Achilles and Patroklos, or Achilles and Hektor, but strangely, perhaps trying to deal with the question of philosophical development which Snell raises, as a model of early "psychic identity." He compares the image in Lacan's mirror to the *psychē* which can exist passively in Hades, almost a *homunculus*, a pre-Platonic *daimōn*. Even so, Simon captures some of the hero's urge to define himself in active terms, to avoid *le corps morcelé* which Lacan so vividly describes as the child's most frightening fantasy: "the split-off or undesirable aspect of the self that may be represented in the *psychē* in Hades is the aspect that must endure passively. It is not unacceptable for a hero to be injured or aggrieved; but to be impotent or passive cannot be endured."[8]

Simon's description of the poetic process is attractive again in its emphasis on the resemblance to primary-process thinking, which we associate with children generally and only with dreams and art and neurosis in adults. He seems, however, to believe in epic as a kind of therapy, a coddling of the reader without his recognition of what is happening, almost as if epic affects in quite the opposite way from tragedy, which, through the raising to consciousness of pre-conscious intimations of unconscious desires, cleanses us not of those desires themselves, but at least of our need to deal with them soon again:

the experience of audience and poet can be considered an artistically controlled blurring of boundaries of the self or as a series of transient experiences of merging with the poem and with its characters . . . this blurring is more characteristic of childhood thinking and dreams than of adult and waking thinking . . . the poem's forms and content co-operate to induce transient modes of thinking and feeling that promise to restore us to a lost childhood state, a state of greater closeness with caring and protecting objects.[9]

This is simply not my experience of the *Iliad*. If anything, the reading of the *Iliad* brings us face to face with the fallacious basis of our own existence and denies us those very "caring and protecting objects" which we normally associate with others, because it shows us that others can never fulfill our desires, and even our images of ourselves are in the hands (and, as words, in the mouths) of others to mutilate and destroy.

I think it is Norman Holland writing on Shakespeare who comes closest to giving us a satisfactory psychoanalytic model for the reader's response, and he then goes on to explain how language is spontaneously produced by the emergence from the unconscious into the pre-conscious of desires, which even then cannot be expressed, since meaning, again, is a structure made up of dynamic relations among the different expressions of desire in the different levels of the mind, derived from the different stages of childhood development.

From a social point of view, then, the important satisfactions in literature are not of the ego's wish for mastery over the moral demands of the super-ego, but rather of the dark impulses of the id, the wildest drives of our earliest childhood, whose dissatisfaction necessarily lingers on. In participating as a group in the substitute gratification offered by art and literature, we gratify these impulses licitly, and we repeat their renunciation (as the work resolves itself); we identify with our cultural group and we reveal the ideals of our particular culture (SE 21. 14). In a very real sense, in our responses to literature, ontogeny recapitulates phylogeny; the individual reaction repeats the cultural subservience to reality.[10]

Again, the psychoanalytic critic seems to find solace, where the sensitive reader can only register anguish and despair. Shakespeare admittedly always sends in a Fortinbras to clean up the stage and bury the dead, but is this ever sufficient to convince us that the chaos of greed, lust, and violence we have witnessed is not, and always will be, seething in our breasts like the witches' cauldron that Macbeth can see at first, but only know at the end? We are slightly better satisfied, however, with Holland's later appeal to the principle of the "eternal return," ontogeny recapitulates phylogeny. Whereas here he uses it to suggest only the compromise formations that are simultaneously the history of the race and of the individual, he later implies its more immediately sensible manifestation in the text itself: "the larger chunks of action: plot, conflict, character configuration, come from the phallic or oedipal stage of childhood retained in the unconscious of the adult; the details of language and characterization seem to come from the earlier oral and anal stages of childhood."[11]

Though Holland's first application to art of the principle that ontogeny recapitulates phylogeny—the work of art reinforces the society's restrictions, so that the adult experiences in art again the limitations he first experienced as a child—congrues with such social and humanistic readings of the *Iliad* as those of Whitman, Havelock, and Redfield—society teaches through its art what it expects of its individuals—this leaves completely unaccounted for our identification with the suffering hero, which only Hegel seems to appreciate, when he paraphrases Homeric formulae in his discussion of art: "The content of the world of imagination . . . gathering round the individuality of some hero, who, however, feels the strength and splendour of his life broken, and mourns the early death he sees ahead of him."[12] In tragedy as in epic the psychological focus is the hero, and it is his world view (altered by our critical perspective, i.e., rendered self-conscious) that we accept as our own. Surely no responsible critic would argue that we are to listen to the tragic chorus' instructions: "Lie low and avoid disaster."

For Holland's second application to art of the principle that ontogeny recapitulates phylogeny, we argue only that for Homeric epic we need to make adjustments backwards, that not only the language, but the characters and plot itself are all pre-oedipal, and that any attempt to read oedipal concerns (like guilt) into the *Iliad* must fail. I suggest for the difference between epic and tragedy something similar to that suggested by Nagy as distinguishing cult from epic. He says that in epic the hero must die, whereas in cult he can be assimilated to the god and worshipped in that "heroic" form. In epic the hero chooses death because he cannot find in society (and the circumstances of society, originally language) space for his full existence; in tragedy the hero chooses death because society has convinced him of his own and society's collective guilt. Tragedy is a compromise formation of epic, just as the Oedipus complex is a compromise formation of primary narcissism.

Devereux begins in advance of Simon, recognizing that "empathy" with Homeric heroes is possible: "It is my thesis that the quality of a work of art—of a Homeric epic for example—is a direct consequence of its psychological realism, which makes interest in, and empathy with, the epic poem's personages and plot possible in the first place." His basic thesis is that Achilles commits suicide by killing Hektor: "the *figure* Achilles faced was far more than Hector in person only. It was also Patroclus impersonating Achilles—and therefore Achilles "himself.""[13]

Devereux therefore not only allows for the psychological plausibility of our identifying with Achilles—something conventional critics and previous psychoanalytic critics have been loath to do—but he recognizes that in Achilles' eyes both Patroklos and, by extension, Hektor also, are doubles of himself, the obvious conclusion to draw from the fact that all three, at one time or another, wear Achilles' armor— Patroklos and Hektor, significantly, when they are killed. (Though Nagy, in his philological and anthropological approach seems close to positing this tripartite identification, he does not in fact make it, being more concerned with the relations between men and gods than those between men and their self-images, nor does he suggest, as we must, that gods themselves, at any rate, are exactly and only that, i.e., men's self-images.)

Unfortunately, Devereux's recognition of Achilles' doubles in Patroklos and Hektor is bound up with his argument for Achilles' guilt over the death of Patroklos:

in attacking *Hector* (clad in *his* former armor) with an almost insane fury and arrogance, Achilles attacked *himself also* because of his guilt over Patroclus' doom. . . . . . In slaying a *Hector* disguised both as Patroclus impersonating Achilles *and* as Achilles himself, an almost insane Achilles punitively slaughters Hector, *so as not to slay himself for the wrong he himself had done to his alter-ego Patroclus.*[14]

The term "alter ego" has been used in previous discussions of the relations between Achilles and Patroklos,[15] but it is of questionable value when creating a critical model from psychoanalytic theory, since it cannot be used with the same precision as the terms "ideal ego,"

"ego ideal," "imago," and "self-object." For clinical terms to have critical significance they must be applied so as to suggest specific stages of development and positions within recognizable topographies. It is in the very paper "On Narcissism"—and Devereux goes on to speak of "a narcissist like Achilles"—and "Mourning and Melancholia" that Freud introduces the concept of the "ideal ego" and the possibility of a libidinal investment of this "object," which later, in Lacan, Mahler, Kohut, and Kernberg, becomes the basis for the whole post-Freudian theory of narcissism, with its concepts of imaginary objects and self-objects.

My contention is that for Achilles Patroklos is only a "self-object," or "partial object," barely distinguished from himself, and, far from feeling guilty for Patroklos' death, Achilles construes that event as the world's most serious and final affront against him, far more painful than Agamemnon's theft of Briseis, who is completely insignificant (in and of herself), if we define significance in terms of libidinal investment of a true object, recognizably distinct from the subject. I hope this objection will not seem too neatly multidimensional, but I find Devereux's discussion of Achilles too much in line with a model taken from ego psychology rather than Freudian depth psychology, and this is particularly inappropriate, in my view, since I do not see in Achilles a fully developed ego.

There is notoriously in the text no suggestion that Achilles feels guilt for the death of Patroklos.[16] Snell can, of course, tell us why: there is no secure center in the character, no self-consciousness of his own integrated being, that can bear such a burden. He rages against the Trojans and Nature not so as to find a "scape-goat upon whom to project his self-reproach" (Devereux), but to punish the world as he sees it for denying him assurance of his own continued existence in the continued existence of his dear friend Patroklos. While it is true that Hektor is an aggressively invested self-object of Achilles, as we shall soon see, and in this sense can be called a scapegoat for Achilles' wrath—if we accept Girard's definition of scapegoat as a double chosen for the mediation of aggressive energy that would otherwise disintegrate its social or individual source—guilt has nothing to do with it, nor with any such crisis in epic poetry, where heroes are obviously, in our eyes, "responsible" for their dear male companions' deaths, but are quite incapable of conceiving such responsibility themselves, nor of being blamed for it by their victims. Think only of Gilgamesh and Enkidu, and Roland and Oliver. The whole point of such poems is to celebrate the hero and so great is the centripetal force he creates that no secondary considerations are possible. We must watch as he struggles to create himself in his own image (often projected onto subordinate characters who are more socialized than he can ever become) and then, as he dies, frustrated of achieving success, in a rage of resentment. This is suicide, but by no means the result of guilt, which is the stuff that tragedy, not epic, is made on.

I.6
FREUD AND HIS FOLLOWERS

 "Interdisciplinary studies" are seldom satisfying because conventionally they tend to use a few insights simplified from one theoretical model against some other model or pre-critical text, i.e., poem, play, or whatever. The best possible result is a brief perception, but then the two intellectual constructs settle back down into their own self-relevent obscurity, having been completely unchanged structurally by the critical operation. It seems to me that to speak, for instance, of anal erotism in the character of Shylock does no great service to either the theory or the character, unless it can be shown that the whole structure of *The Merchant of Venice* is informed by full appreciation of the phenomenon of anal erotism so that the play then seems almost incomprehensible without that appreciation. Otherwise one is simply being clever and entrepreneureal, hardly the serious critic.

What I want to attempt here is a brief description of what I consider to be a critical model, which economically, but not exhaustively, explains our response to the *Iliad*. Though my approach is defined by the psychoanalytic concept of narcissism, I can only suggest the difference between Kohut's position and Kernberg's; also beyond the scope of this study is any sort of integration of either of these relatively empirical American studies with the dazzling conceptual play of Lacan. In other words, I enter into the various debates between Freud and post-Freudian theorists only where the issues touch on the *Iliad*. All I can do is build my own naive definition of narcissism from the various psychoanalytic texts, thus creating a critical model appropriate to the subject of my criticism.

Freud's own discussion of narcissism is focused in the essay of 1914, "On Narcissism: An Introduction." This piece has recently taken a position of importance in the total *oeuvre* second only to the revolutionary larger studies: *The Interpretation of Dreams* (1900), *Beyond the Pleasure Principle* (1920), and *The Ego and the Id* (1923). The most important concept developed in the essay for the theory of psychoanalysis is that there can be libidinal investment of the ego., i.e., that the ego can choose itself for its own object. It is important that early in this very essay Freud draws attention to the development of the ego, so that when he proceeds to compare infantile narcissism (a "normal" developmental stage) with later (if extreme, then perverse) narcissism, we have already laid out before us the ontology of the ego. Clearly, if we speak of the ego choosing itself for its own object at any early stage in childhood development, we are speaking *ex post facto*, in anticipation of the future constitution.[1]

How can the ego libidinally invest itself before it exists? Freud avoids the metaphysical implications of this question (i.e., that the ego is always already there) by directing his attention to ego instincts and their relation with the sexual instincts, as if such instinctual drives have authority independent of their intra-psychic agents. (Of course, *das Ich* and *das Id* are only officially accepted into the Freudian conceptual system nine years later. In all of our discussion we can weigh two ontogenies against each other: the beginnings of psychic functions in each individual's development and the beginnings of these concepts in Freud's development of psychoanalytic theory.)

The sexual instincts are at the outset attached to the satisfaction of the ego-instincts; only later do they become independent of these, and even then we have an indication of that original attachment in the fact that the persons who are concerned with a child's feeding, care, and protection become his earliest sexual objects; that is to say, in the first instance his mother or a substitute for her. Side by side, however, with this type and source of object-choice, which may be called the "anaclitic" or "attachment" type, psychoanalytic research has revealed a second type which we were not prepared for finding. We have discovered, especially clearly in people whose libidinal development has suffered some disturbance, such as perverts and homosexuals, that in their later choice of love-objects they have taken as a model not their mother but their own selves. They are plainly seeking themselves as a love-object, and are exhibiting a type of object-choice which must be termed "narcissistic." In this observation we have the strongest of the reasons which have led us to adopt the hypothesis of narcissism.[2]

Among the analyses of "perverts and homosexuals" here referred to is the famous Schreber case, another work extremely influential in later psychoanalytic theory, especially Lacan's. In this individual Freud found a fascinating combination of megalomania, paranoia, and homosexuality, which he tentatively identified as the psychic residue of an abnormally resolved Oedipus complex. With Ferenczi, his disciple, he concluded, rather simplistically, that paranoia by definition is fear of the discovery of homosexual inclinations, and megalomania an unconscious attempt to fortify the threatened ego against hallucinated attacks of disapproval. All this is later worked out in the "third topography," where the superego is introduced and described as the massively introjected remnant of the Oedipus complex.[3] If we project that conception back upon the earlier discussions of Schreber and narcissism, we see the consistency of Freud's thinking about pre-oedipal and oedipal choice of object. Certainly in the oedipal stage, if the father is as much object of desire as he is model for identification, then the result can be the introjection of a figure who condemns for being desired, i.e., the object of desire, or the model for future objects of desire, is the father rather than the mother, and the father, as representative of the collective opinion of the past, condemns his son for making the wrong choice.[4] If this drama is played out earlier, in the pre-oedipal period, it is not the father as "sexual" object, but the child's choice of himself that disorients his later object-choice. This is not a "sexual" choice, just as the alternative choice of the mother would not be a "sexual" choice, but rather it is a demand made by the ego instincts for the child's own preservation. Strachey, in a long note on his translation of *Anlehnungstypus* as "anaclitic type," explains that Freud here does not suggest that the child chooses between himself as object and a mother he can "lean on," but rather that the choice itself of the mother, if it is made, is a "leaning-on type" of choice, since the child's only interest at this point is self-preservation.

It might seem that we are attempting a distinction here which contradicts Freud's position in this essay and, further, strikes at the very roots of his whole system, i.e., infantile sexuality. We do not deny its operation from birth itself; in fact, our whole study could be subtitled "The Erotic Basis of Ontogeny in the *Iliad*." The distinction that we make—and this is implicit in Freud—is simply between libidinal investment of the self and libidinal investment of another object. Freud posits these two types of erotic choice as simultaneous possibilities, but we insist that there must be some consolidation of the self-image before external object-choice is possible. Freud himself distinguishes autoerotism, which is universal, from the narcissistic choice made by only a few. Sulloway discusses this briefly as one of the "Three Inconsistencies in Psychoanalytic Theory (1910–20)."[5]

I think the best way to see the whole problem is from that perspective which seems so Hegelian in Freud, but which in fact he takes from contemporary theories of biological evolution: any stage of development maintained beyond its normal course is considered a perversion. Thus, below, we shall speak of homosexuality as if it were a fixation in or a regression to the stage of primary narcissism. Certainly the economics of the theory of the libido—the famous figure of the amoeba putting out its pseudopodia to attach a piece of foreign matter—implies that the libidinal investment of a true object is possible only for an integrated ego. The ego which lacks consolidation (secure self-image) must be constantly investing itself with all available libidinal energy in order to remain functional. Achilles is engaged in this very struggle.

The question then arises, how can the child choose himself as object at a point in his development when the very existence of himself is theoretically difficult to assess? Attempts to answer this question account for a large proportion of post-Freudian psychoanalytic research and metapsychology. It is clear that Freud himself had no clear opinion on the matter, and candidly admitted at different points in his career his inability to conceive of the dynamics of this early process: ontogenesis of the ego through the orientation of desire. It has been suggested that Freud lacked a truly dialectical system of thinking, that his concept of negation (*Verneinung*) is the negative pole in Hegel's opposition, which defines the positive (we "know" what the unconscious does not want known), but, of course, there is no transcendent knowledge, either of the unconscious itself, which has no content, nor of a reconciliation between this and what the ego (or superego) allows to be known.

We need to ask Freud whether he recognizes a transcendental subject, or a third movement in the dialectic which defines the notion of the self in terms of the Other. This, of course, is in anticipation of our contention that Patroklos and Hektor both represent seemingly contradictory moments in the notion of Achilles' self (or Achilles' notion of himself). Some sort of resolution is reached, a transcendental moment (or moment to resolve the contradictions of other moments) or ultimate revelation of the notion of Achilles, but not to himself, even in his final confrontation with Priam, only to us who see the action of the *Iliad* from our superior position outside and beyond, looking back self-consciously in appreciation of what is happening to him, because it has already happened to each of us. In face of the ever-present Thetis, we need to know what part the absent Peleus (with his surrogates Phoinix and Priam and Nestor) plays. Is there the slightest suggestion of oedipal conflict in the *Iliad* or are we dealing with the primal drama of the pre-oedipal attempt at ontology (perhaps, rather, the ontic attempt which is pre-oedipal, and later only "realized" through the *logos* of the oedipal conflict)?

Certainly we must make clear that any transcendental "realization" of self we claim for Achilles is conceptually possible only for us and not even for Homer. Because of the narrative structure of the poem we see the pieces of Achilles' psyche coalescing in a self-defining movement. If we speak of Achilles in and of himself in that last interview with Priam, then the only affect we can mention is weariness and confusion and nostalgia. His two doubles are dead: is there anything left to him of them? We have watched his struggle to assimilate them to him, but it has not been successful (and Hegel and Freud tell us why) and he will die from the arrow of the man who stole another man's woman, wounded where his mother failed to protect him, a death both ironic and inevitable, but not tragic: he will not know who he is or why he must die. (*Peripateia* without *anagnōrisis* is not tragic.) We know he is a man who has pursued the image of himself in a world which cannot substantiate that image and that he has died because death is the only end to such unanswerable, ineffable desire.

I must now quote again at great length from Freud's essay "On Narcissism" in order to establish what I believe to be a distinction, in the evolution of his concept of the superego, between the ideal ego and ego ideal. For me it represents the difference between a pre-oedipal image and that oedipal image which Freud later saw as incorporating the whole complex system of identifications and desires which we know as oedipal (or post-oedipal):

We have learnt that libidinal instinctual impulses undergo the vicissitudes of pathogenic repression if they come into conflict with the subject's cultural and ethical ideas. By this we never mean that the individual in question has a merely intellectual knowledge of the existence of such ideals; we always mean that he recognizes them as a standard for himself and submits to the claims they make on him. Repression, we have said, proceeds from the ego; we might say with greater precision that it proceeds from the self-respect of the ego. The same impressions, experiences, impulses and desires that one man indulges or at least works over consciously will be rejected with the utmost indignation by another, or even stifled before they enter consciousness. The difference between the two, which contains the conditioning factor of repression, can easily be expressed in terms which enable it to be explained by the libido theory. We can say that the one man has set up an ideal in himself by which he measures his actual ego, while the other has formed no such ideal. For the ego the formation of an ideal would be the conditioning factor of repression. (SE, 14:93–94)

We pause here to note that Freud is pursuing one of the three themes (according to Sulloway)[6] with which he was preoccupied throughout his life, repression, and that this has little, seemingly, to do with our interest in the intra-psychic positioning of an image for the ego to assimilate towards, let alone with the relations between Achilles and Patroklos. It is also questionable whether Freud's discussion of what seem to be psychic processes in the mature male can have anything to do with the model of childhood development which we shall eventually present as an analogue of the *Iliad*. What we do note, however, is Freud's conception of a dynamic relation between the ideal ego and the "actual" ego. We have already recognized the difficulty in pinpointing the exact stage in childhood development when we can speak accurately of an existent actual ego.

In spite of the fact that Freud's first description of the ideal ego recalls the Homeric *psychē* (as defined by Simon) and the Platonic *daimōn* (i.e., pre-Freudian manifestations of intra-psychic guardians), we insist that he struggles here with a more original notion, that he forces his text into contradiction with its own hypothesis, as threatened from the outset of the essay: "One dislikes the thought of abandoning observations for barren theoretical controversy, but nevertheless one must not shirk an attempt at clarification." Is this "dialogue" between the actual ego and the ideal ego purely monitory, purely in the negative mode of repression? Does the ideal ego only tell the ego that it is not good enough, is not doing the right thing, is not itself?

Freud proceeds to define the relationship between these two "agents" in precisely erotic terms and we begin to see ontogenesis as a function of the identification between identification and desire:

This ideal ego is now the target of the self-love which was enjoyed in childhood by the actual ego. The subject's narcissism makes its appearance displaced onto this new ideal ego, which, like the infantile ego, finds itself possessed of every perfection that is of value. As always, where the libido is concerned, man has here again shown himself incapable of giving up a satisfaction he has once enjoyed. He is not willing to forego the narcissistic perfection of his childhood; and when, as he grows up, he is disturbed by the admonitions of others and by the awakening of his own critical judgement, so that he can no longer retain that perfection, he seeks to recover it in his new form of an ego ideal. What he projects before him as his ideal is the substitute for the lost narcissism of his childhood in which he was his own ideal. (*SE*, 14:94)

There is nostalgia, then, in this formation: the ego, whenever formed, creates an image of itself in its pristine perfection, before compromise sets in, before objects begin to be lost to it (or won and rejected), before there is conscious (verbally articulated) distinction between the principles of pleasure and reality. Can we, perhaps, though Freud himself is inconsistent here and noncommittal later, distinguish between an ideal ego that is perfection, or at least the memory—which may be necessarily false—of the lost perfection of the self-in-formation and this monitory agency which later in the Freudian corpus yields place to the new nomenclature and becomes the superego?[7]

It is frightening to see how quickly Freud slips into discussion of the negative device, forgetting all the excitement, though fraught with frustration, of the desired identification between the two other elements of (the stages of the development of) the ego. Suddenly we are hearing of "conscience," "the critical influence of parents," and "the innumerable and indefinable list of all the other people in his environment—his fellow men—and public opinion" (SE, 14:91). What has become of narcissism? Is it, almost by definition, a stage-specific orientation, which, if maintained, is perverse—or inverse? We return to a consideration of paranoia and the voices that the ego hears, and we see emerge a new concept, "homosexual libido," and a process which seems strangely (perversely) like Adler's "masculine protest," which Freud had earlier in the essay dismissed as an inadequate hypothesis to cover all the neuroses (SE, 14:92).

In this way large amounts of libido of an essentially homosexual kind are drawn into the formation of the narcissistic ego ideal and find outlet and satisfaction in maintaining it. The institution of conscience was at bottom an embodiment, first of parental criticism, and subsequently of that of society— a process which is repeated in what takes place when a tendency towards repression develops out of a prohibition or obstacle that came in the first instance from without. The voices, as well as the undefined multitude, are brought into the foreground again by the disease, and so the evolution of conscience is reproduced regressively. But the revolt against this "censoring agency" arises out of the subject's desire (in accordance with the fundamental character of the illness) to liberate himself from all these influences, beginning with the parental ones, and out of his withdrawal of homosexual libido from them. His conscience then confronts him in a regressive form as a hostile influence from without. (SE, 14:96)

When we finally reach a consideration of the possible influence that recapitulation of the original "choice" between narcissistic and anaclitic objects might have, we begin to understand how the concept of homosexual libido has been introduced: "We say that a human being has originally two objects—himself and the woman who nurses him— and in doing so we are postulating a primary narcissism in everyone, which may in some cases manifest itself in a dominating fashion in his object-choice" (SE, 14:98).

Of course, the manifestation, in a dominating fashion, of homosexual object-choice, is for the narcissistically inclined. When we then come to an attempt to maintain such object-choice in the face of social pressure, Freud has an economic explanation: the subject has originally identified himself with himself (chosen himself as object); he then chooses others like himself as objects, trying to restore the early idealized image of himself. This includes, in oedipal terms, the father, but the father is also the "censoring agent," so we have a very basic kind of "identification with the aggressor." We are back to Schreber, the paranoid, homosexual megalomaniac.

Freud even suggests, in another reference to the Schreber case, that such types are characterized by a tendency "to construct speculative systems," and one thinks of the Platonic *erastēs*. Certainly philosophical speculation must be associated with Lacan's *le stade du miroir*. It is a continuation of that attempt to find the self in the lost perfect image of the self which the original mirror, the mother, provided, a fleeting glimpse of wholeness before recognition of lack and the onset of desire forces one into a system of variations, sexual and sublimated, upon the themes of deprivation and disappointment.

Freud tries to sum up his discussion of the erotic basis of self-esteem in a paragraph that is more suggestive than definitive:

The relations of self-regard to erotism—that is, to libidinal object-cathexes—may be expressed concisely in the following way. Two cases must be distinguished, according to whether the erotic cathexes are ego-syntonic, or, on the contrary, have suffered repression. In the former case (where the use made of the libido is ego-syntonic), love is assessed like any other activity of the ego. Loving in itself, in so far as it involves longing and deprivation, lowers self-regard; whereas being loved, having one's love returned, and possessing the loved object, raises it once more. When libido is repressed, the erotic cathexis is felt as a severe depletion of the ego, the satisfaction of love is impossible, and the re-enrichment of the ego can be effected only by withdrawal of libido from its objects. The return of the object-libido to the ego and its transformation into narcissism represents, as it were, a happy love once more; and, on the other hand, it is also true that a real happy love corresponds to the primal condition in which object-libido and ego-libido cannot be distinguished. (SE, 14:99–100)

Again we note that the argument proceeds simultaneously along conceptual and developmental paths. Whereas we had begun by considering first the ego's investment of its own image of itself, and then moved to the series of its attempts to project that image upon others, now we no longer hear about such purely intrapsychic processes or their interpsychic approximations, but only about love that is freely given to another and received in return, as opposed to love that is repressed and leaves the ego depleted. Freud thus takes for granted that primary narcissism must be abandoned and that homosexuality, which is described as the "natural" heir to primary narcissism, will of necessity be repressed (we recall the model of the "desired father" who condemns), so that the only possible way for the ego to sustain itself in later life is through a reciprocal, heterosexual ("anaclitic") relation with another person.

This development reminds us, of course, of Hegel's insistence that only two self-conscious subjects can establish their mutual reality, that the "master-slave" relationship is unsatisfactory (where the subject absorbs the object) as is as well the "unhappy consciousness" (because its independence is an allusion) and the *schöne Seele*, which tries to project its reality upon the world, is simply suffering from the pathetic fallacy. I do not think it misleading to mix terminologies and suggest that both Freud and Hegel insist upon an investment of the world-in-and-of-itself, since solipsistic orientation of desire is self-destructive, and narcissism is only a stage, phylogenetically and ontogenetically, through which we must pass.

The essay "On Narcissism" as a whole seems to be directed toward the establishment of the ego ideal and its role of denying to the subject certain objects of desire through the operation of the superego (the heir, both in the child's development and in Freud's thinking, to the ego ideal), which creates guilt out of castration anxiety; the narcissistic object is never denied, but compromised in a succession of stages, one of them being the oedipal conflict itself, which validates the mother as object of desire for the son. The original pre-oedipal narcissistic choice is retrospectively reformulated as the secondary, oedipal, anaclitic choice—and ends with the stipulation:

[The ego ideal] binds not only a person's narcissistic libido, but also a considerable amount of his homosexual libido, which is in this way turned back into the ego. The want of satisfaction which arises from the non-fulfillment of this ideal liberates homosexual libido, and this is transformed into a sense of guilt (social anxiety). (*SE*, 14:101–02)

The world as he comes to know it then denies to the child his original choice of himself as object, but he retains this "ideal object" nostalgically constituted: always at the core of his self-consciousness will be a lack, a desire for a former self. This is all so close to Heidegger's description of the human condition that we cannot refuse a comparison, however inadequate. For both thinkers *Angst* and *Schuld* somehow restore the lost authenticity of life. Certainly Freud's castration anxiety—the threatened end of desire—must be associated with Heidegger's validation of the fear of death. Awareness of the being of *Dasein* (its limitation) is the critical concept of "heroic humanism": men in the *Iliad* are superior to the gods because death, as a limit to their existence, gives meaning to their experience.

The world as such must take that original narcissistic object's place, and the world is constituted as object through the intermediacy of the oedipal object, the mother. "Authentic" life can only be lived, then, in the world, as constituted primarily by language, but Heidegger refuses a purely constitutive role to the self-conscious use of language. Again we come to the equation of the child as "literally *infans*" with the human being's only true experience of Being. "Authenticity" is in Heidegger, as in Lévi-Strauss, but a nostalgia for lost innocence, the self as originally constituted or coming-into-being. Only Hegel remained convinced that Being, in the form of Absolute Spirit, *required* (rather than was contradicted by) the philosophical process, which is possible only in that form of language which makes us conscious of the world as Other. Heidegger's recourse to poetic expression is an indication of his dissatisfaction with the subject-object dichotomy. What Hegel had used dialectic to overcome, Heidegger used poetry to deny. In postulating the death drive Freud shows a similar tendency to dissolve the subject. If the oedipal object is the focus of the pleasure principle, then it has the same aim, i.e., reunion with the mother, although unlike the "perverse" regression of the death drive, the pleasure principle fully constitutes the self as subject in relation to its object. In this way we see inhibitions socially imposed as a double-bind: the child is denied both the un-self-conscious bliss of symbiosis and the self-conscious (though unconscious) choice of the oedipal object.

We might say, however, that there is repressed content in the essay "On Narcissism," which emerges in the recognition that the lost stage of narcissism itself is the focus of nostalgic desire, and that it is this nostalgia that makes every subsequent object-choice truly unsatisfactory. Paradoxically, the ego ideal, which is the model against which the ego judges itself, is itself the socially validated correction of the ideal ego, that perfect image of the self, from the forced renunciation of which the ego never recovers. We then recognize that Freud suggests for the pre-oedipal stage (the period of primary narcissism) an originary object-choice (the idealized image of the self) after which all other objects will be second-best, just as he insists that after the oedipal conflict the mother will remain as the model against which all other objects will be found inadequate. What Freud refuses to say—because of his tendency to project the oedipal conflict back into the pre-oedipal period—is that the narcissistic choice of object, because primary, is truly originary of the oedipal choice of object. In other words, the child does not have originally two choices of object—himself and the woman who tends him—but only one, himself, if he is to become a self, and all else is compromise, including the anaclitic choice itself, and certainly the later, analogous, oedipal choice. Loss of "authentic" self at such an early age is loss of Being, and its restoration seems impossible. I think we shall find that this lies as much behind Freud's formulation of the death drive as the biological imperative to repeat or regress. All that psychoanalysis offers in compensation—as opposed to the nostalgia of Lévi-Strauss and Heidegger—is what Hegel offers, self-conscious realization of the loss. Clearly, the *Iliad* is another major text to be considered alongside these models. It also presents man defined only by death and a succession of false objects or partial or self-objects, with no compromise offered in the libidinal investment of the world as Other. Death is here the end of desire for the perfect image of the self, not an inducement to the formation of a community of suffering under the aegis of collective guilt. The *Iliad* is a pre-oedipal drama.

So central is the Oedipus complex to Freud's thinking that he projects it backwards upon the screen of pre-oedipal experience, and so compelling is his influence that psychoanalysts tend to see only that image still, rather than seek behind it a ghost of a different image, a *totally* narcissistic drama played out by the child upon the psychical field which the mother supplies, but in no way involving her (investing her) as object. Even Lacan, whose *stade du miroir* we keep referring to and must eventually face into, though he takes Freud's thinking much further along the path towards the phenomenological beginnings of the ego, sees everything, at that early age, in terms of the oedipal triangle, to which he adds a fourth "member," of course, the ideal of the ego, which is also the child's identification of his ego through the identification of the parental *imago*.[8] Not only does Lacan reckon on the extremely early libidinal investment of the mother, but also, and inevitably, on the aggressive investment of the father.[9] The Oedipus complex is always already there. Only René Girard, who disingenuously denies psychoanalysis as a formative influence upon his thinking, presents us with a triangle which makes sense for early childhood and the *Iliad*: desire is a function of rivalry, suggesting that if the father's presence is not strongly felt by the male child, the mother will never be validated as object of desire. Girard applies this critical model, stripped of its oedipal nomenclature, to French and Russian novels, going so far as to claim that the novel as genre demands the death of the hero because almost by definition the hero must finally recognize the mimetic, i.e., non-originary, nature of desire, and without desire there is only death. In fact, there is a desire for death, another and later Freudian principle, which we must deal with in more detail.[10]

If all this is true, then we must follow all those other critics who have seen in the *Iliad* the first novel, for clearly Thetis is omnipresent, Peleus is absent, and Achilles shows no interest in Thetis, or any other woman, except in the context of rivalry with other men, and seeks death when he is deprived of his dear friend Patroklos, who has provided, as a mirror, the assurance he requires of his own continued existence, a locus of desire, and, of course, in a complex manner yet to be explained, Hektor provides that same assurance.

It is impossible to explain the congestion of Freud's thought in the opening pages of *Beyond the Pleasure Principle* when he describes the *Fort!—Da!* game of his grandson.[11] He is working toward the formulation of the death drive through an examination of the phenomenon of repetition compulsion. The concept of the superego, whereby the entire oedipal experience is introjected by the child to form an intrapsychic agency of almost totally negative operation, is not yet fully developed. Nevertheless, through the ego ideal as defined in the essay "On Narcissism," the child is thought of already as unconsciously—and preconsciously—aware of all the prohibitions of his family and race, and specifically, because of the castration anxiety that initiates the period of latency, psychically aware that he can never possess the mother but must at best be satisfied with a substitute, because the father will not relinquish the mother—nor could the son satisfy her were she available to him—and the father is thus envied to such an extent that he himself, in a way slightly different from that previous, becomes the model for future object-choice.

The constitution of the superego from the oedipal experience is the final capitulation of the child to his existence in a world of delayed gratification and compromise formations. Not only can he hope only for an image of the mother, but he can also hope only for an image of the power of the father. If the phallos reveals anything in contemporary analytic theory, it must mean this distance. Like the actors in Greek comedy and satyr-play who wore leather appendages and did not expose their own genitals (drama is not reality), so the child, through fear of castration, suffers the replacement of that reality (his double desire) by the symbolism of a psychic drama in which he is not even the leading character. This tragedy becomes all the more poignant when we look forward to it rather than backwards from it, by seeing the oedipal drama not as played finally after rehearsal in the pre-oedipal period, but as played first in the oedipal period after the even more painful loss of self in the mirror stage. With the final development of the concept of the superego, then, Freud confronts his grandson's confrontation of the mirror and requires the death drive to be always already in operation, but here the development of Freud's thinking and the development of the child, in their parallelism, distort each other. The father is not a strong presence in the pre-oedipal period, before the development of the superego, and the mother is desired only in her absence.

Sulloway has recently shown how thoroughly Freud's conscious and unconscious dedication to the biological theories prevalent when he was a student continued to form his metapsychology, and this is, of course, particularly true of the theory of the death drive. Is it not equally true that the formulation of the death drive was necessitated by Freud's growing awareness of the contradictions inherent in the dynamics of human desire? Certainly most contemporary Freudian analysts would argue this,[12] and it is this aspect of Freud's intellectual development which has appealed most to contemporary nonanalytic interest. Contemporary literary theorists are familiar with Lacan's distinction between *désir* and *demande,* what we deeply want and need as opposed to what the linguistic structure in which we define ourselves allows us to express. Repetition compulsion is the pathology Freud addresses, and "biological" compulsion to return to inanimate origins is the model to which he assimilates his analysis.[13] Again, though, the subtext is simultaneously erotic and philosophical: "it is the difference in amount between the pleasure of satisfaction which is demanded and that which is actually achieved that provides the driving factor which will permit of no halting at any position attained."[14]

This is how he explains the natural biological process—every organism with its own characteristic route—to death. Again we must predict our own now proximate consideration of Lacan to see with him in this gap between demand and desire the *glissement* of the signifier over the signified. We shall not, however, follow Lacan into further consideration of the phallos as the signifier of signifiers, but rather insist once more that the child's compulsion to repeat is not so much due to genetic encoding or anal sadism or his hallucinations at any stage of himself as the object of his mother's desire or her, necessarily, as his, but rather the attempt to convince himself, specularly, albeit painfully, of his own existence. His demand—because only in the absence of the self as object is desire for the self felt—is for the self that the mirror of his reality projects to him, but his desire is for the self which he always already nostalgically considers his lost authentic self; the mother is only the mirror[15] and the presence of the father need not be nearly so strongly felt as Freudian psychology has always assumed. Without the rivalry of the father, the mother is not constituted as the child's object of desire. Instead, because of her infinite availability, he desires himself and demands from her that image of himself which she alone can provide. Is this not Achilles on the beach calling to Thetis after his argument with Agamemnon? And is it not, too, two hundred years later, Pelops calling to his mother-substitute Poseidon in a similar situation in Pindar's *Olympian I?* As we shall see, not only does ontogeny recapitulate phylogeny, but Greek erotic history recapitulates in its stages, with culture-specificity, our own ontogeny, as we see ourselves develop in it.

P. Slater has studied the absent-father syndrome with a focus primarily upon the phenomenon of misogyny in Athens in the fifth century.[16] He uses the term "oral-narcissistic dilemma" to cover that complex of contradictory desires which characterizes the mother-son relationship when there is no male figure to mediate the inherent tensions between them. The child depends upon the mother for sustenance and self-definition, but it is equally definition as limitation that he fears. Trying to take his absent father's place and placate his mother's resentment of his being male like her husband who has deserted her, he constantly over-achieves. The glory of Hera is that she has perverted Zeus' bastard son into heroism. But what again if the father is not even there in resentment? What if the mother's demands from the son are not for the sexual satisfaction denied her by the father, but only for the son's own fulfillment of his seemingly infinite potential? What, that is, becomes of the son of a goddess who left her mortal husband rather than being left by him? What of the totally benevolent mother whose erotic life has been full, but whose energy is now graciously expended in her son's service? What of the psychosexual context in which active misogyny plays no part, but women are seen simply as passive possessions for men to fight over?

If the *Iliad* is convincing, then we must believe in the psychological reality of a mother who is *tabula rasa* for her son's coming-into-being. Unlike Freud's grandson, Achilles never faces the lack of his mother, nor must he ever use an actual mirror to remind himself of his continued existence. She is always there, and so is not the object of his desire. The object of his desire is himself and his demand is for his dear friend Patroklos. We do not imagine Patroklos, as Achilles' ideal ego, being invested by Achilles' homosexual libido, for two reasons: there is no condemnatory agency to inhibit his love of Patroklos— Achilles has never developed a superego, since he has had no oedipal experience—and homosexuality is inconceivable outside a context of misogyny. I think I am right to insist here on this distinction, though it might be false if we read "homosexual libido" only in terms of its context in the essay "On Narcissism," where it is presented as a protection for the ego against the threat of unanswered desire. The ego invests itself libidinally—or the idealized image of itself—in compensation for the depletion felt in the unsatisfactory investment of an external object. The age of the subject discussed is not clear; presumably he is post-oedipal. I would like to reserve the term "homosexual," as I have the term "guilt," for post-oedipal formations and object-choices. Thus I must, at a later point, carefully qualify my comparison between Achilles' appeal to Thetis in Homer and Pelops' appeal to Poseidon in Pindar. Finally, I hope to establish homosexuality as specific historically in Greek culture, generically in Greek literature (it is not an epic concern) and, of course, developmentally in human experience.

Our attempt, then, is to claim for the *Iliad* a situation comparable to that described by Freud as the child's first experience of himself as his own object, the narcissistic choice of object which we hypothesize as being likely when the mother herself is infinitely available. Guilt, misogyny, and homosexuality have no place there; they are all later and mutually contingent developments. We know, of course, guilt as a product of the normal resolution of the Oedipus complex. The son feels first fear of castration because he would take the mother from the father, and then guilt, the fantasized punishment somehow ratifying the criminality of the desire. Of course, Freud postulates a similar beginning of guilt when the male child takes his father as object: the desired object and condemning agent are the same. Our interest, however, is in the earlier stage, when the self is not yet constituted, and desire is only for the self. There is no place here for guilt. There can be the beginnings of misogyny, of course, as Slater has argued, but only if the son is the target for the mother's resentment of the absent father. This leaves us finally with the possibility of homosexual tendencies being established by the absence of the father, i.e., the son accepting for his own object of desire the mother's object of desire. This is clearly not the case in the *Iliad*, as we shall see. Thetis resents the fact that marriage with a mortal was imposed upon her and feels only pity for the weak and aged Peleus back home in Phthia.

Although Freud concerned himself with the causes and varieties of homosexuality throughout his career, he never claimed that psycho-analysis offered an economic explanation for it. In a footnote added in 1915 to "The Sexual Aberrations," he does describe pederasty as an attempt to recapture the youthful object of the mother's desire, i.e., the mature male seeks in a younger male the image of his own younger

self, presumably thereby reestablishing nostalgically a blissful closeness to the mother.[17] Again, the emphasis on the desire for the lost
intimacy with the mother, and the maturity of the subject himself
make this model inappropriate to the *Iliad*.

We do not, of course, claim that the *Iliad*, in its presentation of the
relationship between Achilles and Patroklos, preserves an accurate
memory of pre-oedipal experience. All memories of all stages of development are "interpreted" by the experience of later stages: thus we
account for the oedipal aspect of the conflict with Agamemnon. Our
insistence on a distinction between pre-oedipal narcissism and post-
oedipal homosexuality has a foundation in Freud's own work, as we
have seen, and we shall see that Lacan and other post-Freudian analysts are much more interested in the former than the latter. Our real
problem comes with texts such as Plato's *Symposium*, where the character Phaidros disputes Aeschylus' interpretation of the relationship
between Achilles and Patroklos. Aeschylus took Achilles for the *erastēs*
and Patroklos for the *erōmenos*, but Phaidros insists that since Achilles
was indisputably the younger and more beautiful of the two, it has to
be the the other way around.[18]

Obviously Aeschylus was right from the fifth-century Athenian perspective, and certainly the more sensitive reader of Homer. He saw
that Achilles was the center of attention in the poem, the "active"
partner as it were. Phaidros applies too stringently the pattern of later
Greek pederasty, not taking into account Patroklos' social and martial
inferiority, which more than offsets his being older than Achilles. The
whole debate, however, is held from a distant literary and historical
and social perspective, which, I maintain, changes the psychological
significance of the original material. Achilles' love for Patroklos is
structurally similar to the love of an *erastēs* for an *erōmenos*, but it is
a different moment in that developing notion. Patroklos is not a true
object, but only a partial object. The whole focus of the *Iliad* is not
on Achilles and Patroklos as a couple, but on Achilles' use of Patroklos
in his struggle to define himself. If it is argued, in turn, as Vlastos
has,[19] that there is something unpleasantly selfish about Platonic love,
and, by association, the whole pattern of Greek homosexuality, that
the *erastēs* has no interest in the *erōmenos* as a separate and equal
human being, but only as a stimulus to his own desire, then, again,

I must admit this as a structural similarity between Homer and Plato. It would be foolish to fall back on the position that the *Iliad* is obviously about more than a homosexual relationship, since it has appeal to a larger audience than those readers of that orientation. The same could be said about Plato. Of course, all of these arguments would seem unnecessary to the reader convinced that the *erastēs-erōmenos* relationship is only of parenthetical interest in the Platonic *Symposium*, *Phaidros*, and other dialogues where it is openly discussed and used as a model for philosophical speculation. I could never be convinced of that; Platonic metaphysics is inconceivable outside that pattern. Plato did not simply take as metaphor from a historical accident of Athenian social life this phenomenon which seems so strange to us; he did not use it just to titillate his youthful and aristocratic audience, the erotic equivalent of sugar-coating the bitter pill of philosophical instruction. It is, rather, integral and original to his thinking. A good indication of this is the difficulty which the neo-Platonist Church Fathers had in adapting Plato's theories to a body of religious dogma that was gradually becoming centered on Mary, the virgin mother, into whose keeping the devotee delivered up his hopes of salvation, i.e., from a narcissistically oriented philosophy ("know thyself") evolved an anaclitic religion ("lose thyself in the mother").

If all of this is already there in Homer, how is Homer different? He is certainly not so different from Plato as Plato is from Augustine, but he is significantly different: his characters in the *Iliad*, paradigmatically represented by Achilles, are engaged in a more "primitive" struggle than the Platonic banqueters.[20] We can say superficially that they are fighting a war and therefore do not have time for such foolishness as Alcibiades indulges in, but depth-psychology demands that we define our common bond with them. They, like us at an early stage in our development, use all their libidinal and aggressive energy to consolidate their egos, and have not the erotic focus or the ontic security to choose a real object outside themselves.

I think if we listen to Lacan describe the struggle of the child between six and eighteen months to achieve this consolidation, we shall recognize Achilles in the *Iliad* and ourselves in Achilles:

The mirror stage is a drama whose internal thrust is precipitated from insufficiency to anticipation—and which manufactures for the subject, caught up in the lure of spatial identification, the succession of phantasies that extends from a fragmented body-image to a form of its totality that I shall call ortho-paedic—and, lastly, to the assumption of the armour of an alienating identity, which will mark with its rigid structure the subject's entire mental develop-ment. Thus, to break out of the circle of the *Innenwelt* into the *Umwelt* generates the inexhaustible quadrature of the ego's variations. This fragmented body—which term I have also introduced into our system of theoretical ref-erences—usually manifests itself in dreams when the movement of the analysis encounters a certain level of aggressive disintegration in the individual. It then appears in the form of disjointed limbs, or of those organs represented in exoscopy, growing wings and taking up arms for intestinal persecutions—the very same that the visionary Hieronymus Bosch has fixed, for all time, in painting, in their ascent from the fifteenth century to the imaginary zenith of modern man. But this form is even tangibly revealed at the organic level, in the lines of "fragilisation" that define the anatomy of phantasy, as exhibited in the schizoid and spasmodic symptoms of hysteria.[21]

Lacan's concept of *le corps morcelé* has twofold resonance for us: it derives from his Hegelian conviction that identification involves aggression, that the image of the self perceived by the self in the other (the mirror) is aggressively invested and therefore suffers disintegra-tion; reciprocal aggression from the alienated image is fantasized so that the self itself disintegrates unless the subject accepts identification with the image and therefore achieves "totality." It also reminds us of Snell's philological analysis of the Homeric conception of the self, and his use of a geometric vase-painting to illustrate the "fragilization" or extraordinary articulation of body parts.

If we follow up both these leads we shall come to some consensus, I think, on what exactly it is that speaks to us in the *Iliad*, or rather what layer of our preconscious or unconscious minds the *Iliad* refers to. First, let us realize that there is good clinical evidence now for the childhood experience of fragilization, which Freud and Lacan con-sidered theoretically. The work of Mahler and Bettelheim in America and Winnicott in England has established that the infantile body-image is indeed fragile, that the child's constant effort is required to "keep himself together" conceptually.[22] Our most frightening evidence of this struggle is from Bettelheim's work with autistic children, who, at the ages of ten or twelve, retain the mental "structures" of *le stade du miroir*, i.e., six to eighteen months. Having been deprived, in Win-nicott's phrase, of "good enough mothering," they simply do not see themselves as integrated beings, and their drawings of themselves, in therapy, exemplify all those nightmare features which Lacan refers to Bosch. The goal of *le stade du miroir*, then, is a consolidated body-image. Lacan and Winnicott, in his more conservative and straightforward manner, stress the importance, in reaching this goal, of the child's acceptance of what the external world "thinks" of his internal constitution. For Winnicott, "the precursor of the mirror is the mother's eyes."[23] Lacan is more concerned to present the mother as Other, the alien world into which the child must move from his fantasy of oneness with the mother (Mahler's "symbiosis and the vicissitudes of individuation"). Lacan stresses that the true ontogeny of the child takes place *in the Other*, in the child-as-subject's contemplation of what the mother thinks of him and his consequent assimilation to that form. To reconcile all this with our pregnant reading of Freud's "On Narcissism," we say simply that the ideal ego pre-exists the ego.

The epic hero, by our definition, seeks not the mother, but the self as reflected by the mother. Although Snell does not emphasize the struggle in the *Iliad* toward integration of the self so much as he does its lack of fulfillment, we must recognize that Achilles, at least, has realized that neither gods nor men can provide him with the true object of his desire. He does not seek oblivion in reabsorption by the mother, but, having been deprived of his ideal ego by the death of Patroklos, he seeks self-annihilation in the Hegelian struggle with the Hegelian other, Hektor. This is Devereux's "suicide" of Achilles, an active, deliberate encounter with his own inability to define himself except in the terms imposed upon him by his peers. It is not the kind of slow slide to oblivion we find in other genres and later periods, especially that of the Romantic poets, who fantasize dreamless sleep at the mother's breast. Achilles breaks the mirror; he does not step back through it into the anaesthetic world of symbiosis. We must recognize polar opposites in Narcissus and Endymion, and then appreciate Achilles' approximation to the narcissistic pole, Keats' Endymion to the anaclitic.

It remains for us to discover whether Kohut and Kernberg, the two contemporary analysts who have studied most intently the phenomenon of narcissism, can tell us about Achilles. We realize that here, unlike the case with Freud and Lacan (who tell us about normal childhood development), and unlike Bettelheim and Mahler (who tell us about abnormal childhood development), we are attempting now to explicate a literary character in terms derived from the psychoanalytic therapy of disturbed adults. It is no more our intention to suggest that Achilles is to be read as a psychopathic type than it has been our intention to suggest that he is arrested in his development or regressed to an earlier stage. This latter distinction is, in fact, relevant to our understanding of the difference between the approaches of Kohut and Kernberg, since the former concerns himself with patients who have succeeded in establishing a secure sense of self in childhood, and later regressed, under traumatic or just generally trying circumstances, to stages prior to that establishment, while the latter is concerned with patients who are now seriously dysfunctional because their development was seriously deficient, and, in fact, belong to that category of cases on the "borderline" between neurotics and psychotics. Kernberg gives us a composite picture of his patients:

These patients present an unusual degree of self-reference in their interactions with other people, a great need to be loved and admired by others, and a curious apparent contradiction between a very inflated concept of themselves and an inordinate need for tribute from others. Their emotional life is shallow. They experience little empathy for the feelings of others or from their own grandiose fantasies, and they feel restless and bored when external glitter wears off and no new sources feed their self-regard. They envy others, tend to idealize some people from whom they expect narcissistic supplies, and to depreciate and treat with contempt those from whom they do not expect anything (often their former idols). In general, their relationships with other people are clearly exploitative and sometimes parasitic. It is as if they feel they have the right to control and possess others and to exploit them without guilt feelings—and behind a surface which very often is charming and engaging, one senses coldness and ruthlessness. Very often such patients are considered to be "dependent" because they need so much tribute and adoration from others, but on a deeper level they are completely unable really to depend on anybody because of their deep distrust and depreciation of others.[24]

The features of this portrait which recall qualities of Achilles are many, but perhaps the basic one is that strange contradiction between apparent strength and actual dependence on others, at least for "tribute," apparent love and actual exploitation of others, superficial charm and profound disdain for others. All of this ambivalence is defined and explained by a lack of guilt, an inability to recognize in other people (his own "self-objects" or "partial objects") self-conscious subjects. We shall come to consider special sections of the poem to illustrate these traits, but we need now only think of Achilles' wrath at the seizure of Briseis and his later wish that she had died before; his extravagant grief over the death of Patroklos, but his ridicule of him while he lived; and, most tellingly, I think, his excellent playing of the role of the benevolent king concerned for his subjects, especially the weaker ones (this recalls his treatment of Kalchas in Book I) during the games in Book XXIII, and the extension of this role to that of gracious host to Priam in Book XXIV (which, of course, recalls his equally gracious reception of the ambassadors in Book IX), until the mask suddenly falls and the absoluteness of his self-absorption is revealed in the chilling threat: "Do as I tell you, old man, or I will kill you here in my tent."

Kernberg is meticulous in his explanation of the formation of such a character and much of what he says lends support to some of our assumptions about Achilles—that he is guiltless, in particular. Having remarked on the narcissistic type's assumption of his right to control and possess others and to exploit them without guilt feelings, he goes on to suggest that the agency, which we have seen is responsible, in the classical Freudian model, for guilt feelings, is poorly developed: "idealized object images which normally would be integrated into the ego ideal and as such, into the superego, are condensed instead with the self concept . . . [there is no normal formation of the super-ego because] realistic parental images derived from oedipal conflicts are missing."[25]

Kernberg does not argue the "absent-father syndrome" as the usual cause for such a failure to develop a superego and thence the capacity for guilt, but it is clear that the lack of differentiation between self and other (as father) is the cause of this and all subsequent failures to respond in any "normal" reciprocal manner to the needs of other people. We need to appreciate here exactly what Kernberg means by "self" and "self-image," since it might appear that throughout our discussion we are simply following him in a contemporary fashion of replacing the Freudian ego with the notion of self, when conceptually there is little to distinguish:

The self is an intrapsychic structure consisting of multiple self representations and their related affect dispositions . . . The self is part of the ego, which contains, in addition, the object representations mentioned before, and also ideal self-images and ideal object-images at various stages of depersonification, abstraction and integration . . . Normal narcissism stems from the libidinal investment in an originally undifferentiated self and object image from which later, libidinally invested self and object images will develop. These will eventually determine an intergrated self, which incorporates libidinally determined and aggressively determined self-images under the predominance of the libidinally determined ones.[26]

At this point I expect Patroklos and Hektor to spring from Kernberg's page wearing Achilles' armor: they are respectively his libidinally and aggressively determined self-images, and therefore it is upon them that his existence depends. One should also think here of Hegel's "other world" of negation, the risk of life to determine life, and above all of the sequence from self-consciousness as subject without self-consciousness as object through the "unhappy consciousness" to the *schöne Seele.*

We must return to Kernberg later for his theory of the replay of this early narcissistic drama in adolescence and mature life, a pattern of repetition which, of course, duplicates Hegel's spiralling dialectic and, with surprising precision, both Devereux's analysis of the Greek preoccupation with sexually undifferentiated physical beauty and our own model of Greek psychohistory. At this point, however, Kohut has a contribution to make, if only to reveal to the mind unaccustomed to psychoanalytic abstractions the essential difference between the narcissistic character and the "normal" character. Kohut waged a battle against the preeminence of drive-theory in psychoanalysis, and this is well documented in a recent collection of his papers with detailed introduction by one of his colleagues.[27] I think this might have greater importance for psychoanalytic practice than it does for psychoanalytic insight into literature, though it is difficult to determine exactly where Kohut thought it would lead him, since he refused to answer his critics, such as Kernberg, and seemed to have been launched upon the formulation of a metaphysics of the self rather than an extension of Freudian psychology.[28]

We must also, however, be grateful to Kohut for publishing a number of analyses conducted on his and his colleagues' (disguised) patients, because they reveal, though no great effort is made to explain this, a significantly persistent strain of homosexuality. This, among the characterizing traits of "narcissistic personality disorders" (Kohut's descriptive phrase for his patients' problems) takes us right back to Freud and his original remark on the potential for pre-oedipal narcissistic object-choice to determine later sexual orientation. Kohut conveniently distinguishes three types of mature object-choice:

We . . . emphasize that there is a crucial difference between (1) the narcissistically experienced, archaic self-object (an object only in the sense of the observer of manifest behaviour); (2) the psychological structures (which are built up in consequence of the gradual decathexis of the narcissistically archaic object) which continue to perform the drive-regulating, integrating, and adaptive functions which had previously been performed by the (external) object, and (3) true objects (in the psychoanalytic sense) which are cathected with object-instinctual investments, i.e., objects loved and hated by a psyche that has separated itself from the archaic objects, has acquired autonomous structures, has accepted the independent motivations and responses of others, and has grasped the notion of mutuality.[29]

If we agree to call Kohut's second category "partial objects," then I think we can begin to build a model against which to measure Achilles' relation with Patroklos. If there seems to be a confusion of inside and outside, it is of the nature of the problem that this be so. Kohut's archaic self-object is to be compared with Freud's ideal ego, that image of infantile perfection which the maturing child refuses to relinquish; the partial object is the projection of this image upon others, especially the father in the oedipal stage; the true object is the post-oedipal object. We speak then simultaneously of development, chronological and psychological, and of affect or experience (is the subject able to recognize an object as another subject?). The result is a three-fold equation between normality and maturity and the Hegelian recognition of one self-consciousness by another.

Kohut's tendency to confuse us arises from his celebration of the self as always already there. He can define the ego, for instance, as the introjection of the pre-oedipal object (on the analogy of the formation of the superego from the introjection of the oedipal object), but then he also defines the ego as "the accepted image of the self," and the self simply as "an archaic formation that can be referred to in analysis," i.e., "as a content of the mental apparatus," but "not an agency of the mind."[30] Nevertheless, when he goes on to distinguish shame as a phenomenon of the relation between the ego and the id, as opposed to guilt, which we identify with the superego, then we find support for our ontogenetic-phylogenetic argument. He even cites Ruth Benedict's *Patterns of Culture*, which had such an influence on Dodds in his distinction of the Homeric society as a shame-culture, from later, fifth-century Greek society as a guilt-culture. Although Kohut's discussion takes place in a footnote, is a bit abstruse, and reads like special pleading, it is worth our consideration:

The notion that shame is in general a reaction of an ego that has failed to fulfill the (perhaps unrealistic) demands and expectations of a strong ego ideal . . .must be rejected, not only on theoretical grounds but especially on the basis of clinical observation. Many shame-prone individuals do not possess strong ideals, but most of them are exhibitionistic people who are driven by their ambitions; i.e., their characteristic psychic imbalance (experienced as shame) is due to a flooding of the ego with unneutralized exhibitionism and not to a relative ego weakness vis-à-vis an overly strong system of ideals. The intense relations of such people to their setbacks and failures, too, are—with rare exceptions—not due to the activity of the super-ego. After suffering defeats in the pursuit of their ambitions and exhibitionistic aims, such individuals experience at first searing shame and then often, comparing themselves with a successful rival, intense envy. This state of shame and envy may ultimately be followed by self-destructive impulses. These, too, are to be understood not as attacks of the super-ego on the ego but as attempts of the suffering ego to do away with the self in order to wipe out the offending, disappointing reality of failure. In other words, the self-destructive impulses are to be understood here not as analogous to the suicidal impulses of the depressed patient but as the expression of narcissistic rage.[31]

Again we see Achilles before us, realizing that his extreme reaction to Agamemnon's mistreatment of him is not due to the loss of status and dignity he might feel he suffers in the face of his peers, but rather, since he is indisputably "the best of the Achaians," so unquestionably above and beyond any ideal they could set up for his behavior, the wrath is purely a function of the internal conflict between the expectations with which his goddess-mother endowed him—the archaic object, his grandiose self, or, even, his ego as introjection of the pre-oedipal object—and this sudden brush with rude, unresponsive reality. Why should Achilles be treated like any other Greek? We, then, of course, readdress the problem of whether Achilles is to be considered an extreme paradigm, an overstatement of the heroic code—shame in its conventional social sense—or a contradiction and transcendence of it. We shall face these (seeming) alternatives in due course. Let us now hear once more from Kohut on his general theme of the inability of the narcissistic personality to invest libidinal energy in a "true object":

In narcissistic personality disorders there is in the preconscious center a sense of an incomplete reality of the self and, secondarily, of the external world. The dynamic source and structural roots of this condition are the fixation on an archaic self-image and the dysfunction and insufficient cathexis of the [pre-] conscious self. [32]

We return to our theme of the mother-son dyad, and the fatherless child's tendency to devalue the mother as object and invest libidinally her image of himself instead. Without libidinal investment of the mother there is no psychological preparation for the investment of the world at large (ultimately the Hegelian self-revelation of Absolute Spirit), and the child remains pathologically self-centered (centered on a pathological self); he is subject to fits of narcissistic rage that can be (appropriately) suicidal. The wrath of Achilles can then be defined as a refusal to accept the compromise inherent in his mixed parentage. He does not yield up the "grandiose self," which is his legacy from his goddess-mother, to the demands of his patrimony, the mundane reality which culminates in death.

I.7

THE ACHILLES COMPLEX

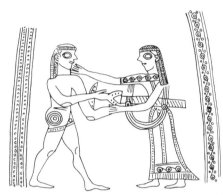 Several assertions we have made about the *Iliad* require support from the text. First, we must check our general impression of the ever-present bountiful mother against specific scenes involving Achilles not only with Thetis, but also with Athene and Hera—indirectly, through Athene and Iris, since they never actually meet. It is here, I think, that our basic premise— Achilles faces in the narrative progress of the poem the loss of what we have all experienced in the early stages of our own development, namely narcissistic preoccupations in the context of unthreatening maternal support and the almost total absence of paternal intervention—will meet with most resistance. It will be said that Achilles is not an eighteen-month-old child and that the whole project is false and facetious on its face. We meet the first objection by referring to memory traces; for the second we must simply argue that the way in which Homer presents Achilles in the context of unquestioning maternal support is the way in which we must understand him, whether it makes sense chronologically or not. His mother is always there helping and his father is never there discouraging, so we have essentially the pre-oedipal (non-oedipal) situation of our hypothesis. This reading also gains support from the father-replacement figures we see in Phoinix and Priam and Nestor, and in Achilles' own memories of Peleus as weak and ineffective: they are all impotent old men who can only talk, not fight.

This consideration of the basic situation leads us inevitably into other areas of concern. What is Achilles' attitude toward women in general, and toward Briseis in particular? Is this the same attitude evident among the other heroes, Greek and Trojan? We have a clear idea of what Helen means to all the men, how Aphrodite manipulates her to arouse their desire, but what is the nature of this desire? Is it for Helen herself as a woman, a true object of desire, or is it desire for the sensation of self-arousal, men's pleasure in the erotic processes of their own bodies, or, in the case of the old Trojan men, their nostalgia for that sense of arousal? We know that this distinction has been made for the effect of Aphrodite's eminence in Sappho's poetry, and we wonder whether it is not equally true of some erotic moments in Homer.[1] Clinically put, it is fascination with one's own penis (phallic pride and exhibitionism) rather than anticipation of the mutual pleasure which the penis can provide both man and woman in intercourse.

Having said all this, what must we then say about Hektor and Andromache? We cannot help noticing that Hektor's relation with his wife and his relation with his mother and Helen herself are different, that he values these women and their function in society, that Helen considers him her friend and protector, just as Briseis considers Patroklos her friend and protector, and that these two women, over whom so many men have fought and died, lament these fallen heroes in terms other than those which they would use to lament their fallen lovers and, finally, that only Andromache in her laments combines, in describing her sense of loss, both friend and lover.

There is, of course, an oedipal moment in the *Iliad*, and this is the confrontation between Achilles and Agamemnon. How important is the woman here and how is she important? Is her value as object of desire or as prize for contention between male rivals? Do we, in fact, have in the conflict over Briseis a suggestion of the struggle that never took place between Achilles and Peleus over Thetis, and in each case can we not assume that the women are not true objects, which the males libidinally invest, but rather are functions of their aggressive investment of each other?

Having decided this question—at least how properly to pose it—we can confront the central problem of the poem, which is Achilles' relations with Patroklos and Hektor, and we have already suggested that these should be read as libidinal and aggressive investments of self-objects (or "partial objects") respectively. (Additional light is cast in these dark corners by the role of Diomedes, so obviously a paradigm of heroic behavior in Achilles' absence, so different in his relations with Agamemnon and his attitude toward war and death.) *We thus posit an "Achilles complex" as the thematic core of the Iliad, and a formative stage in the development of every male child.* If the mother, and after her other women and the world as such, is not validated by "proto-oedipal" conflict, but narcissistic preoccupation continues, then there is no orientation of desire outwards, no libidinal investment of true objects; in fact, there is both libidinal and aggressive investment of self-objects, creating a kind of closed system which must suffer entropy. Or, on another model, without the orientation of desire toward an other outside the self—the mother and her various sublimations and tranferences—there is no true opposition, no tension, to stabilize and define the self. If a dialectical process for the definition of the self through opposition of the seemingly negative moments— negation of the negation—is impossible, and the subject does not become self-conscious of himself as object ("the object is as much ego as object"), then the only possibility is the restoration of an original positive, a self always already there, and this we know does not exist. We are functions of differences and if we cannot libidinally and aggressively recognize-create difference, then our coming-into-being as a process is reversed. Developmentally the Achilles complex is like a running spiral arrested after its first circuit, where, having doubled back upon itself, it dissects itself at a point only slightly in advance of its origin. Ego-instincts (Thanatos) have paradoxically canceled the libidinal instincts (Eros) that could have given life its momentum.

This leaves us with two important abstractions to consider: age and death in the *Iliad*. How are we encouraged by the poet to regard the death of young heroes and the wisdom of old men? Is there not a significant dichotomy between youth, beauty, and action, on the one hand, and age, ugliness, and words, on the other? Why should any young hero want to outlive his active prime? Is there not a prevalent desire in the *Iliad* for early, beautiful death, the sapling felled in its prime? Do these generally developed themes not support the basic plot of the poem, which follows Achilles' progress towards death in defiance of the threat of continued life without definition of himself in his own terms?

Finally, how do we construe the participation of the gods in the action of the *Iliad*? Must we continue to speak of double and triple motivation, even when we have developed a critical model that allows for the externalized imagery of the self? What are the gods of the *Iliad* but more mirrors of the heroes' beauty and prowess? What better example than the Homeric epic could we find of the fallacy of Aristotle's argument for poetry being an imitation of life, of nature at large, decentered and entire? Surely serious poetry is an imitation of the individual's own struggles to define himself, so that the mirror is held up not to static, self-evident Nature, but to man himself in his dialectical attempt to make Nature over in his own image—or break all mirrors in the process.

II
VARIATIONS: TEXTUAL ANALYSIS

II.1
THE VALUE OF WOMEN

We are now equipped with a critical model that will, I believe, prove adequate to the proposition and consideration of the central thematic dilemma of the *Iliad*: Why is it, that in the context of a war fought for a woman, the poet causes us to consider most closely the relations between the central male figure and his dear male companion? Not only is the Trojan War being fought for the sake of Helen, stolen from her husband Menelaos by the Trojan prince Paris—and hence all of Greece has set out on a punitive expedition against all of Troy—but, moreover, the dispute between Agamemnon and Achilles—and the poet tells us in the opening lines of his poem that this brought about the deaths of many Greeks and is the subject of his poem—is over a woman, Briseis, whom Agamemnon expropriates from Achilles, contradicting his own previous distribution of spoils, in compensation to himself for the loss of yet another woman, Chryseis, whose return to her priest-father was required by Apollo.

It is, of course, Achilles' intervention in the crisis precipitated by Agamemnon's refusal to relinquish Chryseis, his calling of the assembly, and his assuring the seer Kalchas of a fair and safe hearing, that lead to Agamemnon's arrogant and defensive move—the seizure of Achilles' woman Briseis—and thus we could consider the whole situation in terms of Realpolitik: who is the leader of the Greek forces at Troy? Has Achilles threatened Agamemnon's hegemony and thus disordered the Greek camp? Although women are involved in these two crucial war-provoking and man-killing circumstances, the poet does not put these women at the center of his poem. Rather he traces the sequence of events which leads to the death of Achilles' dear friend Patroklos and its consequences, the death of Hektor, and the projected and assured death of Achilles himself. How, then, and to what extent are women valued in the *Iliad*?

On the surface level this question can be answered rather straight-forwardly. We are told not only the relative valuation of women, but the basis of this valuation; in the distribution of prizes for the funeral games of Patroklos the standard unit of value is the ox and we find the following allotment for winner and loser, with explanation:

Now Peleides set forth the prizes for the third contest,
for the painful wrestling, at once, and displayed them before the Danaans.
There was a great tripod, to set over the fire, for the winner.
The Achaians among themselves valued it at the worth of twelve oxen.
But for the beaten man he set in the midst a woman
skilled in much work of her hands, and they rated her at four
    oxen.   (23.700–5)

Undoubtedly some women are worth more than four oxen, but can we entirely ignore the clear indication that all women are always po-tentially prizes in conflicts between men? This wrestling match, and the horse race (23.257ff.) in which a woman is also offered, and all the other games celebrated in honor of Patroklos are war games. They are the amiable conflicts of men when men are not fighting other men seriously for cities and plunder, which, of course, includes women. There is no great distance between the wrestling match for the cauld-ron and the woman, and the single combat arranged in Book III to settle the issue of the war, which is the possession of Helen:

αὐτὰρ ᾿Αλέξανδρος καὶ ἀρηΐφιλος Μενέλαος
μακρῆς ἐγχείῃσι μαχήσοντ᾽ ἀμφὶ γυναικί·   (3.253–54)

For warlike Menelaos and Alexandros are to fight
with long spears against each other for the sake of the woman.

Women are allowed essentially two traits, which determine their value: beauty and cleverness. The formulas and epithets seem about equally divided between the two qualities. We hear frequently of women who "know blameless works" (e.g., 23.263, 9.128, 9.270). Women are called "well-girdled" (e.g., 9.366), "deep-girdled" (e.g., 18.122) and "beautifully girdled" (e.g., 7.139), all of which seems to suggest that small waists and large breasts were admired. Women's cleverness at handwork is mentioned several times in similes: when she spins wool (23.759ff.) or dyes ivory (4.141ff.), and the frugality of the poor woman with her scales seems to be both pitied and admired (12.432ff.).

I think we should be reminded at this point of Pucci's perception on Hesiod's treatment of the Pandora myth in *The Works and Days*.[1] Although his concern is the misogyny in that text and our concern is narcissism and male aggression in the *Iliad*, we find in both texts a meditation on the object and the origin of desire. Women are credited in Hesiod with many crafts and allurements; Zeus makes Pandora so that she will seem attractive, but be a bane to men. Nevertheless, she does know how to do many things, such as weaving and cooking. The only problem lies in the contradiction that men did not need these things before Zeus sent women, the implication being that when men lived in the good grace of the gods, before Prometheus as their representative tried to trick the gods into accepting the less attractive portions of meat at their banquets, all things men needed seem to have been spontaneously available to them. Of course, the whole Prometheus myth is a meditation on cooking and dividing and eating meat, paternal possessions (cf. the myth of Oedipus' sons disputing their portions of meat), and paternal authority. When we consider the approximation of dividing the meat at a banquet to dividing the spoils, including women, after a battle—Sarpedon mentions the choice cuts of meat among the perquisites of a warrior-king (12.310–12); cf. Hektor's reproach to Diomedes (8.161ff.)—the similarity of the disputes between Greece and Troy, and Achilles and Agamemnon, on the one hand, and Zeus and Prometheus, on the other, is striking.

If we extend our consideration further, to the myth of Tityos, who suffers the same fate as Prometheus—a vulture eats his liver, which is constantly restored—and this not for taking Zeus' meat, but for attempting to seduce his concubine Leto, then we realize that desire and prerogative as functions of each other are at issue in each of these stories. The liver, after all, in ancient belief, is the organ where sexual passion originates, and the liver is the one organ which can replenish itself. I am not certain that Hekabe's expressed desire to eat Achilles' liver (24.212) can be construed in this context. It almost seems a transference of forces: her desire to punish him is insatiable so that she would eat the organ which creates desire in him, whereas, more straightforwardly, the punishments of Prometheus and Tityos and all the other great sufferers in Tartaros, are to suffer insatiable desire, always for abridging paternal authority. The very phrase "insatiable desire" suggests the absolute identification between hunger and sexual passion. (See below, on *koros* and *korē*.) Thus Zeus the father creates in these son-like figures Tityos and Prometheus insatiable desire: in the first and simplest example, for the lost maternal object; but in the second and more encyclopaedic example, desire for all the paternal prerogatives. The fact that Pandora is a manufactured object of desire, like the phantom Hera that Zeus set before Ixion, and the phantom Helen in Euripides' play, can only be construed as the mythic perception that desire is illusory, the product of rivaly, the object validated by "quasi-oedipal" competition. Without that rivalry and competition there would be no object.

In comparing Hesiod's treatment of the Pandora myth with Homer's treatment of women generally and Achilles' attitude toward them specifically, we look toward a distinction between oedipal and pre-oedipal orientation. Achilles seems to renounce the oedipal object and seek consolation in his relations with Patroklos, whom we identify as his narcissistic (pre-oedipal) self-object. Our final formulation must stress that the validation of the woman as object is a result of oedipal competition, which gives external focus for the opposition engendered by the struggle toward self-definition, a socializing, integrating development that prevents the closed circuitry of investing images of the self with both libidinal and aggressive energy, which is what Achilles does with Patroklos and Hektor. Narcissism without oedipal correction creates a tendency towards suicide; or, dialectical opposition without the restoration of an original positive creates an endless spiral of violence.

Hesiod does not say that men went naked in the world before the crisis precipitated by Prometheus, which ends in the creation of Pandora, i.e., that they did not need the clothes women later could make for them. Clothing is a central theme in Genesis, however, and in other creation myths, where it is emphasized that men did not "need" clothes before they became aware of their difference from women. Hesiod does stress the ease with which men produced food for themselves in their pre-lapsarian world (*Works and Days*, 116–19). This is not the place to extend Pucci's argument to cover various other texts that offer significant analogies, but we should be aware, generally, of the operation in a certain type of creation mythology of the principle that Pucci explicates for Hesiod, i.e., that women are desirable because they fill a lack which did not preexist them. Food and clothing are always important issues here, and we need only think of *Gilgamesh* to call up the whole complex of motifs that have been recently studied as manfestations of conflicts in human development between man's painful progress toward better living conditions and his nostalgia for the lost time when conditions were better without his struggling.

The proposition we are prepared to make in this connection is that the phylogenetic nostalgia for a time of undifferentiated bliss, when all needs are met internally and man is content in union with his god, knowing no lack in himself and recognizing no other in woman, and hence no desire for something different from himself, is simply and individually the ontogenetic nostalgia for the period of symbiosis with the mother when she did not represent to the child a different and desirable object, but rather was felt to be a part of himself.

Complication and contradiction set in when we realize that these same myths conflate those nostalgic feelings for reunion with the mother and equally strong feelings for the establishment of the self independent of the mother. This conflict often expresses itself in terms of misogyny, as in Hesiod: woman becomes the symbol of man's fall from grace with his god. (Another major text in this debate, apart from Genesis, is Shakespeare's *The Winter's Tale*.) His god, as we have suggested above, and will argue more comprehensively below, is, of course, in some manifestations, such as Zeus, the oedipal and post-oedipal father, strong enough to protect the son from the now threatening mother. But he is also, as in the case of Apollo, more nearly the pre-oedipal child's idealized image of himself. This is the essential significance of such myths as the close relationship between Admetos and Apollo, and accounts for the insistence in the Gilgamesh epic on the physical similarity between Gilgamesh and Enkidu (though Enkidu has hair and hooves, as befits a "primitive" image of oneself), who, in plastic art, are depicted in heraldic composition, which might almost be "the state of the mirror." We move easily from here to the relations between Achilles and Patroklos, but first we must continue our examination of the place and function of women in the world of the *Iliad*. We just might discover there an explanation of the paradox implicit in all these texts: that man should "remember" his origin from, and early intimacy with, his mother, as a pre-feminine world where he enjoyed intimacy with a male god.

The particular manner in which women's sexual attraction is described in the *Iliad* signifies an attitude which we must recognize as integral to the entire Homeric world view. Women are often referred to as sexual objects. In Thersites' strange parody of Achilles' great protest against Agamemnon, he mentions not only the various prizes, including women, which the various Greek warriors have won for Agamemnon, but goes on to ask whether Agamemnon wants more, specifically gold, and a young woman "so that you can mingle with her in love and keep her apart by yourself from the others" (2.225ff.). We shall consider shortly the importance of the one-man/one-woman rule, since, again, it lies at the center of the dispute between Agamemnon and Achilles. Agamemnon can claim at the end of the dispute, and at his premature attempt to end it—and it is difficult to say whether this is essential, previously determined as a precaution, fortunate, or simply fortuitous—that he has not "mingled" with Briseis in love (9.132–34, 9.274–76, 19.175–77). Here let us only consider that at each mention of the fact that Agamemnon has not made sexual use of Briseis, the formula is repeated:

"ἦ θέμις ἀνθρώπων πέλει, ἀνδρῶν ἠδὲ γυναικῶν." (9.134)

"as is natural for human people, between men and women."

"ἦ θέμις ἐστίν, ἄναξ, ἥ τ' ἀνδρῶν ἥ τε γυναικῶν." (9.276, 19.177)

"as is natural for people, my lord, between men and women."

The most important statement of what is natural between men and women is made by Thetis, and this is, in and of itself, significant. She makes it, though, in such a way that we realize men do not desire women as any kind of emotional complement or spiritual support, but rather as an outlet for physical energy, and that "mingling with women in love" is part of a general pattern of physical (and perhaps psychological, but specifically physical) hygiene. Thetis speaks to Achilles as he sits in his tent still lamenting Patroklos, though Hektor has been killed, the body burned, and the games celebrated.

"τέκνον ἐμόν, τέο μέχρις ὀδυρόμενος καὶ ἀχεύων
σὴν ἔδεαι κραδίην, μεμνημένος οὔτε τι σίτου
οὔτ᾽ εὐνῆς; ἀγαθὸν δὲ γυναικί περ ἐν φιλότητι
μίσγεσθ᾽."   (24.128–31)

"My child, how long will you go on eating your heart out in sorrow and lamentation, and remember neither your food nor going to bed? It is a good thing even to lie with a woman in love."

Now we must immediately correct the false impression we might have given that we believe women have no value in the world of the *Iliad* except as working possessions and sexual objects. It is quite clear that Andromache means more to Hektor than that, and we shall examine their relationship in another context. We should now reckon with Achilles himself, though, and acknowledge that he claims a great affection for Briseis. When Thetis leaves him on the beach after their first interview, the narrator calls our attention to his hero's sense of loss:

τὸν δὲ λίπ᾽ αὐτοῦ
χωόμενον κατὰ θυμὸν ἐϋζώνοιο γυναικός,
τήν ῥα βίῃ ἀέκοντος ἀπηύρων·   (1.428–30)

. . . she . . . left him
sorrowing in his heart for the sake of the fair-girdled woman
whom they were taking by force against his will.

When the ambassadors come, he explains to them not only his bitterness at the seeming double standard that the Atreidai apply— are they the only men who love their wives?—but goes on to describe precisely his love for Briseis, and to distinguish it from the lesser attachment a man might feel for a woman who was *only* a prize:

. . ."from me alone of all the Achaians
he has taken and keeps the bride of my heart. Let him lie beside her
and be happy. Yet why must the Argives fight with the Trojans?

And why was it the son of Atreus assembled and led here
these people? Was it not for the sake of lovely-haired Helen?
Are the sons of Atreus alone among mortal men the ones
who love their wives? Since any who is a good man, and careful,
loves her who is his own and cares for her, even as I now
loved this one from my heart, though it was my spear that won
    her."   (9.335–43)

We may discover that the later, and to us shocking, amendment
that Achilles makes to this declaration of affection for Briseis defines
the difference between himself and Hektor; or between a war camp
and a city. But for the moment we must simply listen to Achilles on
the subject of his *relative* affection for and dependence upon Briseis,
as opposed to those comrades who have died, and, by implication,
Patroklos in particular:

"Son of Atreus, was this after all the better way for
both, for you and me, that we, for all our hearts' sorrow,
quarrelled together for the sake of a girl in soul-perishing hatred?
I wish Artemis had killed her beside the ships with an arrow
on that day when I destroyed Lyrnessos and took her.
For then not all these too many Achaians would have bitten
the dust, by enemy hands, when I was away in my anger."   (19.56–62)

This is not guilt and its displacement over—developed upon—an
innocent object; rather it is a simple statement of Achilles' own needs
and desires. When Patroklos was alive, he and Achilles slept in the
same tent, each beside his own woman, and Patroklos' woman had
been given him by Achilles (9.663–68). The relations between Achilles
and Patroklos were not homosexual as we have defined that term
above. They were, however, so intimate and such a complete identification that all other human relations, including those with women,
can barely be compared. Now we ask about Achilles' relations with
Patroklos and women, what we always ask about all that concerns
Achilles and the rest of the heroes of the *Iliad*: is he unique in this
respect, or representative?

His polar opposite would seem to be Hektor. Hektor's relation with
Andromache is marriage rather than war-camp concubinage. Indeed,
as has often been pointed out, the basic and most significant contrast
between Hektor and Achilles in general—and we find it now reflected

in their attitudes toward women in particular—is that the former is so forceful and frightening a representative of the war camp and its mentality, while the latter is identified with the city, which we can imagine functioning normally before the siege began: the same contrast, in fact, that Hephaistos develops on the shield for Achilles, though we have already seen that bipolar opposition is a distorting model, for violence animates both scenes. We have also suggested that Hektor's final defeat at the hands of Achilles cannot but convince us that the demands made upon him by his family and his city weaken him in the face of the solely and purely self-committed Achilles. We have even noted his friendship and protective attitude toward Helen, the major theme of her lament for him (24.767–72), as is the major theme of Briseis' lament for Patroklos (19.295–300) his friendly and protective attitude toward her.

Since we already identify Patroklos and Hektor as Achilles' libidinally and aggressively invested self-objects, we might go on to suggest that they share with another hero's double, Enkidu, this protection of defenseless women. We recall that Enkidu engages Gilgamesh in a wrestling match, disputing Gilgamesh's *ius primae noctis* over all the young brides in Ur. Is the hero's double then some kind of socialized (postoedipal) image of himself, as well as being a primitive (pre-oedipal) image of himself? Against all of this we put the poet's characterization of Achilles, most succinctly stated by his dear friend Patroklos to Nestor:

"εὖ δὲ σὺ οἶσθα, γεραιὲ διοτρεφές, οἷος ἐκεῖνος
δεινὸς ἀνήρ· τάχα κεν καὶ ἀναίτιον αἰτιόῳτο."   (11.653–54)

"You know yourself, aged sir beloved of Zeus, how *he* is;
a dangerous man; he might even be angry with one who is guiltless."

This contrast between Achilles and Hektor is extremely important to the whole thematic structure of the poem. With respect to their attitudes toward women, however, there is some congruence. When Hektor speaks to Andromache during his brief return to Troy, he betrays an ambivalence of feeling that makes it possible for us to see him simultaneously as almost unique in his valuation of women, but also representative of the general heroic tendency to regard women as slightly less than human. Indeed, this contradiction in his character is part of its richness and we are reminded of the different ways in which we see Achilles, both as representative of the heroic code generally and as a unique individual.

Briseis' and Andromache's stories are so similar that they might almost be the same woman. Achilles kills all their male relatives— even Briseis' husband—and they find solace only in the men who promise them the security of marriage: Hektor offers himself to Andromache and Patroklos offers Achilles to Briseis. They seem to differ a great deal in their actual status—Andromache always accompanied by two maids wherever she goes, the very pattern of the chaste, dutiful, young noblewoman, while Briseis is rudely transferred from her husband's murderer's bed to that of another warlord. We know, though, that finally this will be precisely Andromache's fate, to be the concubine of the son of the man who killed her husband. Though we desperately want to believe that war is a perversion and women suffer unnaturally in it, the *Iliad* seems to tell us rather that men's aggression is always already there, even in the "normal" life of the city, and that women suffer tangentially, because they are never really what men fight about or really what men desire. If we actually identified Briseis and Andromache, then one could argue at least for this triangulation of desire: Achilles and Hektor dispute the possession of Briseis-Andromache. The *Iliad*, though, presents women as excluded from the essential conflict among men, and the poem even suggests that if they were more immediately involved in that struggle, the struggle itself— men's attempts to define themselves in terms of each other—would not be changed, i.e., that male phallic aggression could not be neutralized by the libidinal investment of female objects, but perhaps only directed upon those objects.

II.2

WHY MEN FIGHT

 Andromache's appeal to her husband (6.406–39) develops along these lines: "stay here within the walls, because going forth to battle outside the walls will guarantee your death; take pity on me and your son; you are husband, father, and brother to me, since Achilles killed all my family; take pity on me and your son and stay within the city walls." Hektor's response seems on first consideration straightforward and sympathetic to Andromache's plight and proposal. He says he has all these things upon his mind, but he must fight, for otherwise he would feel shame (*mal' ainōs aideomai*) before the Trojans and the Trojan women with trailing garments; he knows Troy will fall and it is not the thought of his mother's or his father's suffering that so disturbs him as it is Anromache's own fate:

. . ." when some bronze-armoured
Achaian leads you off, taking away your day of liberty,
in tears; and in Argos you must work at the loom of another,
and carry water from the spring Messeis or Hypereia,
all unwilling, but strong will be the necessity upon you;
and some day seeing you shedding tears a man will say of you:
'This is the wife of Hektor, who was ever the bravest fighter
of all the Trojans, breakers of horses, in the days when they fought
        about Ilion.'
So will one speak of you; and for you it will be yet a fresh grief,
to be widowed of such a man who could fight off the day of your slavery.

But may I be dead and the piled earth hide me under before I
hear you crying and know by this that they drag you captive."   (6.454-65)

There is no denying the genuine sentiment in this address, and yet
there is beneath it the conventional structure of heroic self-reflection:
Andromache living in bondage will be a monument to the shame of
Hektor after his death. So much does he see her as an extension of
himself, so much does he define his role of warrior as centered in a
strange paradoxical fashion on his honor and his wife, that we see
emerge, even in this, the most touching and seemingly timeless moment of the *Iliad*—the farewell of a warrior to his wife—that ethos
which, though not unique to the *Iliad* (cf. e.g., Hotspur's farewell to
his wife in *Henry IV, Part I*, II. iii. 76–120), is so pronounced in the
Iliad. Women are valued only as proof of men's prowess in battle.
Enemies strive to kill men in battle, not to win their women as prizes
valuable in and of themselves, but rather as symbols of their victory
over the vanquished.

We shall come to discuss the stripping of the armor of a dead warrior
as equivalent to castration and admit the seeming absurdity of suggesting that castration might matter to a dead man; so here we suggest
that the victor's taking the vanquished dead man's wife is equivalent
to castration and the same (seeming) absurdity arises: what difference
can it make to a dead man whether he is literally deprived of his wife
or figuratively castrated? The answer is obvious: a man's shame, like
his honor, lives beyond him, and his great terror while alive is that his
wife, in bondage, might be a reproach to him after his death. To speak
of such deprivation—a man's armor and his wife—as castration is not
to speak metaphorically, but metonymically: these "things" are part
of the man, and to lose them, even in death, is painful, shameful
emasculation.

There is no question that men's and women's roles are carefully and
clearly distinguished. At the conclusion of his interview with Andromache Hektor sends her away, back to her quarters, and reminds
himself as well as her that there is a natural order separating them and
their duties:

"ἀλλ᾽ εἰς οἶκον ἰοῦσα τὰ σ᾽ αὐτῆς ἔργα κόμιζε,
ἱστόν τ᾽ ἠλακάτην τε, καὶ ἀμφιπόλοισι κέλευε

ἔργον ἐποίχεσθαι· πόλεμος δ' ἄνδρεσσι μελήσει
πᾶσι, μάλιστα δ' ἐμοί, τοὶ Ἰλίῳ ἐγγεγάασιν."   (6.490–93)

"Go therefore back to our house, and take up your own work,
the loom and the distaff, and see to it that your handmaidens
ply their work also; but the men must see to the fighting,
all men who are the people of Ilion, but I beyond others."

It is as though Andromache had briefly emerged from her passive role
as object over which men fight, but had then been forced to relapse
into that role, to making clothes for those men, especially the shrouds
in which they will be burned or buried. At the same time Hektor has
briefly emerged from his role of man as active in the only meaningful
way men can be active, in war, killing other men. Let us consider now
this kill-or-be-killed philosophy of the *Iliad*, and its constant reference
to women.

Just as we found a paradigm for the valuation of women generally
in the microcosm of the funeral games, so, I think, we find a clear,
simple statement of the dilemma of the warrior in the advice given to
Antilochos by his father Nestor before the chariot race. After many
specific points about handling the horses Nestor sums up the situation:
Antilochos must keep close to the turning point:

"λίθου δ' ἀλέασθαι ἐπαυρεῖν,
μή πως ἵππους τε τρώσῃς κατά θ' ἅρματα ἄξῃς·
χάρμα δὲ τοῖς ἄλλοισιν, ἐλεγχείη δὲ σοὶ αὐτῷ
ἔσσεται·"   (23.340–43)

. . ."yet take care not really to brush against it,
for, if so, you might damage your horses and break your chariot,
and that will be a thing of joy for the others, and a failure
for you."

Gouldner has analyzed this kind of attitude in his study of later
Greek society; he calls it a "zero-sum situation," where no man can
win but by another man losing.[1] Nestor's is a negative statement of
that principle: what is disaster for you will be a delight for your opponents.

In war itself this theme finds constant repetition in the exchange
of boasts between enemies before battle and in the advice given friends.
The formulae are epigrammatic in form and affect because of *figura*

etymologica. In a general description of battle the poet observes:

ἔνθα δ' ἅμ' οἰμωγή τε καὶ εὐχωλὴ πέλεν ἀνδρῶν
ὀλλύντων τε καὶ ὀλλυμένων, ῥέε δ' αἵματι γαῖα.   (8.64–65)

There the screaming and the shouts of triumph rose up together
of men killing and men killed, and the ground ran blood.

Hektor encourages his men in words that express not only the kill-
or-be-killed attitude and delight in the enemies' discomfiture, but also
the complicated relation between a man's ability and his consciousness
of a god's favor, which we must consider at a later stage of the argument:

"Τρῶες καὶ Λύκιοι καὶ Δάρδανοι ἀγχιμαχηταί,
ἀνέρες ἔστε, φίλοι, μνήσασθε δὲ θούριδος ἀλκῆς.
γιγνώσκω δ' ὅτι μοι πρόφρων κατένευσε Κρονίων
νίκην καὶ μέγα κῦδος, ἀτὰρ Δαναοῖσί γε πῆμα·
νήπιοι, οἳ ἄρα δὴ τάδε τείχεα μηχανόωντο
ἀβλήχρ' οὐδενόσωρα· τὰ δ' οὐ μένος ἀμὸν ἐρύξει·
ἵπποι δὲ ῥέα τάφρον ὑπερθορέονται ὀρυκτήν."   (8.173–79)

"Trojans, Lykians and Dardanians who fight at close quarters,
be men now, dear friends, remember your furious valour.
I see that the son of Kronos has bowed his head and assented
to my high glory and success, but granted the Danaans
disaster: fools, who designed with care these fortifications,
flimsy things, not worth a thought, which will not beat my strength
back, but lightly my horses will leap the ditch they have dug them."

Odysseus speaks to himself in words of encouragement:

"ὤ μοι ἐγώ, τί πάθω; μέγα μὲν κακὸν αἴ κε φέβωμαι
πληθὺν ταρβήσας· τὸ δὲ ρίγιον αἴ κεν ἁλώω
μοῦνος· τοὺς δ' ἄλλους Δαναοὺς ἐφόβησε Κρονίων.
ἀλλὰ τίη μοι ταῦτα φίλος διελέξατο θυμός;
οἶδα γὰρ ὅτι κακοὶ μὲν ἀποίχονται πολέμοιο,
ὃς δέ κ' ἀριστεύῃσι μάχῃ ἔνι, τὸν δὲ μάλα χρεὼ
ἑστάμεναι κρατερῶς, ἤ τ' ἔβλητ' ἤ τ' ἔβαλ' ἄλλον."

(11.404–10)

"Ah me, what will become of me? It will be a great evil
if I run, fearing their multitude, yet deadlier if I am caught
alone; and Kronos' son drove to flight the rest of the Danaans.
Yet still, why does my heart within me debate on these things?
Since I know that it is the cowards who walk out of the fighting,

but if one is to win honour in battle, he must by all means
stand his ground strongly, whether he be struck or strike down another."

The notion that death is unavoidable and its particular moment for
each man is determined by his destiny, the gods, and circumstance,
all of which combine to promote one man at the expense of another
(though formerly the winner might have seemed the worse of the two)
is here succinctly expressed and sealed with the kill-or-be-killed com-
monplace, which Odysseus offers himself almost as consolation.

That the man defeated and dead should be a cause of boasting for
the man victorious and alive seems to us extreme, but perhaps not so
strange, and obviously the more famous the defeated—the greater his
reported prowess in battle—the more cause for boasting his defeat and
death gives his killer. Hektor again calls upon his men to have courage
and is excited by the prospect of engaging Agamemnon in single combat:

"Τρῶες καὶ Λύκιοι καὶ Δάρδανοι ἀγχιμαχηταί,
ἀνέρες ἔστε, φίλοι, μνήσασθε δὲ θούριδος ἀλκῆς.
οἴχετ' ἀνὴρ ὤριστος, ἐμοὶ δὲ μέγ' εὖχος ἔδωκε
Ζεὺς Κρονίδης· ἀλλ' ἰθὺς ἐλαύνετε μώνυχας ἵππους
ἰφθίμων Δαναῶν, ἵν' ὑπέρτερον εὖχος ἄρησθε."   (11.286–90)

"Trojans, Lykians and Dardanians who fight at close quarters
be men now, dear friends, remember your furious valour.
Their best man is gone, and Zeus, Kronos' son, has consented
to my great glory; but steer your single-foot horses straight on
at the powerful Danaans, so win you the higher glory."

The double significance of *euchomai/euchos* in all these passages is
important.[2] When a particular god is mentioned, there can be no
question that the whole concept involved is the winning through to
the right to *boast* because a god has answered the winner's *prayer* to
kill his enemy. We have these two statements of the principle in the
preparation for the second trial by single combat to settle the war.
First Hektor announces his intentions:

"εἰ δέ κ' ἐγὼ τὸν ἕλω, δώῃ δέ μοι εὖχος Ἀπόλλων,
τεύχεα σύλησας οἴσω προτὶ Ἴλιον ἱρήν,
καὶ κρεμόω προτὶ νηὸν Ἀπόλλωνος ἑκάτοιο,"   (7.81–83)

"But if I take his life, and Apollo grants me the glory,
I will strip his armour and carry it to sacred Ilion
and hang it in front of the temple of far-striking Apollo."

And then Nestor reproaches the Greeks for not producing a champion, and cites himself in his youth as an example to them:

"καὶ μαχόμην οἱ ἐγώ, δῶκεν δέ μοι εὖχος Ἀθήνη.
τὸν δὴ μήκιστον καὶ κάρτιστον κτάνον ἄνδρα·"   (7.154–55)

"And I fought with him, and Pallas Athene gave me glory.
Of all the men I have killed this was the tallest and strongest."

The gods are given credit for answering a man's prayer, so that he remember (or discover for the first time) his own (god-given) excellence, and can therefore kill his opponent, which will give him cause to boast. Conflated and syncopated, this means that the successful hero needs his enemy as much as he needs the god's support, and both relations define him as a hero, the defeated enemy as proof of the god's favor, but, of course, both enemy and god as means of asserting himself. In this way we see that for the Homeric hero war and religion are closely combined in an attempt to define the self, just as one becomes aware, at Delphi and Olympia, that later, in the sixth and fifth centuries, religion and athletic competition were combined to produce an ideal of masculine excellence, which is, in fact, what the Greeks seem always to have worshiped in themselves.

We suspend for the time development of our embarrassingly anatomical argument on this economy of violence, but we cannot disbelieve it entirely: the rape of women and the castration of men are in the battlefield mentality of the *Iliad* equivalent. The world of the *Iliad* is phallo-centric in the sense that men abuse women and other men to assure themselves of their own continued capacity to dominate. The phallos is a symbol of the penis, not that organ itself, just as the woman is a symbolic object of desire and not the true object. The Homeric hero seeks to define and play his role in this complicated phallic drama, always and only concerned with himself, and that is, of course, precisely what he loses in the death of his comrades and himself. This is pretty straightforward Lacanian psychology, and its Hegelian foundation is secure. I only hope that the inescapable difference between true objects and compromise formations is clear and, too, that my only heresy begins with the insistence that in the *Iliad* the "true" object is the self and not the mother (or any replacement for her).

Perhaps we can hear something of a prophecy of the later development of Greek athletics and religion in the famous speech of Sarpedon to Glaukos. We can certainly hear a clear statement of the necessity for the hero to risk his life to prove his existence (as in Hegel's *Phenomenology*), and marvel at the economy and, paradoxically, the altruism of the whole code. Glory is all, and men must be content to feed themselves to it as well as to batten upon it:

"ὦ πέπον, εἰ μὲν γὰρ πόλεμον περὶ τόνδε φυγόντε
αἰεὶ δὴ μέλλοιμεν ἀγήρω τ᾽ ἀθανάτω τε
ἔσσεσθ᾽, οὔτε κεν αὐτὸς ἐνὶ πρώτοισι μαχοίμην
οὔτε κε σὲ στέλλοιμι μάχην ἐς κυδιάνειραν·
νῦν δ᾽ ἔμπης γὰρ κῆρες ἐφεστᾶσιν θανάτοιο
μυρίαι, ἃς οὐκ ἔστι φυγεῖν βροτὸν οὐδ᾽ ὑπαλύξαι,
ἴομεν, ἠέ τῳ εὖχος ὀρέξομεν, ἠέ τις ἡμῖν."   (12.322–28)

"Man, supposing you and I, escaping this battle,
would be able to live on forever, ageless, immortal,
so neither would I myself go on fighting in the foremost
nor would I urge you into the fighting where men win glory.
But now, seeing that the spirits of death stand close about us
in their thousands, no man can turn aside nor escape them,
let us go on and win glory for ourselves, or yield it to others."

Once we realize that men exist to fight, exist because they fight, are men and not women or gods when they do fight—Hektor says to Andomache *polemos d'andressi melēsei* (6.492) and Poseidon says to Hera *polemos d'andressi melēsei* (20.137)—then we can raise again the question of women's value to men and men's dependence upon each other, both as companions in war and as enemies.

We know that men fight for women: not only do the Greeks fight to regain Helen, but Achilles refuses to fight because Agamemnon has taken Briseis. To this we must add the true devotion of Hektor to Andromache: he fights to save her from slavery. This last principle is stated generally and positively by the poet himself when he distinguishes, as will all later writers on military valor and inspiration, between the besiegers and the besieged:

Οἱ δ' ἄρα δεῖπνον ἕλοντο κάρη κομόωντες 'Αχαιοὶ
ῥίμφα κατὰ κλισίας, ἀπὸ δ' αὐτοῦ θωρήσσοντο.
Τρῶες δ' αὖθ' ἑτέρωθεν ἀνὰ πτόλιν ὁπλίζοντο,
παυρότεροι· μέμασαν δὲ καὶ ὣς ὑσμῖνι μάχεσθαι,
χρειοῖ ἀναγκαίῃ, πρό τε παίδων καὶ πρὸ γυναικῶν.   (8.53–57)

Now the flowing-haired Achaians had taken their dinner
lightly among their shelters, and they put on their armour thereafter,
and on the other side, in the city, the Trojans took up
their armor, fewer men, yet minded to stand the encounter
even so, caught in necessity, for their wives and their children.

More frequent is the negative statement of this principle, i.e., rather than the men thinking of themselves fighting for the sake of saving their own women, they think of themselves as fighting in order to take away the women from their enemies. Again, one might argue that the real distinction is between besiegers and besieged, the former more savage and brutal than the latter, but there are corrections to that contention in the text, showing that universally men fight to possess other men's women, and, more perverse, to force those men to acknowledge their loss, even beyond death.

Nestor follows Odysseus in rebutting Agamemnon's proposition to give up the war effort and return to Greece, and he proposes an oath or prohibition against further discussion:

"τῶ μή τις πρὶν ἐπειγέσθω οἰκόνδε νέεσθαι,
πρίν τινα πὰρ Τρώων ἀλόχῳ κατακοιμηθῆναι,
τείσασθαι δ' Ἑλένης ὁρμήματά τε στοναχάς τε."   (2.354–56)

"Therefore let no man be urgent to take the way homeward
until after he has lain in bed with the wife of a Trojan
to avenge Helen's longing to escape and her lamentations."

The actual oath for the single combat is even more chilling, suggesting again the potential of the shame and suffering consequent upon defeat to be extended beyond death:

"ὧδέ σφ' ἐγκέφαλος χαμάδις ῥέοι ὡς ὅδε οἶνος,
αὐτῶν καὶ τεκέων, ἄλοχοι δ' ἄλλοισι δαμεῖεν."   (3.300–1)

"first, let their brains be spilled on the ground as this wine is spilled now,
theirs and their sons', and let their wives be the spoil of others."

(*Damnēmi*, translated here "to be the spoil of," should suggest servi-
tude on the analogy of "tamed" animals, and therefore sexual bondage.)

Hektor claims that Patroklos boasted that he would sack Troy and
take their women (16.830) and Achilles wants the Trojan women to
cry (18.122). Perhaps the episode that ties all these motifs together
most neatly is the death of Othryoneus:

. . . a man who lived in Kabesos,
who was newly come in the wake of the rumour of war, and had asked
Priam for the hand of the loveliest of his daughters,
Kassandra, without bride price, but had promised a great work for her,
to drive back the unwilling sons of the Achaians from Troy land
and aged Priam had bent his head in assent, and promised
to give her, so Othryoneus fought in the faith of his promises.
Idomeneus aimed at him with the shining spear, and threw it,
and hit him as he came onward with high stride and the corselet
of bronze he wore could not hold, the spear fixed in the middle belly.
He fell thunderously, and Idomeneus vaunting cried out:
"Othryoneus, I congratulate you beyond all others
if it is here that you will bring to pass what you promised
to Dardanian Priam, who in turn promised you his daughter.
See now, we also would make you a promise, and we would fulfil it:
we would give you the loveliest of Atreides' daughters,
and bring her here from Argos to be your wife, if you joined us
and helped us storm the strong-founded city of Ilion.
Come then with me, so we can meet by our sea-faring vessels
about a marriage; we here are not bad matchmakers for you."   (13.363–82)

This situation and the way in which the poet presents it has resonance with other crucial situations in the poem itself, and with many
myths outside it, as well as with the conventional manner in which
men mention women as part of their boast before or after killing other
men. Most notable is the similarity with Achilles' own situation. Not
only is he promised by Agamemnon's ambassadors to him in Book IX
that he might have one of Agamemnon's daughters to marry if only
he would return to the battle, but there is a prior episode in the myths
about the Trojan expedition, and elaboration on the sacrifice of Iphi-
geneia by Agamemnon at Aulis, which explains Klytaimnestra's jour-
ney to Aulis to bring her daughter to her husband, not for the purpose
of sacrifice, but for the purpose of marriage with Achilles. Also, of

course, there is the myth that after the fall of Troy Agamemnon chose Kassandra for his own and arrogantly introduced her into his household upon his return to Argos, thus precipitating his own murder at Klytaimnestra's hands, she claiming that thus she avenges her daughter who was sacrificed.

I do not claim precisely that the Othryoneus passage in the *Iliad* suggests the poet's knowledge of these episodes, which we find fully developed first in fifth-century tragedy. I do think that the story of Othryoneus is a paradigm for the value of women in war. They are prizes, of course, as we have seen, and we can readily see the extension of that type of narrative in various directions. The rape of Helen is the cause of the Trojan War. The pan-Hellenic expedition to reclaim her was preordained by her surrogate father Tyndareus at the time when there was pan-Hellenic competition for her as bride. He caused all the suitors to swear that they would acquiesce in his decision— based upon their demonstrated prowess in various athletic competitions and talent contests—and collectively avenge any man's attempt to take wrongful possession of her. Helen is, then, in the action of the *Iliad*, formerly the prize in a bride-contest and currently the prize in a huge war game. She is both the means of binding together one group of men in a common cause for war, and the creation of instant and intractable enmity between that group of men and the other group of men which centers around her abductor. We need to consider two exceptional circumstances here: first, the rape of a man's wife seems to be one of only two crimes that cannot be paid off with *apoina* ("blood price"), the other being the killing of a relative; second, the bond of guest-friendship between the warriors on the opposite sides in the conflict is a stronger prerogative than the claim of either king on the loyalty of their warriors or of any oaths they might have sworn. We shall finally argue that gifts, women, and words are the three media of exchange that bind men together, that each has value only thus, as a social medium, and that Achilles rejects all three.

II.3
THE PRICE OF RAPE AND MURDER

 One might expect the two terms *poinē* and *apoina* to have antithetical meanings, punishment and nonpunishment respectively. Such a distinction seems in fact to hold true in a large number of cases, where *poinē* has reference to a death for a death, but *apoina* recognizes the possibility that payment can be made instead. There are two crucial passages, however, where the two terms are clearly reversed. Let us begin by considering the various passages where *apoina* is used in reference to what one man must pay another for the return of a woman.

Clearly this is an issue central to the *Iliad*, since Agamemnon refuses *apoina* from Chryses for his daughter Chryseis until Kalchas interprets Apollo's intention to continue killing Greeks unless he does so, and Achilles refuses *apoina* from Agamemnon in addition to the return of Briseis and the oath that he has not had sexual intercourse with her. In the first instance the formula *pherōn t'apereisi' apoina* ("bringing countless gifts") and its relatives *aglaa dechthai apoina, ta d'apoina dechesthai* ("to accept the [glorious] gifts"), etc., are repeated so as to introduce an important word-theme at the opening of the poem: 1.13, 1.20, 1.23, 1.95, 1.111, 1.372, 1.377. We later hear Thersites, perversely echoing Achilles' own accusation against Agamemnon, use the term in a different sense, as booty in general, rather than ransom in particular (2.230). From then on we hear the term used as "ransom" for a captured male relative, e.g., when Adrastos begs Menelaos not to kill him but to take *apoina* (6.46). So, too Peisandros and Hippolochos beg Agamemnon (11.131); Dolon begs Odysseus (10.380). We know that Achilles has accepted *apoina* for Andromache's mother (6.427) and for Isos and Antiphos, two sons of Priam whom he caught watching sheep (11.106); Agamemnon later meets them in battle and kills them. This situation is repeated in the shocking episode of Achilles' second meeting with Lykaon, whom he had previously sold into slavery but, when Lykaon begs Achilles to accept *apoina* for him, he is told that no Trojan will live to be ransomed after Patroklos' death (21.99). The first time we hear of *apoina* for a dead man, rather than a living man or woman, is in Achilles' response to Hektor's plea that his body be returned for ransom (22.349). Then, throughout Book XXIV *apoina* is the term used for the gifts brought by Priam to Achilles' tent. Strange indeed is Achilles' appeal to the dead Patroklos not to resent his having accepted *apoina* for Hektor's body (24.594).

We seem to feel the true and original force of *poinē* in those passages where one man is killed in vengeance for having killed another man. Thus Akamas boasts over Promachos that, by having killed Promachos, he has avenged his brother (*kasignētoio ge poinē* (14.483)), whom Promachos had previously killed, and Akamas goes on to moralize the situation:

. . . . . . "τῶ καί τίς τ' εὔχεται ἀνὴρ
γνωτὸν ἐνὶ μεγάροισιν ἄρης ἀλκτῆρα λιπέσθαι."   (14.484–85)

". . . therefore a man prays he will leave behind him
one close to him in his halls to avenge his downfall in battle."

We hear a similar sentiment expressed by Sarpedon, when he appeals to Glaukos to protect his body from being stripped of its armor:

"σοὶ γὰρ ἐγὼ καὶ ἔπειτα κατηφείη καὶ ὄνειδος
ἔσσομαι ἤματα πάντα διαμπερές, εἴ κέ μ' 'Αχαιοὶ
τεύχεα συλήσωσι νεῶν ἐν ἀγῶνι πεσόντα."   (16.498–500)

"For I shall be a thing of shame and a reproach said of you
afterwards, all your days forever, if the Achaians
strip my armour here where I fell by the ships assembled."

We hear that Meriones kills Harpalion, the son of King Pylaimenes, who receives no *poinē* for him (13.659); that Patroklos kills many Trojans as a *poinē* for all the Achaians killed (16.398); and, most dreadfully, that Achilles sacrifices twelve young Trojans as a *poinē* for Patroklos

(21.28). Thus, we think usually of *poinē* as death for death, whereas *apoina* suggests gifts offered in recompense for death caused or offense given. However, in a figurative use of the term *poinē* there is the suggestion that it can consist of material ojects—Zeus is glad to give Hektor the armor of Achilles and Patroklos as a *poinē* for the fact that he will not return from battle (17.207)—and in Ajax' speech to Achilles in Book IX he questions the intensity of Achilles' wrath, saying a man even takes *poinē* (which must mean gifts here, to be analogous to the immediate situation) for the death of a child or a brother (9.633-36). Of course, in the first case there is terrible irony in the use of *poinē* for the granting of Achilles' armor to Hektor, since it is the armor which binds Hektor, Achilles, and Patroklos in death; in the second case, Ajax seems to define the very nature of the relationship between Achilles and Agamemnon: he cites the case of murder which can be arbitrated, which must be a murder outside the family; Achilles refuses arbitration, the implication being that he considers Agamemnon's theft of Briseis the equivalent of shedding kindred blood.

Ajax specifies that his hypothetical killer could, after paying the price, remain in his own country. We compare this with the several cases in which heroes are said to have had to flee their homes after killing members of their own families, such as Epeigeus (16.570ff.), and Patroklos (23.85ff.). It is not clear whether the poet is aware of kindred murder as the reason for Bellerophontes fleeing to King Proitos (6.156ff.), or of the antagonism between Meleager and his mother Althaia (9.553ff.), but the poet himself suggests the awe in which such men were held when he says Priam appears like one of them to Achilles:

ὡς δ' ὅτ' ἂν ἄνδρ' ἄτη πυκινὴ λάβῃ, ὅς τ' ἐνὶ πάτρῃ
φῶτα κατακτείνας ἄλλων ἐξίκετο δῆμον,
ἀνδρὸς ἐς ἀφνειοῦ, θάμβος δ' ἔχει εἰσορόωντας,
ὡς Ἀχιλεὺς θάμβησεν ἰδὼν Πρίαμον θεοειδέα· (24.480-83)

As when dense disaster closes on one who has murdered
a man in his own land, and he comes to the country of others,
to a man of substance, and wonder seizes on those who behold him,
so Achilleus wondered as he looked on Priam, a godlike man.

If we add to this constellation of passages just one more use of the term *poinē* and one more myth as told by one of the ambassadors to

Achilles, I think we can see the full range of social and familial crises that are covered in the poem, and in the whole Homeric concept of what can be paid for and for what a man must die. We hear that Aeneas' horses are descended from the horses Zeus gave Tros as *poinē* for his rape-seduction of Ganymede (5.266). If there were a clear distinction between *poinē* as death-vengeance and *apoina* as ransom or blood price, then we would have expected *apoina* to be used here, since the situation is similar to that in Book I. Chryses offers *apoina* to Agamemnon for the return of his daughter, whom Agamemnon would have as his concubine, but later, of course, it is Agamemnon who must not only return the girl to her father, but make offerings to Apollo in addition. Perhaps it is even implied that the Greek dead from the plague are the *poinē* for Agamemnon's refusal to give up the girl, the offerings to Apollo being *apoina*. It is not certain that Andromache's mother would have become any Greek's concubine if Achilles had not accepted *apoina* for her but, again, the suggestion is that a woman can be ransomed. Is it possible, however, if the woman has become her abductor's concubine? Would Achilles have accepted Briseis back if Agamemnon had not been able to swear that he had not had sexual intercourse with her? The terminology is not consistent and some of the situations are too complicated to offer clear corroboration of precise principles, but a vague pattern emerges.

First, the basic family unit is, with its conventional extensions, extremely important. Thus, Diomedes and Glaukos will not fight, though they are sworn to enmity, because their fathers were bound by the ties of guest friendship. So, too, though murder committed by a member of one family against a member of another family can be paid for with gifts, intrafamilial murder cannot be disguised or dismissed in this way, and the murderer tends to go abroad to seek sanctuary and ablution in the court of a foreign king. Violence, then, outside the family, can be dealt with by the exchange of gifts, and families can be bound together by the exchange of gifts.

Do erotic situations follow the same laws? Phoinix is expelled by his father and cursed with childlessness for having sexual intercourse with his father's mistress at his mother's insistence (9.447ff.). We cannot tell whether the poet is aware of the version in which Amyntor blinds his son for that quasi-incestuous crime, but if we compare the Phoinix myth in all its detail and variations with the myth of Oedipus himself (23.678f.), then the equivalence of blindness and castration becomes apparent: the man who usurps his father's place in his "mother's" bed will be punished with expulsion from the family and impotence. Another myth in the *Iliad* that impinges on this center of concern is, of course, Bellerophontes and his reported seduction of Proitos' wife, followed by his dismal end as a crippled beggar; and, of course, outside the *Iliad*, we hear of Pelops' curse on Laios for having seduced or raped his son Chrysippos. I do not mean that there is a *simple* cause-and-effect relationship between Bellerophontes' non-rape of Anteia and his ending his life as a cripple. I will suggest that the crime he is accused of by Anteia is "oedipal," that mutilated feet, like blindness, are symbolic of castration (cf. Oedipus himself) and that Bellerophontes' attempt to fly to Olympos is also an "oedipal" affront (cf. Phaethon and Ikaros). It is significant that Pelops suffers from Laios what Oinomaus suffers from Pelops: the violent, or inexcused, or unpaid for, rape of one's child. In the case of Oinomaus, we should specify that he suffers for his attempt to keep his daughter for himself, when Pelops beats him at his own chariot race. The father has the same sexual prerogative over his children—both male and female, in the Greek material—as he has over his wife. All of this rests firmly on the basic framework of the *Iliad* when we recall that Paris was a guest in Menelaos' house when he seduced and raped Helen. If we can see the host *in loco parentis* to the guest—this is particularly clear with the younger Bellerophontes and the older Proitos, the younger Paris and the older Menelaos—then the crime behind the Trojan War begins to look like incest.

I am not sure that this is where I want the argument to conclude. What I want to emerge from this consideration of compensation for violence is a difference between intra-familial and inter-familial relations, or, more familiarly put, the basic taboos against kindred murder and incest as opposed to the more expiable crimes of simple (nonrelated) murder and sexual expropriation. We might require here Lévi-Strauss' observation that women serve as means of exchange in primitive societies, to bind separate families together, as in the institution of gift-giving. It is certainly tempting to refer here to Achilles' own comparison between a war fought for a woman and what he seems to consider the more conventional, and sensible, kind of war—that fought for sheep and cattle (1.154ff.). We began our whole discussion of the value of women in the *Iliad* with the relative assessment that at least one woman, though no doubt an inferior one, was valued at only four oxen, and would go to the loser in the wrestling match (23.700ff.). Perhaps we have gone as far as we can in this investigation, without the examination of other complexes of formulae and situations, in saying simply that violence results between men over the theft of objects which have some intrinsic value in and of themselves— cattle for meat and hide, women for skills and sex—but that this valuation is exponentially increased by the very fact of these commodities' being stolen. Moreover, such affronts, when they involve actual murder, can be paid for, if the two parties are not closely related by blood or sacred friendship. When, however, the theft of a woman is "incestuous" and the murder is of a kinsman, the violence is inexpiable: someone else must die, and so on and on, as in the houses of Atreus and Laios.

All of these structures come together in the crucial insight of Achilles' long reply to Odysseus' speech in Book IX:

"οὐ γὰρ ἐμοὶ ψυχῆς ἀντάξιον οὐδ' ὅσα φασὶν
Ἴλιον ἐκτῆσθαι, εὖ ναιόμενον πτολίεθρον,
τὸ πρὶν ἐπ' εἰρήνης, πρὶν ἐλθεῖν υἷας Ἀχαιῶν,
οὐδ' ὅσα λάϊνος οὐδὸς ἀφήτορος ἐντὸς ἐέργει,
Φοίβου Ἀπόλλωνος, Πυθοῖ ἔνι πετρηέσσῃ.
ληϊστοὶ μὲν γάρ τε βόες καὶ ἴφια μῆλα,
κτητοὶ δὲ τρίποδές τε καὶ ἵππων ξανθὰ κάρηνα·
ἀνδρὸς δὲ ψυχὴ πάλιν ἐλθεῖν οὔτε λεϊστὴ
οὔθ' ἑλετή, ἐπεὶ ἄρ κεν ἀμείψεται ἕρκος ὀδόντων."   (9.401–9)

. . . "For not
worth the value of my life are all the possessions they fable
were won for Ilion, that strong-founded citadel, in the old days
when there was peace, before the coming of the sons of the Achaians;
not all that the stone doorsill of the Archer holds fast within it,
of Phoibos Apollo in Pytho of the rocks. Of possessions
cattle and fat sheep are things to be had for the lifting,
and tripods can be won, and the tawny heads of horses,
but a man's life cannot come back again, it cannot be lifted
nor captured again by force, once it has crossed the teeth's barrier."

The only way to construe *palin elthein* (408) is as epexegetical infinitive with both *leistē* and *heletē*, so that Achilles' point is appreciable only within the context of the *Iliad*. Whereas Catullus uses the sun rising and setting for his comparison to human life—*nox est perpetua una dormienda* (5.6)—the Homeric statement is based on the economy of theft: a man cannot steal back his own life. *Life is outside the system of mutual validation represented by the exchange, peaceful or warlike, of women and animals and artifacts. Life is an absolute value inexpressible in language*—itself a medium of exchange—except in this kind of negative example: "Life is not plunderable back."

Although I have no illusion that my simplistic view of this complex matter will be accepted here, at this point in its evolution, I must warn the reader that I am going finally to suggest that all of this violence is oedipal and that it is for this very reason that Achilles feels alienated from it. Generally in the *Iliad* women have only a social value, as a means of exchange, because other men value them, and especially so when they are disputed. For Achilles, I do not think they have even this value, because he is not social. He has almost no bonds with the socially structured world of humanity, since he is more a god than a mortal, more closely aligned with his mother than with his father, though not in the conventional oedipal manner, and this means that he is more concerned with himself than with any object in the world, such objects being conventionally only socially validated, whether they be material or sexual.

We can certainly see the father's place in all this. By denying the son possession of the mother he simultaneously teaches the son to value the mother and other women like her and, more generally, to accept the displacement of his desire from one object (the mother) onto other objects (money, political power, other men's women, etc.). It is not without "significance" that the son's oedipal experience is simultaneous with his acquisition of language, from about eighteen months until six years. As Lacan has shown, language displaces gratification from the original, inexpressible object of desire, to the object that can be expressed in the language which the society the child must enter supplies him with: *désir* and *demande* are not only not the same, but exist only as functions of their difference from each other. My difference from Lacan (and, I must admit, from Freud) is in positing a period, or particular circumstances, when the mother is not valued, both because she is always already there and because the father is not there to compete with the son for her. The results of this experience I call the Achilles complex: only the narcissistic image of the self is invested as an object, and, more generally, the world as social and linguistic structure is not recognized or appreciated.

If we can accept these conditions, then can we wonder at Achilles' response to the embassy? Even before he has lost his dear friend Patroklos, he has received a severe blow to his previous conception of his place in the world. Three men come from Agamemnon (whom we must see as casting an oedipal shadow over Achilles' world for the first time) and speak to him in languages he refuses to understand and offer him gifts that have no value to him. These heroes cannot understand the absolutism of Achilles' refusal, but they and all the other Greeks and Trojans share with him a preoccupation with self-assertion and self-recognition. Again, the principle in operation is desire, since they seek what they lack, a locus of identity.

Our appreciation of the *Iliad* depends upon our ability to reexperience this struggle-into-being. The dynamics of the literary process are such that the intensity of Achilles' struggle might be filtered through the compromised response of the other heroes, just as in tragedy we might sometimes listen to the chorus when the hero seems to have receded beyond our reach. Nevertheless, in epic as in tragedy, our focus must always be upon the hero, for not even the gods— certainly not the gods—can tell us what he is suffering. It is the quality of his suffering that is our interest in both genres. Speaking phylogenetically, the epic hero lacks an integrated sense of self and depends upon his fellows to validate his sense of reality (shame), while the tragic hero has developed sufficient individuality to bear his burden of guilt. Ontogenetically we say that the epic hero represents for us pre-oedipal experience characterized by narcissistic rage, whereas the tragic hero represents the bitter renunciation of the oedipal object.

II.4
MEN IN PAIRS

Although we recognize the universality of the Oedipus complex and see in it the absolute basis for all human society and therefore find in the *Iliad* some indication of its operation, we insist that far more important to the whole world view of the *Iliad* is the urge on the heroes' part to define themselves in terms of themselves—outside of the society which gives them scope for their activity—and hence the centrality of Achilles to the poem and the necessity to appreciate what we tentatively call the Achilles complex. We mean by this, of course, narcissism, the attempt to recapture the lost image of completion and perfection, which under certain circumstances is the infant's first experience of himself. These circumstances are, primarily, an all-sufficient mother, and one of the paradoxical consequences of her constant presence and unquestioning love is the child's libidinal investment of his own image as she projects it to him, rather than investment of her herself. Just as important as the everpresent mother is the absent father. Clearly we are describing the childhood of Achilles as represented in the mature experience of Achilles in the poem. For the other heroes we have less information and less clearly defined characteristics.

We see, of course, in Patroklos Achilles' image of himself, and yet we realize that this is by no means a relationship that can be explained in conventional terms, neither our modern structures for homosexual orientation (or object-choice), nor the ancient (e.g., Platonic) structures for the preference shown by mature Greek males for barely postpubescent boys, i.e., pederasty. We can easily settle the debate be-

tween the Platonic Phaidros and Aeschylus over whether Achilles is
erastēs and Patroklos erōmenos, or vice versa (Symposium, 180), but
these are not the proper terms for the Iliad. Let us look instead precisely at the relationship as depicted in the poem, in the context of
other similar but not nearly so extreme relationships of love and dependence that exist between other heroes.

We know that Patroklos came to the court of Peleus because he had
killed a man, presumably a relative, in his own country (23.85ff.).
From Nestor we hear at great length about his own arrival there, some
years later, with Odysseus, in gathering the pan-Hellenic force for the
expedition against Troy. For some reason Patroklos' father Menoitios
is also in attendance and advises his son in these words:

"τέκνον ἐμόν, γενεῇ μὲν ὑπέρτερός ἐστιν Ἀχιλλεύς,
πρεσβύτερος δὲ σύ ἐσσι· βίῃ δ' ὅ γε πολλὸν ἀμείνων.
ἀλλ' εὖ οἱ φάσθαι πυκινὸν ἔπος ἠδ' ὑποθέσθαι
καί οἱ σημαίνειν· ὁ δὲ πείσεται εἰς ἀγαθόν περ."   (11.786–89)

"My child, by right of blood Achilles is higher than you are,
but you are the elder. Yet in strength he is far the greater.
You must speak solid words to him, and give him good counsel,
and point his way. If he listens to you it will be for his own good."

Briefly alluded to here is a general conception basic to the whole
argument of the Iliad, and one we must discuss at greater length in
another section of this study. For now, let us simply acknowledge the
identification between youth and physical strength, martial prowess,
etc. (Achilles), on the one hand, and on the other maturity and good
counsel, restraint and caution (Patroklos). If we recall our "under"-
reading of Freud "On Narcissism," we will recognize, perhaps, in
Patroklos Achilles' ego ideal, that monitoring aspect of his intellectual
and emotional consciousness, which, were we to follow Freud through
to his final topography of the mind and allow that Achilles has experienced anything like an Oedipus complex and its normal resolution,
we would call the superego. I think all this is possible, and indeed does
inform the reader's appreciation of the relation between Achilles and
Patroklos. To some extent, certainly in the central section of the poem,
when he delivers Nestor's advice to Achilles, Patroklos does serve as
a mediating agent between the outside world, which we might with
some trepidation call reality, and the inner world of Achilles' own

struggle to define himself. Beyond this, though, I insist that we also recognize in Patroklos Achilles' ideal ego, that image of his lost childhood. Patroklos is to Achilles what Enkidu is to Gilgamesh and Oliver to Roland: not the hero's more powerful, or older, or more authoritative (i.e., oedipal) self-correction, but rather his assurance of his own continued existence as first and best.

When one thinks of pairs of men in the *Iliad* other than Achilles and Patroklos, those that immediately spring to mind are Odysseus and Diomedes in the much maligned Book X, and the seemingly inexplicable dual forms of Book IX, when the three ambassadors reach Achilles' tent (182–98). In this latter case we must believe either that an earlier version excluded Phoinix, and the duals' reference is then to Ajax and Odysseus; or that their reference is to the heralds, for the most part, recalling the similar use of the form and conventional use of the heralds in the taking of Briseis (1.327ff.); or, that Odysseus is omitted, because of his traditional enmity with Achilles.[1] On the former problem, that of the authenticity of Book X, we shall say nothing but that Diomedes and Odysseus are also mentioned in the dual at 11.320ff. and 19.47: they seem to be a conventional pair. Another conventional pair is that of the two Ajaxes, e.g., 7.164. Nagy has called our attention to the significance of ("cognates" of) *therapōn* as "double" in other languages and literatures which delimit societies and cameraderies similar to those in the *Iliad*.[2] It has long since been noted that the Homeric warrior is helpless without a *therapōn* to drive his chariot. The reverse is equally true: after the death of Othryoneus at the hands of Idomeneus, Asios comes forward to save the body from being pulled away and stripped of its armor, but Idomeneus is "too quick with a spearcast," and Asios, too, is felled, "as when an oak goes down or a white poplar / or like a towering pine tree" (13.389–90). Then we have a picture of the helpless, nameless companion, here referred to not as *therapōn* but as *hēniochos*:

ὣς ὁ πρόσθ' ἵππων καὶ δίφρου κεῖτο τανυσθείς,
βεβρυχώς, κόνιος δεδραγμένος αἱματοέσσης.
ἐκ δέ οἱ ἡνίοχος πλήγη φρένας, ἃς πάρος εἶχεν,
οὐδ' ὅ γ' ἐτόλμησεν, δηΐων ὑπὸ χεῖρας ἀλύξας,
ἂψ ἵππους στρέψαι, τὸν δ' Ἀντίλοχος μενεχάρμης
δουρὶ μέσον περόνησε τυχών· οὐδ' ἤρκεσε θώρηξ
χάλκεος, ὃν φορέεσκε, μέση δ' ἐν γαστέρι πῆξεν.   (13.392–98)

So he lay there felled in front of his horses and chariot,
roaring, and clawed with his hands at the bloody dust. Meanwhile
the charioteer who was close behind him was stricken in the wits
and shrinking from the hands of the enemy did not have daring
to turn the horses about, but Antilochos stubborn in battle
pinned him through the middle with a spearstroke,
and the corselet of bronze he wore could not hold, the spear fixed in the
     middle belly. . . .

This is in contrast to the role usually played by the companion as
charioteer, as in the passage where Kebriones gives advice to Hektor:

"Hektor, you and I encounter the Danaans at the utmost
edge of the sorrowful battle, but meanwhile the rest of the Trojans
are driven pell-mell upon each other, the men and their horses.
The Telamonian Aias drives them; I know him surely
for he carries the broad shield on his shoulders. So let us all
steer our horses and chariot that way, since there the horsemen
and the foot-ranks more than elsewhere hurling the wicked war-hate
against each other, are destroying, and the ceaseless clamour has
     risen."   (11.523–30)

Again, at 12.75ff., we learn that the companions are specifically char-
ioteers, that their function is primarily to position their lords in the
battle so that they can fight effectively either from the car, or leaving
it, on foot, but with the car always there for their escape, if they are
wounded, or for their quick remove to another area of the battlefield
if they are needed there.

We hear in 7.148ff. that Lykourgos left his armor to his companion
when he grew old, so perhaps we should take as conventional a difference in age: the *therapōn*, like the feudal page or squire, was usually
the younger attendant upon his lord. We know, of course, that this
is not true in the case of Achilles and Patroklos, but the fact that
Achilles' social superiority to Patroklos, not to mention his martial
superiority, offsets his youth in the relationship might have a parallel
in the sets of hero and companion, where the former is the legitimate
child of a king and the latter a bastard, e.g., the sons of Priam at
11.103-4: "The bastard Isos was charioteer / and renowned Antiphos
rode beside him."

Not only do we consistently find hero and companion mutually and
vitally dependent upon each other in battle—and, of course, off the
battlefield, where we see the companion feeding the hero and tending

his wounds—but also we notice the negative of all this, that is, that just as men fight successfully in pairs, they tend to die in pairs. The *aristeia* of Agamemnon begins with the slaying of Bienor, "shepherd of his people," and Oïleus his companion (*hetairos*) and charioteer (*plēxippos*) (11.91–93). We have already mentioned Isos and Antiphos, whom Agamemnon slays immediately thereafter, as soon as he has stripped the armor from the bodies of Bienor and Oïleus. Then, immediately, he kills Peisandros and Hippolochos, sons of Antimachos, who are driving their chariot together. Then, after the narrative intrusion of Zeus sending Iris to Hektor, Agamemnon continues his slaughter with the two sons of Antenor, Iphidamos and Koön. Their passion is the most touching of any series, since it is explicitly stated that the latter dies trying to avenge the former:

When Koön, conspicious among the fighters, perceived him,
he who was Antenor's oldest born, the strong sorrow
misted about his eyes for the sake of his fallen brother.
He came from the side and unobserved at great Agamemnon
and stabbed with his spear at the middle arm, underneath the elbow,
and the head of the glittering spear cut its way clean through.
Agamemnon the lord of men shuddered with fear then
but even so did not give up the attack or his fighting
but sprang at Koön, gripping a spear that struck with the wind's speed.
Now Koön was dragging his father's son, his brother Iphidamas,
by the foot back eagerly, and cried out on all the bravest,
but as he dragged him into the crowd, Agamemnon thrust at him
with the smoothed bronze spear underneath the knobbed shield, and
    unstrung him,
then came up and hewed off his head over Iphidamas.
There under the king, Atreus' son, the sons of Antenor
filled out their destiny and went down to the house of the death
    god.   (11.248–63)

Several points could be made about this sequence of three double killings, all brothers. The conventional critic would remark on the pathos and irony of the narrative pattern, that there is contradiction between the two more effective similes: Agamemnon is a lion who devours the young of the doe while she watches in helpless terror (11.113–21), but then, when he himself is wounded, the pain descends upon him as upon a woman in childbirth (11.267–74). I would rather call attention to the fact that all the brothers die in tandem and that finally, when Agamemnon feels his strength ebbing, he relies upon his own companion-charioteer to take him out of the battle to safety. The whole passage, then, is a study in dependence, how men fight and die in pairs, and though I would admit that the pairing is particularly concentrated here, I would insist that it is nevertheless paradigmatic of the whole poem. We find it again, for instance, at 11.749ff., and 21.90ff.

We often hear heroes calling upon a companion to come to their aid or thinking to themselves that their situation requires a companion's help. Thus Deïphobos, seeing Idomeneus kill Asios, aims at the killer, but hits another hero Hypsenor, and vaunts over him:

"Asios lies not now all unavenged. I think rather
as he goes down to Hades of the Gates, the strong one,
he will be cheerful at heart, since I have sent him an escort."   (13.414–16)

We then see Hypsenor's companion Antilochos bestride the body and protect it with his shield, while Idomeneus pursues and kills a third Trojan (after Othryoneus and Asios), Alkathoös, and his vaunt to Deïphobos is that he has exchanged three for one and it is time for Deïphobos himself to face him and find out how great is the strength of a son of Zeus. Whereupon Deïphobos hesitates:

Δηΐφοβος δὲ διάνδιχα μερμήριξεν,
ἤ τινά που Τρώων ἑταρίσσαιτο μεγαθύμων
ἂψ᾽ ἀναχωρήσας, ἤ πειρήσαιτο καὶ οἶος.   (13.455–57)

. . . the heart in Deïphobos was divided,
pondering whether to draw back and find some other high-hearted
Trojan to be his companion, or whether to attempt him singly.

There is, then, even a verb to express the need for accompaniment, the lack a Homeric hero feels when he is alone: hetairizō in the active voice signifies "to be a companion to" and in the middle "to take as a companion."

Perhaps it will be claimed that all we have done here is illustrate the obvious fact that men in battle need help from each other and that the successful effort in battle requires cooperation. Indeed, shortly, I shall examine the use of a particular verb which does stress this need in such a way that we feel the attraction of anonymity. Here, however, we see men stepping out in the front of battle and facing their enemies on what at first seems a one-to-one basis, but is then revealed always to be in fact a hero with the support of his *therapōn* or *hetairos*. Homeric heroes fight in pairs and die in pairs and this feature of the poem, rather than being shunted aside as a peculiarity— even a corruption—of Aegean Bronze Age military tactics, must be recognized as a manifestation of the heroic temperament. The individual functions in a closed, highly structured society which supplies him with the support and encouragement he requires to meet that society's demands primarily through the institutionalization of the dual relationship of companionship. *The Homeric hero requires his mirror in another closely related hero (or subordinate) to assure himself of his own "actual" existence.* We do not for a moment forget that this axiom has a negative corollary: that the hero denies to his companion (especially his subordinate) any usurpation of his own particular function: Achilles warns Patroklos not to take his glory from him. Nagy has shown us what happens when *therapōn* assimilates to hero and hero assimilates to god. It is that crisis of undifferentiation which Girard has also articulated. We shall deal with all this later in our consideration of subject and object in the *Iliad*, active and passive, fighter and fought-over, etc. For now, let us only set in our minds the helplessness of abandonment which the hero without companion suffers. There is no better example than Antilochos careening in and out of the battle after the death of Patroklos, for whom he served as charioteer:

He would dash in, like a vulture among geese, with his horses,
and lightly get away out of the Trojans' confusion
and lightly charge in again in pursuit of a great multitude,
and yet could kill no man when he swept in the chase of them.
He had no way while he was alone in a separate chariot
to lunge with the spear and still keep in hand his fast-running
    horses.   (17.460–65)

The hero in the *Iliad* does not exist as such if he cannot kill. We have seen this truth spelled out for us in those formulas such as *olluntas t'ollumenas te*. We have recognized in this tension between killing and being killed the Hegelian insistence on the risk of death as the only validation of life for the truly self-conscious subject. Now, let us only see in Antilochos' senseless course in and out, ineffective after the loss of Patroklos, a visual and actual realization of that psychic *aporia* which will beset Achilles when he hears the news of his dear friend's death. As in all cases, Achilles is the extreme statement of heroic reality: continued existence without the constant assurance of a companion is impossible. We see this come literally true when Athene tricks Hecktor into facing Achilles. Hektor is confident in his fighting ability as long as he thinks his brother Deïphobos stands beside him there outside the walls, but when he realizes that this confidence is based upon a delusion caused by a god he knows that death is upon him.

If we bring this brief discussion of interdependent pairs of men in the *Iliad* back to its beginning, where we argued for the greater importance of the pre-oedipal experience of narcissism to an appreciation of the poem—greater, that is, than oedipal experience—then we might refer to Lévi-Strauss for some comment on the universality of this kind of mirroring as a social phenomenon. Strangely enough, his consideration of men's pairing in primitive culture is contained in his contradiction of Freud's myth of oedipal attack in the primal horde. In his general discussion, then, of exogamy as a means of binding families together rather than a way of escaping incest, he quotes several previous studies, including those of Montaigne and Margaret Mead:

[Seligman] cites the institution of blood brotherhood as expressed by the *henamo* relationship among the natives of New Guinea. . . . The brother-in-law is ally, collaborator and friend; it is the term given to adult males belonging to the band with which an alliance has been contracted. In the same band, the potential brother-in-law, i.e., the cross-cousin, is the one with whom, as an adolescent, one indulges in homosexual activities which will always leave their mark in the mutually affectionate behavior of the adults. . . . Furthermore, objects found in a series, such as hut posts, the pipes of a Pan-pipe, etc., are said to be "brothers," or are called "others," in their respective relationships, a terminological detail which is worth comparing with Montaigne's observation that the Brazilian Indians whom he met at Rouen called men the "halves" of one another, just as we say "our fellow men". . . . Mead's Arapesh informants had difficulty at first in answering her questions on possible infringements of the marriage prohibitions. . . . The ethnographer pressed the point, asking what they would think or say if, through some eventuality, this impossibility [brother-sister incest] managed to occur. Informants had difficulty placing themselves in this situation, for it was scarcely conceivable: "What, you would like to marry your sister! What is the matter with you anyway? Don't you want a brother-in-law? Don't you realize that if you marry another man's sister and another man marries your sister, you will have at least two brothers-in-law, while if you marry your own sister you will have none? With whom will you hunt, with whom will you garden, with whom will you go to visit?[3]

The situation generally, and therefore the situation in the *Iliad*, is suddenly outlined with awesome clarity: men define themselves in terms of other men, and women are only a means of strengthening and formalizing men's relations with each other. The phylogenetic-ontogenetic parallels could not be clearer: the relations of brothers-in-law recapitulate the perhaps homosexual relations of adolescent "blood-brothers," which in turn recapitulate the beginning of con-sciousness in the infantile experience of narcissism. Montaigne's in-formation of the cannibal calling men the "halves" of one another explicates Aristophanes' myth in Plato's *Symposium*. This is the begin-ning of men's desire, and Plato validates the mature version of it, male homosexuality, which most closely approximates that beginning. Again we run the risk of offending everyone by suggesting that Homer recaptures a "primitive" stage in human development, but how can we refuse the revelations consequent upon such a suggestion? The indications are inescapable that "under-developed" societies contain clearer traces of those stages in human development through which we all pass.

This is not to say that Achilles and Patroklos represent to us, as do some Brazilian Indians, our own adolescent experiences of homosex-uality. Though perhaps it is in the Brazilian Indian's identification of the cross-sex object of his desire in maturity with the same-sex object of his desire in adolescence—the brothers and sisters might remind us of Shakespeare's Sebastian and Viola—that we find an illustrative parallel for the relationship between Achilles and Patroklos, lying down each with his own woman (and Achilles gave Patroklos the woman he lies with), but being emotionally dependent upon each other in a way which is impossible to imagine between Achilles and Briseis. Rather it is to recognize that in this, as in so much else that anthropology and ethnology have shown us, our overdeveloped societies camouflage so much that is essential to us. So insistent are we on heterosexual monogamy as the basis of family life, and family life as the basis of society generally, that we deny our early and continuing dependence for self-definition on "similars" as well as "others." Morally we have been forced to renounce our narcissism along with all other aspects of the polymorphous perversity of childhood. We shall come finally to see Achilles as the model for Nietzsche's "blond beast," and perhaps this will convince us that not only has Judaeo-Christian humanism forced us to misread ourselves, as Nietzsche maintained, but it has forced us to misread the *Iliad* as well.

II.5
"MIXING" IN LOVE AND WAR

Many of these features of the erotic and aggressive life of the heroes come together in the narrative expressed by one verb, *mignumi*. In many of its appearances it seems colorless, hardly more suggestive than *eimi* or *ekhō*, e.g.,

οὐδέ   ποτε   Τρῶες   Δαναῶν
ἐδύναντο φάλαγγας
ῥηξάμενοι κλισίῃσι μιγήμεναι ἠδὲ νέεσσιν.   (15.408–09)

nor again had the Trojans strength to break the battalions
of the Danaans, and *force their way into* the ships, and the shelters.

or

ῥεῖα διακρίνωσιν, ἐπεί κε νομῷ μιγέωσιν,   (2.475)

easily separate them in order as *they take* to the pasture

where the subject is shepherds, the object sheep, and the finite verb—though it perhaps suggested itself to the poet in a formulaic framework of which we have little trace, but which originally was based on the contrast between mixing and separating—now seems like filler. Occasionally it means little more than "lie with or among," but its strength is still felt so that the situation described suggests that strange combination of intimacy and hostility that characterizes the whole poem and lies as a primary ambivalence at the root of the verb:

"πῶς γὰρ νῦν, Τρώεσσι μεμιγμένοι ἱπποδάμοισιν
εὕδουσ', ἢ ἀπάνευθε;"   (10.424–25)

"How, then, are these sleeping? And are *they mixed* with the Trojans, breakers of horses, or apart?"

ἀλλὰ γλῶσσ' ἐμέμικτο, πολύκλητοι δ' ἔσαν ἄνδρες.   (4.438)

but their talk *was mixed*, who were called there from many far places.

ἀλλ' ὅτε δὴ τάχ' ἔμελλε μιγήσεσθαι φυλάκεσσι   (10.365)

But when he was on the point of *reaching* the Achaian pickets.

ἀλλ' ὅτε δὴ Τρώεσσιν ἐν ἀγρομένοισιν ἔμιχθεν,   (3.209)

Now when these *were set* before the Trojans assembled.

(Said of Menelaos and Odysseus within the walls of Troy.) Sometimes *mignumi* carries great force, and is used in conventional, but still shocking figures, e.g.,

ἥ τε κόμη τό τε εἶδος, ὅτ' ἐν κονίῃσι μιγείης.   (3.55)

nor your locks, when *you rolled* in the dust, nor all your beauty.

and

φθεγγομένου δ' ἄρα τοῦ γε κάρη κονίῃσιν ἐμίχθη.   (10.457)

and Dolon's head still speaking *dropped* in the dust.

Most of the verb's occurrences are closely divided between the two types of relationship. Thus there is the basic euphemism for the sexual act: *migē philotēti kai eunēi* "he mixed with her in love and in bed" (6.25, cf. 21.143, 6.161, 6.165, 2.232, 24.131, 3.445, 15.33, 14.295). I think there is even a suggestion of the erotic in Thetis' plaint "*aideomai de misgesth' athanatoisin*" (I am ashamed to mix among the immortals) (24.90–91). It reminds us of her once almost intimate relations with Zeus and Hephaistos. We shall discuss below her strange relation with Hera. Thus the briefly told tale of Bellerophontes at the court of King Proitos warns us of the potential disaster implicit in a woman's own desire, that it can manifest itself in transference onto its own object so that two men are brought into a conflict immediately displacing and canceling a previously and elaborately sacred intimacy:

αὐτὰρ Γλαῦκος τίκτεν ἀμύμονα Βελλεροφόντην·
τῷ δὲ θεοὶ κάλλος τε καὶ ἠνορέην ἐρατεινὴν
ὤπασαν· αὐτάρ οἱ Προῖτος κακὰ μήσατο θυμῷ,

ὅς ῥ' ἐκ δήμου ἔλασσεν, ἐπεὶ πολὺ φέρτερος ἦεν,
'Αργείων· Ζεὺς γάρ οἱ ὑπὸ σκήπτρῳ ἐδάμασσε.
τῷ δὲ γυνὴ Προίτου ἐπεμήνατο, δῖ' 'Αντεια,
κρυπταδίῃ φιλότητι μιγήμεναι· ἀλλὰ τὸν οὔ τι
πεῖθ' ἀγαθὰ φρονέοντα, δαΐφρονα Βελλεροφόντην.
ἡ δὲ ψευσαμένη Προῖτον βασιλῆα προσηύδα·
"τεθναίης, ὦ Προῖτ', ἢ κάκτανε Βελλεροφόντην,
ὅς μ' ἔθελεν φιλότητι μιγήμεναι οὐκ ἐθελούσῃ."   (6.155–65)

and Glaukos in turn sired Bellerophontes the blameless.
To Bellerophontes the gods granted beauty and desirable
manhood; but Proitos in anger devised evil things against him,
and drove him out of his own domain, since he was far greater,
from the Argive country Zeus had broken to the sway of his sceptre.
Beautiful Anteia the wife of Proitos was stricken
with passion to lie in love with him, and yet she could not
beguile valiant Bellerophontes, whose will was virtuous.
So she went to Proitos the king and uttered her falsehood:
"Would you be killed, o Proitos? Then murder Bellerophontes
who tried to lie with me in love, though I was unwilling."

(The alternatives are clearer in the Greek: "You should either die yourself, Proitos, or kill Bellerophontes," which calls for comparison with all those formulae about "killing and being killed" in battle.)

This story can indeed be appreciated as paradigmatic of the whole plot of the *Iliad* if once we accept the premise that women can serve both as functions of men's aggression against each other—men need something to fight over, anything—and as unreal causes of that aggression, especially when inter-familial and intra-familial relations are confused. We should not be surprised to see the battle between the Lapiths and the Centaurs sculpted into so many later temple pediments: marriages are occasions when such confused relations are most worrisome, and it is here that one should expect the violence of men's appetites to break forth. We shall shortly consider Menelaos' meditation on libidinal and aggressive *koros*.

In hearing of Anteia's demand on Proitos we immediately think of Herodotos' story of Gyges and Kandaules and contemplate the twofold phenomenology of myth: it simultaneously shapes all human experience into its own predetermined patterns (Persian history becomes Greek mythology) and it originally delineates itself from the constantly recurring patterns of human experience (Greek mythology is "true" and adequately explains dynastic revolutions in Persia). We recall that the theme of *cherchez la femme* as an explanation of all war is constant in the opening chapters of Herodotos' history; he cites Io, Europa, and Medea, as well as Helen. In both his telling of the Gyges–Kandaules story and Homer's telling of the Bellerophontes–Proitos story, the great impact comes from the oedipal nature of the triangle: the king's wife is compromised by the hallucinated lust of the king's subordinate. (We know the motif generally by its Old Testament example, "Joseph and Potiphar's wife.") Why is it that only one man can live when two men have "known one woman's nakedness"? Is it partly because sexual possessions are one of the few means men have of distinguishing themselves from each other? Why is the man in a subordinate position so continuously tempted to usurp his master's place in his wife's bed? Clearly, in these examples there is a tripartite identification: to take the king's wife is to take his life, is to take his right to rule. Can we indeed go further than Freud and Rank, who simply attest to the universality in human life and literature of the incest motif, especially its oedipal form? "Kill or be killed," says Anteia to Proitos, and this is the imperative under which all Homeric heroes seem to function. But is she then the *prophasis* or the *aitia* for their violence? Of course, in her case the seduction was a lie and Proitos refrained from violence, but the potential is frighteningly there in those *sēmata lugra*, which one is inclined to regard as Derrida's traces, the suspicion and violence that is always already there, on Freud's magic writing tablet, in the stitching of Othello's mother's handkerchief. Is this violence oedipal or is it narcissistic (Achillean)? Is it oedipal in Herodotos, but narcissistic in Homer? What else does Homer say about it?

The erotic and aggressive uses of *mignumi* mix in its use as a description of the predicted consequences of the fall of Troy or, less convincingly, the defeat of the Achaians, as they make their oaths and pour their libations:

"ὧδέ σφ' ἐγκέφαλος χαμάδις ῥέοι ὡς ὅδε οἶνος,
αὐτῶν καὶ τεκέων, ἄλοχοι δ' ἄλλοισι δαμεῖεν." (3.300–1)

"First, let their brains be spilled on the ground as this wine is spilled now theirs and their sons', and let their wives be the spoil of others."

The variant reading from Eustathios is *megeien* at the end of 301: "let their wives mix (in love) with others." Agamemnon swears his oath (that he has not "mixed in love" with Briseis) at 9.133; it is repeated by Odysseus to Achilles at 9.275, and Agamemnon swears it once more at 19.176. What difference does it make, as Achilles himself wonders aloud (9.336ff.), whether Agamemnon has had carnal knowledge of Briseis? The great issue is his own (Achilles') life, and the lives of the other Achaians. Is Helen, or Briseis, or any other woman, or anything, worth fighting for? Must men fight? Will they always find an excuse? They seem to want to mix in violence with each other as much as they want to mix in love with women.

Τηλεμάχοιο φίλον πατέρα προμάχοισι μιγέντα
Τρώων   (4.354–55)

the very father of Telemachos *locked* with the champion Trojans

ὣς μεμαὼς Τρώεσσι μίγη κρατερὸς Διομήδης.   (5.143)

such was the rage of the strong Diomedes as he *closed* with the Trojans

ἀρᾶται δὲ τάχιστα μιγήμεναι ἐν δαῒ λυγρῇ·   (13.286)

but his prayer is *to close* as soon as may be in bitter division

πατροκασιγνήτοιο μιγήμεναι ἐν παλάμῃσι.   (21.469)

to close and fight in strength of hand with his father's brother.

εἴκελον ἀστεροπῇ· τῷ δ' οὐ θέμις ἐστὶ μιγῆναι   (14.386)

. . . as glitters the thunderflash none may *close* with.

θεσπεσίῳ δ' ὁμάδῳ ἁλὶ μίσγεται, . . .   (13.797)

[Zeus' thunderbolt] with gigantic clamour *hits* the sea.

ὣς τῶν μισγομένων γένετο ἰαχή τε πόνος τε.   (4.456)

such, from the *coming together* of men, was the shock and the shouting.

(Note also the epithet *misgagkeian* ("where mountain glens meet"), 4.453.

ἢ αὐτοσχεδίῃ μεῖξαι χεῖράς τε μένος τε.   (15.510)

to close and fight with the strength of our hands at close quarters

σύν ῥ' ἔπεσον, σὺν δέ σφι βαρεῖαι χεῖρες ἔμιχθεν.   (23.687)

and *closed*, so that their heavy arms were crossing each other

Τυδεΐδης δ' ἐξαῦτις ἰὼν προμάχοισιν ἐμίχθη,   (5.134)

. . . . while Tydeus'
son *closed* once again with the champions, taking his place there

Τυδεΐδης δ' αὐτός περ ἐὼν προμάχοισιν ἐμίχθη,   (8.99)

the son of Tydeus, alone as he was, *went among* the champions.

αὐτὸς δ' αὖτ' ἐξαῦτις ἰὼν προμάχοισιν ἐμίχθη.   (13.642)

and turned back himself *to merge* in the ranks of the champions

. . . αὐτὸς δ' αὖτις ἰὼν προμάχοισιν ἐμίχθη.   (15.457)

. . . then himself *went back* into the ranks of the champions.

Clearly the heroes both want to emerge from the anonymity of the
battle and stand in the first rank to invite single combat with an enemy,
and they simultaneously require (usually)—note the use of *autos* in
the last three examples—the assistance of a comrade, and occasionally
they lose their sense of themselves and their prowess, and slip back
into the mass of men fighting behind them, their own fellows, and the
verb is the same for this regression and emersion:

Ἕκτωρ δ' ὦκ' ἀπέλεθρον ἀνέδραμε, μίκτο δ' ὁμίλῳ,   (11.354)

But Hektor sprang far away back and *merged* among his own people

. . . ὁ μὲν αὖτις ἀνέδραμε, μίκτο δ' ὁμίλῳ,   (16.813)

. . . but ran away again, and *lost himself* in the crowd . . . .

This last is said of Euphorbos who, after wounding Patroklos with
a spearthrust, when Apollo has already stripped Patroklos of his armor,
still cannot face the hero in single combat. Men are only men when
they mix with the foremost fighters; when they mix with the crowd,
and with women in love, they lose themselves. It is the same paradox
we have faced in Achilles' relations with Patroklos: the object of desire
is despised for its passivity, its failure to maintain an aggressive posture—Achilles likens Patroklos to a young girl crying (16.7–11). The
object of desire is also feared, because the subject might assimilate to
its pattern of passivity or the object might usurp the subject's place.
Achilles warns Patroklos not to storm the gates of Troy because that
is his, Achilles', glory (16.83–90). Achilles must be preeminent; when
he goes to shout at the ditch *oude es Akhaious/misgeto* (18.215–16)
"nor mixed [he] with the other Achaians."

I think finally that it is Menelaos who puts violence and desire together and explains to us—as it is, of course, his place to do—what drives men on to take each other's wives and lives. He himself will immediately "mix himself, though alone, with the foremost fighters" (13.642), but first he develops the sense of another word, seeking its *etymos logos*, and that is *koros*, which, as we shall see, cannot but be associated by sound and sense in this context with *korē*. It is the sort of passage Peabody has explicated in Hesiod, and we follow the directions of Nagy and Nagler in attempting to see the traditional formulas working themselves out in this single example (a momentary manifestation of a notion that must always remain without complete or original expression), rather than having some historical development hypothesized for it.

"λείψετέ θην οὕτω γε νέας Δαναῶν ταχυπώλων,
Τρῶες ὑπερφίαλοι, δεινῆς ἀκόρητοι ἀϋτῆς,
ἄλλης μὲν λώβης τε καὶ αἴσχεος οὐκ ἐπιδευεῖς,
ἣν ἐμὲ λωβήσασθε, κακαί κύνες, οὐδέ τι θυμῷ
Ζηνὸς ἐριβρεμέτεω χαλεπὴν ἐδείσατε μῆνιν
ξεινίου, ὅς τέ ποτ' ὕμμι διαφθέρσει πόλιν αἰπήν·
οἳ μευ κουριδίην ἄλοχον καὶ κτήματα πολλὰ
μὰψ οἴχεσθ' ἀνάγοντες, ἐπεὶ φιλέεσθε παρ' αὐτῇ·
νῦν αὖτ' ἐν νηυσὶν μενεαίνετε ποντοπόροισι
πῦρ ὀλοὸν βαλέειν, κτεῖναι δ' ἥρωας Ἀχαιούς.
ἀλλά ποθι σχήσεσθε καὶ ἐσσύμενοί περ Ἄρηος.
Ζεῦ πάτερ, ἦ τέ σέ φασι περὶ φρένας ἔμμεναι ἄλλων,
ἀνδρῶν ἠδὲ θεῶν· σέο δ' ἐκ τάδε πάντα πέλονται·
οἷον δὴ ἄνδρεσσι χαρίζεαι ὑβρισταῖσι,
Τρωσίν, τῶν μένος αἰὲν ἀτάσθαλον, οὐδὲ δύνανται
φυλόπιδος κορέσασθαι ὁμοιίου πτολέμοιο.
πάντων μὲν κόρος ἐστί, καὶ ὕπνου καὶ φιλότητος
μολπῆς τε γλυκερῆς καὶ ἀμύμονος ὀρχηθμοῖο,
τῶν πέρ τις καὶ μᾶλλον ἐέλδεται ἐξ ἔρον εἶναι
ἢ πολέμου· Τρῶες δὲ μάχης ἀκόρητοι ἔασιν."   (13.620–39)

"So, I think, shall you leave the ships of the fast-mounted Danaans,
you haughty Trojans, *never to be glutted* with the grim war-noises,
nor go short of all that other shame and defilement
wherewith you defiled me, wretched dogs, and your hearts know no fear
at all of the hard anger of Zeus loud-thundering,
the guest's god, who some day will utterly sack your steep city.
You who in vanity went away taking with you my *wedded*
wife, and many possessions, when she had received you in kindness.
And now once more you rage among our seafaring vessels

to throw deadly fire on them and kill the fighting Achaians.
But you will be held somewhere, though you be headlong for battle.
Father Zeus, they say your wisdom passes all others'
of men and gods, and yet from you all this is accomplished
the way you give these outrageous people your grace, these Trojans
whose fighting strength is a thing of blind fury, nor can they ever
be glutted full of the close encounters of deadly warfare.
Since there is *satiety* in all things, in sleep, and love-making,
in the loveliness of singing and the innocent dance. In all these
things a man will strive sooner to win satisfaction
than in war; but in this the Trojans cannot *be glutted.*"

This is obviously a major "thematic" speech, both in the conventional sense of theme as point or issue of a literary work (or, by analogy with musical composition, a basic pattern constantly returned to), and in Peabody's sense of a complex of words which may or may not be etymologically connected but of which the poet makes an *etymos logos*, worrying them into relation with each other because he feels them to be related. Behind Menelaos' hostile meditation on the character and motivation of the Trojans lies an original identification between food and sex, which we know, of course, from erotic literature of all periods, and everyday speech. Beyond the essential association by sound of *koros* and *korē* in all their forms, there are the similar formulas with their conceptual similarity. The Trojans *oude dunantai/ phylopidos koresasthai* even though normally among men *pantōn men koros esti, kai hypnou kai philotētos*. We recall Thetis' advice to Achilles: *agathon de gynaiki per in philotēti/misgesth'* (24.130–31). We see already in Homer the beginnings of the *mēden agan* theme, which will finally be codified by Aristotle in his tripartite ethics: a moderate amount of sexual activity is essential to man's well-being (like food and drink), but (as with food and drink) man should have enough and not tend toward excess.

Normally one should get enough of food and drink, and we are frequently told when this point is reached at banquets; usually the formula used turns on the word for sexual love:

αὐτὰρ ἐπεὶ πόσιος καὶ ἐδητύος ἐξ ἔρον ἔντο

(1.469, 2.432, 7.323, 9.92, 9.222, 23.57, 24.628)
But when they had put away their desire for eating and drinking.

Once, when Odysseus advises Achilles to allow the Achaians to eat before they enter battle, he uses the verbal form of *koros* instead:

ὃς δέ κ' ἀνὴρ οἴνοιο κορεσσάμενος καὶ ἐδωδῆς   (19.167)

But when a man has been *well filled* with wine and with eating.

Once, in a simile, it is used of a donkey which young boys have allowed to get into good pasture:

σπουδῇ τ' ἐξήλασσαν, ἐπεί τ' ἐκορέσσατο φορβῆς·   (11.562)

by hard work they drive him out when his is *glutted* with eating.

Frequently this verb is used in boasting, as a threat to the opponent of the desecration his body will suffer after death:

ἤ τις καὶ Τρώων κορέει κύνας ἠδ' οἰωνοὺς   (8.379)

or see, if some Trojan *give* the dogs and the birds *their desire.*

ὅς κε τάχα Τρώων κορέει κύνας ἠδ' οἰωνούς,   (17.241)

who presently *must glut* the dogs and the birds of Troy.

. . . ἀτὰρ Τρώων κορέεις κύνας ἠδ' οἰωνοὺς   (13.831)

yet then you *will glut* the dogs and birds of the Trojans.

Andromache fantasizes even worse for Hektor's body:

αἰόλαι εὐλαὶ ἔδονται, ἐπεί κε κύνες κορέσωνται,   (22.509)

the writhing worms will feed, when the dogs *have had enough* of you.

The same verb is used in an extraordinary image by Patroklos, when he has killed Kebriones, and Kebriones "dives" out of his chariot like a man diving for oysters:

πολλοὺς ἂν κορέσειεν ἀνὴρ ὅδε τήθεα διφῶν,   (16.747)

he *could fill the hunger* of many men, by diving for oysters.

If we think, however, that the word, in its nominal and verbal forms is essentially concerned with the satiation of the appetite when food is eaten, then we realize this use had been extended to other areas where there are appetites, such as for grieving—Priam says to Hekabe that if they held Hektor's body in their arms

τῷ κε κορεσσάμεθα κλαίοντέ τε μυρομένω τε,   (22.427)

might so *have glutted* ourselves with weeping for him and mourning.

and fighting, as above in Menelaos' speech

φυλόπιδος κορέσασθαι ὁμοίου πτολέμοιο.   (13.635)

be glutted full of the close encounters of deadly warfare.

and once more

αἶψά τε φυλόπιδος πέλεται κόρος ἀνθρώποισιν,   (19.221)

when there is battle men have suddenly their *fill* of it.

and, then, again, when Hektor asks Poulydamas why he advises retreat to the city

ἦ οὔ πω κεκόρησθε ἐελμένοι ἔνδοθι πύργων;   (18.287)

Have you not all *had your glut* of being fenced in our outworks?

There is one strange use, as if in personification of a part of the body; the woodsman stops felling trees

οὔρεος ἐν βήσσῃσιν, ἐπεί τ᾽ ἐκορέσσατο χεῖρας   (11.87)

in the wooded glens of the mountains, when his arms and hands *have grown weary.*

The denominal adjective *akorētos*, used twice by Menelaos

Τρῶες ὑπερφίαλοι, δεινῆς ἀκόρητοι ἀϋτῆς,   (13.621)

you haughty Trojans, *never to be glutted* with the grim war-noises

ἦ πολέμου· Τρῶες δὲ μάχης ἀκόρητοι ἔασιν."   (13.639)

But [in battle] the Trojans *cannot be glutted*

is never used of food, but always of war:

ἀμφὶ σέ, Πηλέος υἱέ, μάχης ἀκόρητον Ἀχαιοί,   (20.2)

around you, son of Peleus, *insatiate* of battle

εἴ περ ἀδειής τ᾽ ἐστὶ καὶ εἰ μόθου ἔστ᾽ ἀκόρητος,   (7.117)

and even though he is without fear, and can never be *glutted* with rough work . . .

ἐς δ' ἐνόησ' Αἴαντε δύω, πολέμου ἀκορήτω,   (12.335)

and saw the two Aiantes, *insatiate* of battle . . .

or, once, in contrasting true insatiable desire for war, with cowardly pretense thereof:

'Αργεῖοι ἰόμωροι, ἀπειλάων ἀκόρητοι,   (14.479)

You Argives, arrow-fighters, *insatiate* of menace

There is no agreement on the exact significance of *kouridios*, but the fact that it is used in the *Iliad* four times as an epithet of *alochos* (1.114, 7.392, 13.626, 11.243), once of *posis* (5.414) and once of *lechos* (15.40) makes it quite clear that its range is restricted to legal marriage, that its derivation is from *korē*; therefore, I suggest that it suggests the essential conceptual tie between virginity and legal marriage. Menelaos' outburst is that of the wronged husband, but his way of expressing himself shows a deep and complex system of beliefs about the relations between men and women and war, i.e., about the basic problems of the *Iliad*. The outrage perpetrated against him by Paris was oedipal, as we have said, insofar as the host is *in loco parentis* to the guest. Menelaos sees it all in terms of physical appetites and their excess, moving first from war (*autē*, used metonymically) to the *lōbē* and *aischos* of the rape itself. This is intensified by the verbal form of *lōbē*, which is turned back against its noun to make of it an internal accusative. The Trojans are dogs; perhaps we think of the dogs who at least are satiated by the meat of dead men's bodies. He appeals to Zeus *xenios* and speaks of his *khalepē mēnis*, obviously a key term. The expression "you went away taking my wife and many possessions, *epei phileesthe par autēi* (627) "even though you had been received by her in kindness (literally "loved by her")" is very strange. It clearly refers here to the rites of guest friendship, but it seems lexically and even morphologically, or syntactically, ambiguous enough to suggest that Menelaos doubts whether Helen, his *kouridios alochos*, went altogether unwillingly. *kai essumenoi per Arēos* (631) "though you be so headlong for battle" is almost equivalent to *deinēs akorētoi autēs* (621) "never to be glutted with the grim war-noise." Then Menelaos prays directly to Zeus and again characterizes the Trojans as insatiable in all respects, this time in tricola that have resonance through separate formulaic systems:

οὐδὲ δύνανται
φυλόπιδος κορέσασθαι ὁμοιΐου πτολέμοιο.   (634–35)

. . . nor can they ever
be glutted full of the close encounters of deadly warfare

τῶν πέρ τις καὶ μᾶλλον ἐέλδεται ἐξ ἔρον εἶναι
ἢ πολέμου· Τρῶες δὲ μάχης ἀκόρητοι ἔασιν.   (638–39)

. . . In all these
things a man will strive sooner to win satisfaction
than in war; but in this the Trojans cannot *be glutted.*

We can easily establish that Menelaos is the most sensitive of all the
Greeks (even more so than his brother Agamemnon) to shame, in the
eyes of his war-companions. He associates appetite for women and
appetite for war in a close complex of thematic expression. He has
been deprived of his woman. I think we shall discover that this makes
him like a woman. What Paris has done to him is inexpiable, not only
because it is an oedipal crime, but also because it is a form of castration
(ironically, the punishment the son expects from the father for the
crime of desiring the mother). Menelaos, in speaking of the Trojans,
reverses Paris' own priorities: Paris' appetite for sex seems insatiable,
but he tires quickly of war; in this he is unlike the other warriors,
Greek and Trojan. If we look briefly at *glēnē*, a strange epithet that
Hektor uses against Diomedes, and compare this usage with the later
similar usage of *korē*, we might be able to see more clearly the relations
between sex and violence in the *Iliad*. Let us only recall from this
discussion of *mignumi* and *koros* that though the formula systems
reveal sex and violence to be mutually conceived—men "mix" in love
and war; men have "appetites" for love and war—violence seems originary, and sex only one of its expressive modes.

II.6
WOMEN AS REFLECTIONS IN THE EYES OF MEN

Hektor, in abusing Diomedes, who withdraws from battle when he sees Hektor approach, combines many of the attitudes we have traced in other situations and formulaic systems into one strange epithet:

"Τυδεΐδη, περὶ μέν σε τίον Δαναοὶ ταχύπωλοι
ἕδρῃ τε κρέασίν τε ἰδὲ πλείοις δεπάεσσι·
νῦν δέ σ᾽ ἀτιμήσουσι· γυναικὸς ἄρ᾽ ἀντὶ τέτυξο.
ἔρρε, κακὴ γλήνη, ἐπεὶ οὐκ εἴξαντος ἐμεῖο
πύργων ἡμετέρων ἐπιβήσεαι, οὐδὲ γυναῖκας
ἄξεις ἐν νήεσσι· πάρος τοι δαίμονα δώσω." (8.161–66)

"Son of Tydeus, beyond others the fast-mounted Danaans honoured you
with pride of place, the choice meats and the filled wine-cups.
But now they will disgrace you, who are no better than a woman.
Down with you, *you poor doll.* You shall not storm our battlements
with me giving way before you, you shall not carry our women
home in your ships; before that comes I will give you your destiny."

Instead of fighting over a woman Diomedes has become a woman, and worse than a woman: *kakē glēnē* is rendered by Lattimore as "you poor doll." Though it means literally, and seemingly originally, the pupil of the eye, it is glossed by Rufus Medicus as *to eidolon to en tōi opsei* (*LSJ, ad loc.*) "the image in the eye," and hence "puppet" or "girl." (The nonfigurative use is found at *Odyssey* 9.390: *autmē/ glēnēs kaiomenēs* of the blinding of Polyphemos: "the steam from the eye being burned.") We should be fascinated to learn that this same triad of meanings is available in later Greek for *korē* and in Latin for *pupilla*. Plato explains about *korē*:

> Did you ever observe that the face of the person looking into the eye of another is reflected in the visual organ which is over against him, and which is called the *korē*, as in a mirror—there is a sort of image of the person looking? Then the eye looking at another eye, and at that in the eye which is most perfect, and which is the instrument of vision, will there see itself . . . But looking at anything else in man or in existence, and not to that which is like, it will not see itself? . . . Then if the eye is to see itself, it must look at the eye, and at that part of the eye in which the virtue of the eye resides; and this, I suppose, is right? . . . And if the soul, my dear Alcibiades, is ever to know itself, must she not look at the soul in which her virtue resides, and which is like herself? (*Alcibiades* I:132e–133b. Jowett, tr.)

This recalls the famous passages on mirror imagery in the *Symposium* and the *Phaidros*, which we shall discuss below, but now we must try to appreciate the linguistic tendency to identify eyes, women, and insignificance. We recall, of course, that Achilles calls Patroklos a little girl crying to be picked up by her mother when he returns from his interview with Nestor in Book XVI.

"τίπτε δεδάκρυσαι, Πατρόκλεες, ἠΰτε κούρη
νηπίη, ἥ θ' ἅμα μητρὶ θέουσ' ἀνελέσθαι ἀνώγει,
εἰανοῦ ἁπτομένη, καί τ' ἐσσυμένην κατερύκει,
δακρυόεσσα δέ μιν ποτιδέρκεται, ὄφρ' ἀνέληται·
τῇ ἴκελος, Πάτροκλε, τέρεν κατὰ δάκρυον εἴβεις." (16.7–11)

. . . "Why then
are you crying like some poor little girl, Patroklos,
who runs after her mother and begs to be picked up and carried,
and clings to her dress, and holds her back when she tries to hurry,
and gazes tearfully into her face, until she is picked up?
You are like such a one, Patroklos, dropping these soft tears."

What of himself does Achilles see in Patroklos, in Patroklos' eyes, when they sit apart by themselves and talk? It must be his own weakness; it must be the diminished, effeminized, socialized image of himself that Hektor accuses Diomedes of having become. Patroklos is like a young girl in this respect. Certainly we do not claim, with Shakespeare's Thersites, that he is Achilles' "male varlet," "his masculine whore" (*Troilus and Cressida* V.i. 18–20). We are amazed, however, at the insistence on Patroklos' body being *gymnos*, lying there on the field being fought over, Ajax astride it, protecting it like a mother lion protects her young, and we remain fascinated by Devereux' insistence that Patroklos' death was caused by a blow, which technically, if not in this, then in a previous version of the narrative, castrated him.

If we look at this complex of action and epithets we might be able to move our discussion of the Homeric hero's concept of himself one step forward, to admit, perhaps, that there is some fascination for him in his own potential weakness, almost as though he could see in his women and in his image of himself reflected in the eyes of friends and enemies, and in his premonition of his own body stripped and mutilated, something reassuring, some end to the constant struggle he mounts to keep himself active and in control. In short, I think we will find in the Homeric hero's fascination with his own impotent image the operation of Freud's notorious death instinct, though I think we shall also have to adapt that theory to a text which seems to present it not as a constant developing force in human experience, but rather as a sudden reversal. When the individual's insistence on his own completion and perfection cannot be maintained by society, he retraces the steps of his own development, determining not to accept a compromised existence.

II.7

NAKED MEN AS WOMEN

I quote at some length from Devereux:

When Patroclus finally encounters Hector in the fray, Apollo must stun him and strip him of his armor, so as to enable Hector to slay his dazed and disarmored opponent with a spear-thrust in the "nethermost belly." The word *keneōn* is so translated by Lang, Murray, Rouse, and Mazon. *LSJ* gives "hollow between rib and flank," but also simply "a hollow." These greatly diverging translations suggest that the ambiguousness of the wording is due to a bowdlerization. The "hollow" in question can only be the crotch: a *horizontal* thrust could probably not have driven the *bronze* point of the spear "clean through"; the lower spine or pelvic bone would have stopped it. A downward thrust would, however, have permitted the tip of the spear to re-emerge in the crotch. But if *that* were the real meaning, a less ambiguous anatomical term would have sufficed even for the prudish Homer. This leads me to assume that the model which Homer had bowdlerized described an upward thrust, piercing the crotch and permitting the spear's tip to re-emerge from the body above the upper rim of the pelvis, near the kidneys.

Now, such a thrust at the genitals, while efficient and natural enough in combat, tends because [of] its resemblance with castration, to elicit special horror. As will be indicated below, Homer states that, by wounding men in *that* area, Ares (here "war") is "most cruel to wretched mortals." But it is also exceedingly probable that being wounded in the crotch was deemed to be somehow disgraceful, though perhaps not in the sense in which a wound in the back—implying cowardice—was deemed disgraceful.[1]

There is something here to offend everyone: the reliance on translations; the supposition that Homer is "prudish" and following an anatomically precise model;[2] the seemingly constant psychoanalytic concern with the genitals, especially their mutilation. I am not entirely convinced, on the basis of 16.820–21:

ἀγχίμολόν ῥά οἱ ἦλθε κατὰ στίχας, οὖτα δὲ δουρὶ
νείατον ἐς κενεῶνα, διαπρὸ δὲ χαλκὸν ἔλασσε.

. . . and with the spear stabbed him
in the depth of the belly and drove the bronze clean through

that Patroklos has been literally castrated, if only because in the very passage Devereux refers to:

Μηριόνης δ' ἀπιόντα μετασπόμενος βάλε δουρὶ
αἰδοίων τε μεσηγὺ καὶ ὀμφαλοῦ, ἔνθα μάλιστα
γίγνετ' Ἄρης ἀλεγεινὸς ὀϊζυροῖσι βροτοῖσιν.   (13.567–69)

but as he went back Meriones dogging him threw the spear
and struck *between navel and genitals* where beyond all places
death in battle comes painfully to pitiful mortals.

the genitals are specified unambiguously, so Homer is not prudish, and if he had meant castration he could and perhaps would have said so. What confirms for me, however, the essential truth of Devereux' argument—which I take to be that Patroklos has suffered "symbolic castration" (a term I hope to define a bit further on)—is Homer's insistence on his first being stripped of his armor by Apollo so that afterwards, when first Euphorbos and then Hektor thrust their spears at him, he is *gymnos*: it is said of Euphorbos, as we have previously noted:

ὁ μὲν αὖτις ἀνέδραμε, μίκτο δ' ὁμίλῳ,
ἐκ χροὸς ἁρπάξας δόρυ μείλινον, οὐδ' ὑπέμεινε
Πάτροκλον γυμνόν περ ἐόντ' ἐν δηϊοτῆτι.   (16.813–15)

. . . but [he] ran away again, snatching out the ash spear
from your body, and lost himself in the crowd not enduring
to face Patroklos, *naked as he was*, in close combat.

As the battle rages for his body, the heroes say in horror, as they have said of no other fallen hero, that Patroklos' body is naked; first Menelaos speaks to Ajax:

"Αἶαν, δεῦρο, πέπον, περὶ Πατρόκλοιο θανόντος
σπεύσομεν, αἴ κε νέκυν περ Ἀχιλλῆϊ προφέρωμεν
γυμνόν· ἀτὰρ τά γε τεύχε' ἔχει κορυθαίολος Ἕκτωρ."

(17.120–22)

"This way, Aias, we must make for fallen Patroklos
to try if we can carry back to Achilleus the body
which is naked; Hektor of the shining helm has taken his armour."

Then, Menelaos speaks to Antilochos:

"ἀλλὰ σύ γ' αἶψ' Ἀχιλῆϊ θέων ἐπὶ νῆας Ἀχαιῶν
εἰπεῖν, αἴ κε τάχιστα νέκυν ἐπὶ νῆα σαώσῃ
γυμνόν· ἀτὰρ τά γε τεύχε' ἔχει κορυθαίολος Ἕκτωρ."

(17.691–93)

"Run then quickly to Achilleus, by the ships of the Achaians,
and tell him. He might in speed win back to his ship the dead body
which is naked. Hektor of the shining helm has taken his armour."

And finally Antilochos delivers the horrible message to Achilles:

"ὤ μοι, Πηλέος υἱὲ δαΐφρονος, ἦ μάλα λυγρῆς
πεύσεαι ἀγγελίης, ἣ μὴ ὤφελλε γενέσθαι.
κεῖται Πάτροκλος, νέκυος δὲ δὴ ἀμφιμάχονται
γυμνοῦ· ἀτὰρ τά γε τεύχε' ἔχει κορυθαίολος Ἕκτωρ."

(18.18–21)

"Ah me, son of valiant Peleus, you must hear from me
the ghastly message of a thing I wish never had happened.
Patroklos has fallen, and now they are fighting over his body
which is naked. Hektor of the shining helm has taken his armour."

Menelaos even makes the connection, which we might think explains
this peculiar concern over the body's having been stripped, a not
uncommon occurrence; he speaks again to the two Ajaxes:

"κεῖνον μὲν δὴ νηυσὶν ἐπιπροέηκα θοῇσιν,
ἐλθεῖν εἰς Ἀχιλῆα πόδας ταχύν· οὐδέ μιν οἴω
νῦν ἰέναι μάλα περ κεχολωμένον Ἕκτορι δίῳ·
οὐ γάρ πως ἂν γυμνὸς ἐὼν Τρώεσσι μάχοιτο."   (17.708–11)

"Now I have sent the man you spoke of back to the fast ships
on his way to swift-footed Achilleus, yet think not even
he can come now, for all his great anger with Hektor the brilliant.
There is no way he could fight naked against the Trojans."

To argue that it is Achilles' honor which is at stake, since it is his
armor which has been taken as a trophy by Hektor, by no means
answers Devereux' argument that Patroklos has suffered castration: the
man who has no armor cannot fight; the man who cannot fight is not

a man. Hektor himself, as we would expect, supplies the missing links in this chain of thought when he contemplates his alternatives in facing Achilles. We know from his previous conversation with Andromache (6.441ff.) that he is conscious of shame before the women of Troy; this continues to determine his course of action:

"αἰδέομαι Τρῶας καὶ Τρῳάδας ἑλκεσιπέπλους,
μή ποτέ τις εἴπῃσι κακώτερος ἄλλος ἐμεῖο·
''Εκτωρ ἧφι βίηφι πιθήσας ὤλεσε λαόν.'"   (22.105–7)

"I feel shame before the Trojans and the Trojan women with trailing robes, that someone who is less of a man than I will say of me: 'Hektor believed in his own strength and ruined his people.'"

He then considers the principle of kill-or-be-killed, take glory from another or give it to him, that economy of self-definition through violence which we have previously identified as phallic pride:

. . . "ἐμοὶ δὲ τότ' ἂν πολὺ κέρδιον εἴη
ἄντην ἢ 'Αχιλῆα κατακτείναντα νέεσθαι,
ἠέ κεν αὐτῷ ὀλέσθαι ἐϋκλειῶς πρὸ πόληος."   (22.108–10)

. . . "and as for me, it would be much better
at that time, to go against Achilleus, and slay him, and come back,
or else be killed by him in glory in front of the city."

He then acknowledges the possibility of offering terms to Achilles, the return of Helen and many rich gifts besides (all the same terms that Agamemnon finally had to offer Chryses, and then Achilles: Hektor cannot, of course, claim that Helen has not had sexual intercourse with Paris), but breaks off this line of thought in recognition of the man he has to deal with, a recognition Agamemnon never truly makes:

"ἀλλὰ τίη μοι ταῦτα φίλος διελέξατο θυμός;
μή μιν ἐγὼ μὲν ἵκωμαι ἰών, ὁ δέ μ' οὐκ ἐλεήσει
οὐδέ τί μ' αἰδέσεται, κτενέει δέ με γυμνὸν ἐόντα
αὕτως ὥς τε γυναῖκα, ἐπεί κ' ἀπὸ τεύχεα δύω."   (22.122–25)

"yet still, why does the heart within me debate on these things?
I might go up to him, and he take no pity upon me,
nor respect my position, but kill me *naked* so, as if I were
a woman, once I stripped my armour from me."

The extraordinary range of meaning in *aideomai*, from shame, to pity, to awe, prepares us for *gymnos*: the man without weapons, who is unable to fight, is not a man, but, lacking precisely *aidoia* ("male genitalia"), it seems, he is a woman. Can we relate this back to *glēnē* and *korē*? The man who does not fight—Hektor's accusation against Diomedes—is just a reflection in another man's eye, a non-man, a girl (8.164). Diomedes, in turn, rebukes Paris, who has grazed his right hand with an arrow (Paris had hoped to hit him *neiaton es keneōna* —11.381— "in the nethermost belly"; these heroes want not only to deal death to each other, but to cause pain and shame):

"τοξότα, λωβητήρ, κέρᾳ ἀγλαέ, παρθενοπῖπα,
εἰ μὲν δὴ ἀντίβιον σὺν τεύχεσι πειρηθείης,
οὐκ ἄν τοι χραίσμῃσι βιὸς καὶ ταρφέες ἰοί·
νῦν δέ μ' ἐπιγράψας ταρσὸν ποδὸς εὔχεαι αὔτως.
οὐκ ἀλέγω, ὡς εἴ με γυνὴ βάλοι ἢ πάϊς ἄφρων·
κωφὸν γὰρ βέλος ἀνδρὸς ἀνάλκιδος οὐτιδανοῖο.
ἦ τ' ἄλλως ὑπ' ἐμεῖο, καὶ εἴ κ' ὀλίγον περ ἐπαύρῃ,
ὀξὺ βέλος πέλεται, καὶ ἀκήριον αἶψα τίθησι.
τοῦ δὲ γυναικὸς μέν τ' ἀμφίδρυφοί εἰσι παρειαί,
παῖδες δ' ὀρφανικοί· ὁ δέ θ' αἵματι γαῖαν ἐρεύθων
πύθεται, οἰωνοὶ δὲ περὶ πλέες ἠὲ γυναῖκες." (11.385–95)

"You archer, foul fighter, lovely in your looks, *eyer of young girls*.
If you were to make trial of me in strong combat with weapons
your bow would do you no good at all, nor your close-showered arrows.
Now you have scratched the flat of my foot, and even *boast* of this.
I care no more *than if a witless child or a woman*
had struck me; this is the blank weapon of a useless man, no fighter.
But if one is struck by me only a little, that is far different,
the stroke is a sharp thing and suddenly lays him lifeless,
and that man's wife goes with cheeks torn in lamentation,
and his children are fatherless, while he staining the soil with his red blood
rots away and there are more birds than women swarming about him."

We know all these points from passages cited in previous parts of this argument: a man is no man unless he fights; he is a woman; the bow is the weapon not of a man, but of a woman, since it is used from a protected place in the throng of fighters rather than in the front line of battle, where men "distinguish" themselves in single combat (we might compare here the simile of Teukros, shooting his bow and running behind Ajax' shield, like a child into its mother's arms—8.270f.); the blow of a strong man is death-dealing; his victim's wife will disfigure herself in grief and his children will be orphans (like Astyanax, begging his bread from other heroes at the table, until they shoo him away, since his father is not dining among them—22.485ff.); his body will not be tended by women, but the birds and dogs will eat him. The surface psychology of these taunts is clear—to distract the opponent before the competition takes place, to cause him to question his ability—and is known in all sorts of contexts, e.g., the modern sporting arena. The depth psychology is different, and more culture-specific, or at least genre-specific. These men have only the identity given them by the action of battle; they cannot think of themselves as fathers, husbands, or men with occupations ("meaningful work") outside that context. Most fundamentally their definition of themselves is erotic and aggressive, based entirely upon their interaction with other men. Women are not sufficiently valued to break the pattern of this male violence, although it is often in their name that the battles are being fought, and their grief that extends beyond their men's deaths and immortalizes the men's shame. Men exist only when they fight and they cannot fight without armor; even Achilles can only stand at the ditch and shout, not enter the battle, until Thetis returns with new armor for him (18.128ff.; 18.188ff.).

That the battlefield is where men live, and are more than men, godlike, is echoed in a negative statement by a late (perhaps final) reincarnation of Achilles, Alexander of Macedonia, who claimed descent through his mother Olympias from Neoptolemos, and, of course, Zeus as his father. He confided to his companions that "sleep and the act of generation chiefly made him sensible that he was mortal" (Plutarch, *Alexander* 22, Dryden, tr.). We recall that food, sleep, and sex with a woman are the essentials Thetis mentions to her son (24.129–31). These the body requires, but the spirit requires battle and for that a man must be armed. Alexander died shortly after his dear friend Hephaistion (both apparently from overeating), with whom he had been raised. He had told his companions when they first reached the site of Achilles' tomb on the Hellespont that Achilles was fortunate in two things, to have Patroklos as his friend while he lived, and Homer as poet to sing his praises after he died (Plutarch, *Alex.* 15). Alexander was known for his control of his passions, particularly where women were concerned.

May we trace back to Achilles that long tradition in Greek culture which separated from normal commerce with women those elite forces on whom the defense of the cities depended, Sparta's Spartiates and Thebes' "Immortals"? The simplistic assumption is inescapable: men's highest function is martial, and for this he must deprive himself of the company of women; it is not only that sexual intercourse debilitates, but that men who spend time with women become like women, and therefore lose their male spirit for battle with other men. Almost contemporary with Alexander, "the last Achilles," is a ludicrous statement of this system of beliefs in Menander's *Dis Exapaton*, which we know from Plautus' translation *Bacchides*. A young man tries to resist the blandishments of a courtesan:

Should I then enter that arena, where a man only works up a sweat in
    demeaning himself?
Should I exchange there my sword for a turtle-dove?
Should someone take from me there my baldric and give me a tankard?
Should I be equipped with a finger-bowl instead of my helmet,
A festive garland instead of my battle insignia,
Dice instead of my spear, a soft cloak instead of my cuirass,
A couch for my shield and a whore for my horse?   (68–72)

The paradox is unresolvable and almost inexpressible: men turn erotic energy into aggressive energy, but always the equipment appropriate for war is seen as that appropriate for sex, so that to be stripped of his armor is to be castrated. Odysseus will not undress and put aside his sword to get into bed with Circe, lest she "take advantage of his nakedness and render him useless and effeminate (*anēnora*)" (*Od.* 10.341).

That there is no consolidated sense of self which can sustain the Homeric warrior from one violent encounter to another is made manifest by the sensitivity of the heroes to such abuse. We recall Diomedes' response to Hektor's previous taunt, when Hektor had called him a *glēnē*. Diomedes had already confided to Nestor his fear of such abuse, and Nestor had tried to console him, reassure him of his martial prowess and, predictably, it is the number of Trojan women lamenting their husbands killed by Diomedes that is Nestor's final proof:

Τὸν δ' ἠμείβετ' ἔπειτα βοὴν ἀγαθὸς Διομήδης·
"ναὶ δὴ ταῦτά γε πάντα, γέρον, κατὰ μοῖραν ἔειπες·
ἀλλὰ τόδ' αἰνὸν ἄχος κραδίην καὶ θυμὸν ἱκάνει·

Ἕκτωρ γάρ ποτε φήσει ἐνὶ Τρώεσσ' ἀγορεύων·
'Τυδεΐδης ὑπ' ἐμεῖο φοβεύμενος ἵκετο νῆας.'
ὣς ποτ' ἀπειλήσει· τότε μοι χάνοι εὐρεῖα χθών."
   Τὸν δ' ἠμείβετ' ἔπειτα Γερήνιος ἱππότα Νέστωρ·
"ὤ μοι, Τυδέος υἱὲ δαΐφρονος, οἷον ἔειπες.
εἴ περ γάρ σ' Ἕκτωρ γε κακὸν καὶ ἀνάλκιδα φήσει,
ἀλλ' οὐ πείσονται Τρῶες καὶ Δαρδανίωνες
καὶ Τρώων ἄλοχοι μεγαθύμων ἀσπιστάων,
τάων ἐν κονίῃσι βάλες θαλεροὺς παρακοίτας."   (8.145–56)

Then in turn Diomedes of the great war-cry answered:
"Yes, old sir, all this you have said is fair and orderly.
But this thought comes as a bitter sorrow to my heart and spirit;
for some day Hektor will say openly before the Trojans:
"The son of Tydeus, running before me, fled to his vessels."
So he will vaunt; and then let the wide earth open beneath me."
Nestor the Gerenian horseman spoke to him in answer:
"Ah me, son of brave Tydeus; what a thing to have spoken.
If Hektor calls you a coward and a man of no strength, then
the Trojans and Dardanians will never believe him,
nor will the wives of the high-hearted Trojan warriors,
they whose husbands you hurled in the dust in the pride of their
   manhood."

These themes are familiar to us by now, but their conjunction is
giving them greater significance: a man is accused of being appearance
and not reality, word and not deed, woman and not man. His only
reassurance that all of this is not true is the number of men he has
in fact killed, and the women who weep for them. Women can only
weep; they cannot avenge; they cannot even protect. In all the discussion of nakedness, until the death of Hektor, we know from context
that the point is the vulnerability of the flesh, not its actual cover; i.e.,
we are concerned with armor, not clothing. In the few instances in
the poem where the epithet *gymnos* or its verbal derivatives are used
of heroes other than Patroklos and Achilles and Hektor—that triumvirate who share the same armor and whose quotient of shame and
glory is finite and mutually determined—parts of the body are specified. Thus many men are stabbed in the back—

ἠμὲν ὅτεῳ στρεφθέντι μετάφρενα γυμνωθείη   (12.428)

wherever one of the fighters turning aside *laid bare*
his back . . .

and Teukros stabs Glaukos—

ᾗ ῥ' ἴδε γυμνωθέντα βραχίονα, . . .   (12.389)

where he saw the arm was *bare* of defense . . .

and Menelaus stabs Thoas and Patroklos stabs Pronoos—

στέρνον γυμνωθέντα παρ' ἀσπίδα, . . .   (16.312, 16.400)

in the chest where it was *left bare* by the shield. . . .

An important transition in the development of this "theme" of nakedness, vulnerability, and "castration" is Achilles' confrontation with
Lykaon; he sees him

γυμνόν, ἄτερ κόρυθός τε καὶ ἀσπίδος, οὐδ' ἔχεν ἔγχος,   (21.50)

naked and without helm or shield, and he had no spear left.

Achilles wonders, of course, whether the men he has previously
killed are coming back to life, an association between nakedness and
death that has already applied to Patroklos and continues with the
association between nakedness ("castration") and women, which is
finally articulated by Hektor. Of course, there is close resemblance
between Lykaon as he begs for mercy and Hektor as he considers
doing so, and just as Diomedes seems to have answered Hektor's rebuke with a rebuke to Paris—i.e., the poet "transposes" situations so
that important principles can be articulated—Hektor seems to have
been witness to the Lykaon scene before he makes his decision not
to face Achilles *gymnos*, seems to have heard Achilles' harsh word
upon him. Later Hektor will fear lest a worse man blame him for
Troy's fall (22.106f.), and to Lykaon Achilles says:

"ἀλλά, φίλος, θάνε καὶ σύ· τίη ὀλοφύρεαι οὕτως;
κάτθανε καὶ Πάτροκλος, ὅ περ σέο πολλὸν ἀμείνων.
οὐχ ὁράᾳς οἷος καὶ ἐγὼ καλός τε μέγας τε;   (21.106–8)

"So, friend, you die also. Why all this clamour about it?
Patroklos is dead, who was better by far than you are.
Do you not see what a man I am, how huge, how splendid?"

There is an absolute hierarchy of heroism as it approaches divinity.
We know now from Nagy that it is this very approximation which
determines death for the hero in epic and thereby defines him as such.
To that perception we add that men consider themselves men purely

with reference to their martial equipment and that consideration is indisputably phallic, i.e., we are seldom in the *Iliad* forced to witness actual castration. When it happens it is a fantasy of Priam and his dogs will do it, not his enemies (22.66–76). Usually it is rather the association of the male member with youth and energy and martial effectiveness, through the medium of the arms and weapons themselves. We hesitate even to call this "phallic symbolism," a phrase which Lacan has shown us to be redundant: man is seldom faced with the actual threat of castration; rather he fantasizes this act of violence against his own body, perpetrated not by his own father, but by some image of a hostile father, which will reduce him to the status of the mother, whom he desires, she who clearly (and actually) lacks a penis.[3] This is the denoument of the oedipal drama, but we have claimed that this is not played out in the *Iliad*, or if by other heroes, not by Achilles, who does not desire a woman, refuses to fight for a woman (his own or Menelaos') and will die because he fights to avenge the death of his dear male companion.

We argue then that castration-anxiety, in its imagistic and symbolic manifestations in the *Iliad* (i.e., using Lacan's distinction between the visual image and the linguistic sign, which is essentially Freud's distinction between primary-process thinking and secondary-process thinking),[4] is generally pre-oedipal, even non-oedipal: the woman is not the real object of desire, so, though there is the constant threat of assimilation to her pattern of weakness and passivity—through desire for the woman, the man becomes like a woman, which is a phenomenon we see the beginnings of in both Hektor and Paris, and perhaps even in Patroklos—the real threat is to the continued existence of the self as perceived in constant violent action. Zeus is not *le nom du Père*; if the poem were structured by oedipal anxiety we would expect a vindictive paternal figure. The phallos is an image of the penis; the weapons of the Homeric hero are symbols of the penis; Homer's poetry gives us visual images of symbolic castration in its use of the term *gymnos*. The Homeric identification between nakedness and castration prefigures the double meaning of the term *hopla* in later Greek, both "armor" and "male genitalia." We know it best from Aristophanes, particularly in the description at the end of the *Acharnians* of the discomfiture of the warrior Lamachos.

That women have nothing to do with castration is suggested by

Andromache herself, for she laments that she cannot cover Hektor's body although she has clothes for him at home:

"νῦν δὲ σὲ μὲν παρὰ νηυσὶ κορωνίσι νόσφι τοκήων
αἰόλαι εὐλαὶ ἔδονται, ἐπεί κε κύνες κορέσωνται,
γυμνόν· ἀτάρ τοι εἵματ' ἐνὶ μεγάροισι κέονται
λεπτά τε καὶ χαρίεντα, τετυγμένα χερσὶ γυναικῶν."   (22.508–11)

"But now, beside the curving ships, far away from your parents,
the writhing worms will feed, *when the dogs have had enough of you,*
on your naked corpse, though in your house there is clothing laid up
that is fine-textured and pleasant, wrought by the hands of women."

Again we are in the realm where food and sex (*koros, korē*) are associated, and furthermore, as with the hallucination of Priam, also in that realm castration and the eating of human flesh are associated, and though in these passages the final connection with cannibalism is not explicit, we shall have to face other passages where it is. Meanwhile we remind ourselves that though men fight for women in word (i.e., in the symbolic realm), in "fact" they fight for their own images of themselves, and these images must be kept fully armored ("uncastrated"), not like the *gymnos* body of Patroklos, or the *gymnos* and mutilated body of Hektor. Women cannot provide the arms men require; a man must be given these by his father, a male companion, or a god; or he must win them in battle from another man. The phallic community is exclusive of women, who can only cover a dead man with useless clothing, not protect him with armor for martial action.

It cannot go unnoticed that the conventional terms of Freudian psychology, even as explicated by Lacan, have failed us, because we have found the Freudian order of things inverted in the *Iliad*. How can we speak of weapons as phallic symbols, of the stripping of armor as castration, when our argument has arrived at the point of insisting that violence is originary in the *Iliad*, and sexual relations only its "sublimated," "displaced" expression? Can we claim to have taken the sexually based psychology of Freud and "placed it on its head; or rather turned [it] off its head, on which it was standing and placed upon its feet?" The crucial issue is the relation between the Achilles and Oedipus complexes, so now we turn to our consideration of the role of the mother in the *Iliad*.

II.8

THE MOTHER-GODDESSES

If all that we have said about the relative irrelevance of women is true, how is it that the goddesses play such a large and commanding role in the *Iliad*? We have accounted theoretically for the central position of Thetis in our basic premise: the mother is so available to her son that he never desires her, and hence the woman as Other—and indeed the whole world as different from himself, and therefore to be dealt with as an other and not as an extension of himself—is never realized by him. Does this apply to the other goddesses and the other heroes? A partial answer to this question is simply that, from Achilles' point of view, which is the point of view of the poem, all goddesses are Thetis: they all provide him with the comfort and support he requires and in such a spontaneous manner that he never feels the lack of their comfort and support and hence never desires them or feels attracted to the "female principle" they represent. I shall make two brief attempts at this problem: first, by citing a recent study that shows the syncretism in cult and myth between Thetis and Metis and Tethys; second, with some references to the text where the cooperation of Thetis, Hera, and Athene is clearest.

Detienne has shown consistent confusion between Thetis and Metis, and the identification of both with "cunning intelligence," throughout archaic poetry and the older myths on which this poetry is a meditation.[1] The myths of the births of Athene and Achilles are, of course, similar, in that they suggest the possibility of oedipal revolution. Thetis is consistently identified with crafts as are Metis and Athene: she seems to have taught Hephaistos smithery after rescuing him (*Iliad* 18.395ff.). Thetis also figures in cosmogonies, shaping things at the beginning of the world or, confused with Tethys, as the *genesis pantessi*. Why did Zeus marry and incorporate Metis? Hesiod tells us (*Theogony* 887–900): "Metis knows more things than any other god or mortal man. . . . [Lodged within him she will enable him] to know in advance everything that will bring him either good or bad fortune." Nagy has argued that implicit throughout the *Iliad* (in the context of its tradition), and explicit in the *Odyssey*, is antagonism between Achilles and Odysseus, the former representing *biē*, the latter *mētis*, and finally he mystifies us with a meditation on heroic immortality, suggesting (with a reference to Detienne) that Thetis is a figure of *mētis* whereas Achilles is only the *biē* of wind and fire: hence he ends up as ashes in an urn on the Hellespont.[2]

I believe that we have again here in Nagy (as we have discovered previously with Austin and Redfield, serious crtics who have fallen into the simplicity of bi-polar opposition) the thought that by invoking the gods of structuralism he has said something about Homer. I do not deny that men think in opposites and negations, though I have suggested before, following Greimas and Jameson, that human thinking, especially in literary texts, tends to be much more complicated than that. I do question, however, the efficacy for literary criticism of hypostatizing such opposed abstracts as *biē* and *mētis*. Where is their existence? Certainly not in the poem. They exist only in the symbolic realm of our attempt to deal with concrete complexities of the poem. What Homer presents to us is a mother-goddess and her child-hero, a basic contradiction that can end only in death and despair, and we respond to this presentation with all the shock of recognition, because, though we have never been to Troy, we have experienced symbiosis with the mother (our own brief intimation of immortality) and then the vicissitudes of individuation.

Thetis certainly seems to know all things. We remember that had not Prometheus warned Zeus he would have made Thetis pregnant with a god-child to overcome him, continuing the oedipal cycle begun with Kronos' overcoming Ouranos, and continuing with Zeus overcoming Kronos. In each of these first two conflicts the god-father had denied the birth of his son and the goddess-mother had raised him apart to take his father's place, Gaia and Rhea behaving like fully conscious Iokaste's, though their sons, of course, did not then marry their mothers, but their mothers' younger images in their sisters. Thetis seems indeed to know all about her son's destiny, and about each event that affects him before it happens. When he calls upon her after his argument with Agamemnon, she asks what troubles him and he seems almost impatient with her pretense of ignorance, though willing to tell all as it happened:

"οἶσθα· τίη τοι ταῦτα ἰδυίῃ πάντ' ἀγορεύω;"   (1.365)

"You know; since you know why must I tell you all this?"

In the course of the narrative, though, we realize that Thetis herself might have known about the death of Patroklos and yet did not tell her son. The poet himself makes this quite clear; he stops in the midst of his description of the battle around Patroklos' body to consider Achilles and the impact the news of his dear companion's death will have upon him:

. . . . But the brilliant
Achilleus did not yet know at all that Patroklos had fallen.
Since now the men were fighting far away from the fast ships
under the Trojan wall, and Achilleus had no expectation
that Patroklos was dead, but thought he was alive and close under
the gates, and would come back. He had not thought that Patroklos
would storm the city without himself, nor with himself either;
for often he had word from his mother, not known to mortals;
she was ever telling him what was the will of great Zeus; but this time
his mother did not tell Achilleus of all the evil
that had been done, nor how his dearest companion had
    perished.   (17.401–11)

It is almost as though she had not known it would matter to him; that, having gone to Zeus and claimed from him the favor of glorifying her son by destroying the Greeks in his absence (a favor due to her acquiescence in the wretched marriage to a mortal man which he forced upon her after his realization that were he himself to have a child by her, there would be oedipal strife), she had fulfilled all her son's wishes. Did Achilles not want the Greeks to die, and is Patroklos not a Greek? When he calls upon her again, after hearing of Patroklos' death, again she asks the disingenuous question:

. . . "Why, then,
child, do you lament? What sorrow has come to your heart now?
Speak out, do not hide it. These things are brought to accomplishment
through Zeus: in the way that you lifted your hands and prayed for,
that all the sons of the Achaians be pinned on their grounded vessels
by reason of your loss, and suffer things that are shameful."   (18.72–77)

The exchange that follows is crucial to the whole poem, and therefore to our understanding of the relation between Thetis and Achilles, which, it seems, is central to the main problem the poem faces, for here the son tells the mother that all she has done for him, all the glory she has given him, is not enough. By implication he goes further: all that she will do for him, the glorious armor she will give him, will not be enough; since Patroklos is dead, all is death, and he, too, Achilles, must die.

How can we fail to respond to the pathos of this confrontation in precisely the terms in which it is presented to us? There is no need here of hypostatized abstractions. The all-bountiful mother has not been able to protect her son against the loss of the image of himself that alone can sustain him in the world. That image has now been absorbed and disintegrated (stripped and mutilated) by the world, hostile to all men, because it generates in all men the desire for establishing and protecting themselves in conflict with all other men. The logic of the exchange is straightforward: not only does Achilles recapitulate his past history, his dependence upon Patroklos, and Peleus, but he damns his own destiny, wishes reversed his own birth, defining precisely his heroic identity as his origin in the union of goddess and mortal man. Had Peleus married a mortal woman there could have been no Achilles, at least no hero who is torn between divine aspirations and the certainty of mortality. Going further, we can even claim that Achilles defines himself matrilineally:

"My mother, all these things the Olympian brought to accomplishment.
But what pleasure is this to me, since my dear companion has perished,
Patroklos, whom I loved beyond all other companions,
as well as my own life. I have lost him, and Hektor, who killed him,

has stripped away that gigantic armour, a wonder to look on
and splendid, which the gods gave Peleus, a glorious present,
on that day they drove you to the marriage bed of a mortal.
I wish you had gone on living then with the other goddesses
of the sea, and that Peleus had married some mortal woman.
As it is, there must be on your heart a numberless sorrow
for your son's death, since you can never again receive him
won home again to his country; since the spirit within does not drive me
to go on living, and be among men, except on condition
that Hektor first be beaten down under my spear, lose his life
and pay the price for stripping Patroklos, the son of Menoitios."
   Then in turn Thetis spoke to him, letting the tears fall:
"Then I must lose you soon, my child, by what you are saying,
since it is decreed your death must come soon after Hektor's."   (18.79–96)

We might simply compare the armor Achilles receives as his patrimony and the armor his mother is now to beg for him from Hephaistos
to affirm our conviction that the mother is the all-important figure in
the *Iliad*, presenting ourselves once more with the paradox that the
mother (and all women after her), for the very reason of her constant
presence and beneficence, is never desirable. It might confuse somewhat the sexual issues involved to introduce this analogy, but at least
we shall see the dynamics of the two situations more clearly, if we
compare Homer's version of Achilles' seeking aid from his mother to
kill Hektor and Pindar's version of Pelops' seeking aid from Poseidon
to win Hippodameia away from Oinomaus (*Olympian* I). We must
accept, first, that Poseidon is a father-substitute for Pelops, replacing
the vicious Tantalos; then, of course, we must accept Pindar's construction of the relationship, that Poseidon was *erastēs* to Pelops'
erōmenos.[3] In both cases the "parent" will lose the child through filling
the child's wish, not unlike those other myths where the mortal child
or beloved asks the divine parent or lover for a destructive show of
affection. e.g., Phaethon and Helios, Semele and Zeus. Pelops will
be henceforth unavailable for Poseidon's caresses. In neither case is
the all-good parent, of whichever sex, considered the ultimate object
of desire, but always just a means to an end, and that end is, strangely,
an object of the opposite sex from the all-good parent.
   If we pursue this comparison and try to find in it some indication
of the sexual (and familial and social and political) changes that have

taken place historically between Homer and Pindar (generically between epic and lyric), we have to see in Pindar a first expression of
the belief that men move through stages of sexual orientation: passive
homosexual (*erōmenos*), active homosexual (*erastēs*), and finally heterosexual husband to produce legitimate offspring. By presenting the
Pelops-Poseidon relationship in analogy with the Ganymede-Zeus relationship, Pindar suggests an extremely important determination:
Ganymede we assume to be extremely youthful, fixed, as it were, in
the stage of development when he is sexually attractive to the pederastic Zeus; Pelops, having outgrown the role of *erōmenos* (the first
bloom of beard is on his cheeks), and without ever having assumed
the role of *erastēs*, passes directly on to the stage of heterosexuality,
the socially demanded role of husband and father. To project this
scheme back upon Achilles we must take for granted our basic premise
that in the *Iliad* we have only a narcissistic premonition of the later
pattern of *erastēs-erōmenos* relationships. Achilles will not fight for
Briseis or Helen, which we can take as representative of socially demanded outlets for his libidinal and aggressive energy, but he fights
and dies to avenge Patroklos's death. Achilles, constantly under the
influence and protection of Thetis and the other maternal goddesses,
simply refuses to mature and accept the sexual and political role society
demands of him.

We begin our consideration of the roles of Athene and Hera in
conjunction with that of Thetis by recalling the straightforward treatment given the perplexing problem of the relations between gods and
men in the *Iliad* by Willcock.[4] He establishes two extreme poles for
divine intervention or activity in the poem and locates most of the
gods' "moments" between them. One extreme, which he calls alle-
gorical, is where Hephaistos simply is fire (2.426), or Ares war (7.241).
The other extreme is represented by the physical participation of a
god in human action, such as Athene restoring to Achilles his spear
(22.276f.) and to Diomedes his whip (23.389f.). He discourages the
rationalizing approach, which, though it can seem to deal adequately
with Athene grabbing Achilles by the hair of the head (1.197f.) (mental
or emotional activity externalized as a god's intervention), faces contradiction in the purely physical moments just mentioned. Through
consideration of seeming contradiction in the mention of gifts given

by the gods to men—Pandaros' bow is a gift of Apollo (2.827), but some bowyer made it (4.105ff.); Andromache's headdress is a gift of Aphrodite (22.470), but she probably made it herself—Willcock presents the paradox of certain men functioning effectively because gods favor them and gods favoring them because they function well; beginning and ending with the "aid" given Achilles by Athene in his battle with Hektor, Willcock warns:

In our desire for a fairness that is not true to life, we so easily forget that Achilleus was bound to win. Hektor never had a chance. Achilleus was a far better fighter. Aias and Diomedes could deal with Hektor with some ease, as is shown elsewhere in the *Iliad*, and probably so could Agamemnon. And Achilleus was certainly better than any of these. So he did not need the assistance of Athene at all. Indeed, it is precisely because he did not need her help that he gets it; Athene helps him because he is going to win.[5]

This is salutary in that it reconciles Homeric appearance with our reality, without forcing our reason upon his religion. It remains, nevertheless, metaphysical: the myth makes Achilles best and therefore destined to beat Hektor, so Athene is simply part of the plan, which has all been worked out in the mind of Zeus (and prior to that by the Fates at the births of the heroes: are they, too, maternal figures?).

Modern readers, however, do not believe in the gods (whatever our attitude toward "fate") and we do not understand myth. Nevertheless, if, with Willcock's help, we can once get past our impulse to moralize— "it is not fair for Athene to help Achilles"—then we see sense in this and many other episodes in the *Iliad* and yet do not know whence that sense comes. I think it is phenomenological; I think that in every instance where a god helps a hero we recognize the operation of that psychic mechanism whereby men suddenly become aware of themselves and their abilities. Willcock deals with this possibility, in passing, by labeling some divine manifestations "Moments of Enhanced Awareness" and, most importantly, seeing Athene as the most obvious example of this phenomenon: "But what is the function of Athene? What in her case is parallel to sexual attraction for Aphrodite, and killing for Ares? The answer, at least in the *Iliad*, is winning, success, and specifically Greek success."

I have suggested above that I consider Fränkel's reading of Aphrodite in Sappho's lyrics almost precisely applicable to a "good enough" reading of Aphrodite in Homer's epic, i.e., the sudden immanence of sexual attraction, and not so much a choice of true object of desire (love *for* another) as fascination with the operation of desire upon oneself, the subject. The male in Homer is always the subject, so we are justified in speaking here of phallic pride or, in the full redundancy of the expression, phallic fascination. We certainly do not think Helen is sexually stimulated when Aphrodite sends her in to Paris in Book III; rather she is being forced by her servile position, as his hostage, to satisfy his sexual needs, which are strangely acute after his combat with Menelaos. This close conjunction of erotic and aggressive activity—two men fighting over the same woman and then one man enjoying the spoils—is, of course, significant. But why should the loser enjoy the spoils? It seems almost that Homer wants us to see Achilles as one extreme of the heroic code and Paris the other, with Hektor caught somewhere in the middle. Paris makes only love, not war; Achilles makes only war, not love; Hektor does both and is the first to perish.

If at any point in the poem, in the presentation of any character, Homer wants to distance us from the heroic material so that we can contemplate it "objectively," this episode in Book III and the character of Paris are our clearest indications. Because Paris is so closely associated with Aphrodite, though, he seems almost above the human concerns of Achilles (his individual honor and early death) and Hektor (his city's dependence upon him, and the wife and child he will leave behind). Certainly when Paris leaves Troy with Hektor at the end of Book VI, and Homer compares him to a stallion galloping out to his favorite pasture, we associate his animal spirits with his sexuality and thereby with his proximity to divinity (Aphrodite). He simply does not bear the weight of the world upon him, as does Hektor at that moment (the social world) and Achilles always (the world which refuses to mirror his excellence).

Is it then the quality of sexual passion, and of those peculiarly subject to it, to be lifted above the human condition, while other aspects and affects of human experience, other gods and goddesses than Aphrodite, and their particular favorites, are more mundane and immediate? I think that this is indeed the case, and that if we look closely at the roles of Hera and Athene we shall find that they are allied in support of the Greek cause, but their most important shared characteristic is that they create self-consciousness momentarily in their favorites. I insist on the qualification "momentarily" because I am using "self-consciousness" in the full Hegelian sense, and the great distinction I see between Homeric man and philosophical man is that the former can experience flashes of recognition, when he suddenly sees himself as integrated and responsible, but these moments are sporadic, and his self-concept suffers disintegration at other moments, whereas philosophical man has a consistent identity, which is subject to disintegration only in moments of trauma, religious ecstasy, or madness.

We have already suggested that when Athene appears to Achilles in Book I, she appears in three modes: the real, the imaginary, and the symbolic. Willcock is more concerned with the latter two, since the process here is mental rather than physical. But, at this moment, to deny Athene a physical reality that is allowed her elsewhere—as when she helps Achilles in the duel with Hektor—is inconsistent. In each case we can see the action both from the protagonist's point of view and as removed spectator. Achilles on both occasions feels Athene's presence and attributes to her his mental and physical functioning: she causes him to sheathe his sword and she causes his spear to return to his hand. The spectator wonders why Achilles did sheathe his sword (when he so clearly intended to draw it and kill Agamemnon) and how Achilles did retrieve his spear? The answer to both questions is "Athene caused this to happen." As we have suggested before and shall often have cause to repeat, the point of view of the narrator is essentially the same as that of Achilles in the full sweep of the poem—he is indisputably the best of the Achaians—and in the parts of the poem where he is not in control of the action, when some other hero fills that place (significantly) for him—as in the Diomedeia, Patrokleia, etc.—there is a similar uniformity of point of view: the poet and the hero see things in the same way, only in some fine degree does the poet see things more clearly. In this very subtle sense we are justified in speaking of Homeric irony. It exists in that narrow gap between the hero's phenomenology and the poet's phenomenology, however each may construe reality behind illusion. We shall consider shortly the phenomenology of war itself and try to define finally the different ways in which a hero sees himself vis à vis his companion in terms of his

energy and his god. Now, however, we are more particularly concerned with the divine chain of command:

ἦος ὁ ταῦθ' ὥρμαινε κατὰ φρένα καὶ κατὰ θυμόν,
ἕλκετο δ' ἐκ κολεοῖο μέγα ξίφος, ἦλθε δ' Ἀθήνη
οὐρανόθεν· πρὸ γὰρ ἧκε θεὰ λευκώλενος Ἥρη,
ἄμφω ὁμῶς θυμῷ φιλέουσά τε κηδομένη τε·   (1.193–96)

Now as he weighed in mind and spirit these two courses
and was drawing from its scabbard the great sword, Athene descended
from the sky. For Hera the goddess of the white arms sent her,
who loved both men equally in her heart and cared for them.

Is this simply the myth entire speaking through the psychology of
the particular moment? We all know that Hera favors the Greeks and
hates the Trojans, so we would expect her to avoid dissension between
the first two men in the Greek camp, even though it is Athene who
actually limits their quarrel to words, it being her sphere of influence
where such decisions are made. We do not note any particular intimacy
between Athene and Achilles, not such as that between Athene and
Odysseus in the *Odyssey*. Certainly there is a difference in tone and
affect between this rather formal encounter in the *Iliad*—ready though
Achilles is to argue his case through before yielding to the goddess'
advice—and the jocular exchanges between Athene and Odysseus in
Phaiacia and Ithaka.

We should remain aware of the fact that it is Hera who has caused
Achilles to call the assembly where the release of Chryseis would be
discussed (1.54ff.). Later it is Hera who stops the rout after Agamemnon's perverse test of his men's resolve (2.155). We wonder whether
there is any significance in the epithet "Argive" shared by Hera and
Helen (4.8, 19). When we hear that Hera would eat Priam raw, we
have some indication not only of her hatred for the Trojans but also
of her primitive nature (4.35). We are not surprised, however, that
Hera always yields to Zeus (8.407, 8.421f., 8.427ff.). While suspending
our attempt to distinguish carefully between the female qualities perceived in Hera, and those in Athene and Thetis, we can question the
significance of Hephaistos serving both Hera and Thetis in their service
of the Greeks. (Aphrodite's gift of the girdle in this same attempt to
deceive Zeus is like Aphrodite's gift of a headdress to Andromache on
her wedding day: Aphrodite will be involved in any erotic endeavor,

no matter what its consequences.) That Hera is deceptive is underlined by her seduction of Zeus; more frequently she is simply overbearing, as when she slaps Artemis and neither Apollo nor Leto dares stop her. When Zeus asks Artemis who hit her, the answer is a characterization of Hera:

> "σή μ᾽ ἄλοχος στυφέλιξε, πάτερ, λευκώλενος Ἥρη,
> ἐξ ἧς ἀθανάτοισιν ἔρις καὶ νεῖκος ἐφῆπται." (21.512–13)

"It was your wife, Hera of the white arms, who hit me,
father, since hatred and fighting have fastened upon the immortals."

(I think *ex hēs* refers to Hera: "because of whom (Hera) hatred and fighting have fastened upon the immortals.")

Perhaps the two most extraordinary passages dealing with Hera, and suggesting the close bonds that tie her to Thetis, are where she insists that Hektor is not to be honored equally with Achilles because Hektor was nourished with mortal woman's milk (24.58)—we think of the myth (probably much later) that has Hera attempting to suckle Herakles, thus claiming this hero for her own, but he bites her nipple and spews out the milk, all of which accounts for the Milky Way—and her great speech to Poseidon and Athene on the necessity of Achilles' being constantly aware that the greatest of the gods are concerned with his welfare. Other gods acknowledge the privileged position of Zeus' concubines, such as Hermes in the theomachia:

> "Λητοῖ, ἐγὼ δέ τοι οὔ τι μαχήσομαι· ἀργαλέον δὲ
> πληκτίζεσθ᾽ ἀλόχοισι Διὸς νεφεληγερέταο·
> ἀλλὰ μάλα πρόφρασσα μετ᾽ ἀθανάτοισι θεοῖσιν
> εὔχεσθαι ἐμὲ νικῆσαι κρατερῆφι βίηφιν." (21.498–501)

"Leto, I will not fight with you; since it is a hard thing
to come to blows with the brides of Zeus who gathers the clouds. No,
sooner you may freely speak among the immortal
gods, and claim that you were stronger than I, and beat me."

After claiming the immortal's right of victory for Achilles, Hera goes on to claim an almost maternal affection for and authority over Thetis:

> "Ἕκτωρ μὲν θνητός τε γυναῖκά τε θήσατο μαζόν·
> αὐτὰρ Ἀχιλλεύς ἐστι θεᾶς γόνος, ἣν ἐγὼ αὐτὴ
> θρέψα τε καὶ ἀτίτηλα καὶ ἀνδρὶ πόρον παράκοιτιν,
> Πηλέϊ, ὃς περὶ κῆρι φίλος γένετ᾽ ἀθανάτοισι.

πάντες δ' ἀντιάασθε, θεοί, γάμου· ἐν δὲ σὺ τοῖσι
δαίνυ' ἔχων φόρμιγγα, κακῶν ἔταρ', αἰὲν ἄπιστε."   (24.58–63)

"But Hektor was mortal, and suckled at the breast of a woman,
while Achilleus is the child of a goddess, one whom I myself
nourished and brought up and gave her as a bride to her husband
Peleus, one dear to the hearts of the immortals, for you all
went, you gods, to the wedding; and you too feasted among them
and held your lyre, o friend of the evil, faithless forever."

We attribute this fondness to gratitude, of course; Thetis did not become Zeus' concubine, so Hera took great pleasure in playing the maternal role in her marriage to a mortal man. It is this union that Thetis claims makes her the most wretched of goddesses (18.429–61), not only because her husband is now crippled with old age, but because her son is caught in the contradiction between immortal excellence and mortal limits. Probably the best description of this, the heroic dilemma, is given by Hera herself, when she compares Achilles to Aeneas, and insists how important it is that Achilles should always be aware of her presence and Poseidon's presence and Athene's presence. It summarizes our impression of Hera as already, in Homeric characterization, predicting the frustrated resentful woman whom Slater has so definitively placed at the peak of later Greek misogyny. In its vicious cycle we see her both as the manifestation of male fears of the mature female, and as the justification of those fears; i.e., because Greek men come to hate and fear women, Greek women become hateful and fearsome. In the Homeric Hera this is all still only implicit.

Much more explicit is her representation of the maternal role, identifying as she does a mother's early tendance of her male child with his later estimation of himself and therefore his potential for performance. She has already lost most of her earth-mother qualities, and her own actual offspring are notoriously distorted by her influence: Hephaistos literally crippled and Ares personifying her *eris* and *neikos*. Her concern for her "foster" children, though, is sincere, and when she speaks we feel not only the power of divinity (Zeus' wedded wife), but also the power of the real mother to determine the son's self-consciousness:

"φράζεσθον δὴ σφῶϊ, Ποσείδαον καὶ 'Αθήνη.
ἐν φρεσὶν ὑμετέρῃσιν, ὅπως ἔσται τάδε ἔργα.

Αἰνείας ὅδ᾽ ἔβη κεκορυθμένος αἴθοπι χαλκῷ
ἀντία Πηλείωνος, ἀνῆκε δὲ Φοῖβος Ἀπόλλων.
ἀλλ᾽ ἄγεθ᾽, ἡμεῖς πέρ μιν ἀποτρωπῶμεν ὀπίσσω
αὐτόθεν· ἤ τις ἔπειτα καὶ ἡμείων Ἀχιλῆϊ
παρσταίη, δοίη δὲ κράτος μέγα, μηδέ τι θυμῷ
δευέσθω, ἵνα εἰδῇ ὅ μιν φιλέουσιν ἄριστοι
ἀθανάτων, οἱ δ᾽ αὖτ᾽ ἀνεμώλιοι οἵ τὸ πάρος περ
Τρωσὶν ἀμύνουσιν πόλεμον καὶ δηϊοτῆτα.
πάντες δ᾽ Οὐλύμποιο κατήλθομεν ἀντιόντες
τῆσδε μάχης, ἵνα μή τι μετὰ Τρώεσσι πάθῃσι
σήμερον· ὕστερον αὖτε τὰ πείσεται ἅσσα οἱ Αἶσα
γιγνομένῳ ἐπένησε λίνῳ, ὅτε μιν τέκε μήτηρ.
εἰ δ᾽ Ἀχιλεὺς οὐ ταῦτα θεῶν ἐκ πεύσεται ὀμφῆς,
δείσετ᾽ ἔπειθ᾽, ὅτε κέν τις ἐναντίβιον θεὸς ἔλθῃ
ἐν πολέμῳ· χαλεποὶ δὲ θεοὶ φαίνεσθαι ἐναργεῖς." (20.115–31)

"Poseidon and Athene, now take counsel between you
and within your hearts as to how these matters shall be accomplished.
Here is Aineias gone helmed in the shining bronze against
Peleus' son, and it was Phoibos Apollo who sent him.
Come then, we must even go down ourselves and turn him
back from here, or else one of us must stand by Achilleus
and put enormous strength upon him, and let him not come short
in courage, but let him know that they love him who are the highest
of the immortals, but those who before now fended the fury
of war, as now, from the Trojans are as wind and nothing.
For all of us have come down from Olympos to take our part
in this battle, so nothing may be done to him by the Trojans
on this day. Afterwards he shall suffer such things as Destiny
wove with the strand of his birth that day he was born to his mother.
But if Achilleus does not hear all this from gods' voices
he will be afraid, when a god puts out his strength against him
in the fighting. It is hard for gods to be shown in their true shape."

This is a maternal attitude, and is the attitude of the mother of the gods (at least of some of them; obviously one must speak figuratively to stretch her authority as wide as Zeus') toward the greatest of the Greek heroes. She is his surrogate mother, taking Thetis' place here and elsewhere, initiating action beneficial to him and generally regarding him (in feudal terms) as her champion. In this speech especially the peculiarly filial-maternal quality of the relationship between Greek heroes and their goddess-protectresses becomes apparent, and not, even so, only in general terms of affection and support, but particularly in terms of seeing and knowing oneself in the mirror of the mother's eyes.

I shall grant here, and later when I come to discuss this passage again in relation to the overall phenomenology of war, that there is ambiguity in *khalepoi de theoi phainesthai enargeis: phainesthai* is construed with *khalepoi*, whether it is considered middle or passive in form and meaning. The real question arises with the reference of *khalepoi*; for whom is there difficulty in the gods' appearance, the men to whom they appear or the gods themselves? Either sense fits the context, since Hera's concern is that Achilles' awareness of his gods will weigh against his (and Aeneas') awareness of his (Aeneas') gods: Achilles' gods are stronger. I think Lattimore translated *phainesthai* as a passive to suggest the latter; i.e., that men have the difficulty. One naturally assumes that the gods have no difficulty of any kind.

There is a comparable passage, though, which suggests that the former reading is preferable. The Oilean Ajax speaks to the Telamonian Ajax, alerting him to the fact that it was Poseidon, disguised as Kalchas, who has just spoken to them. He says he could tell by the figure's legs as he walked away: *arignōtai de theoi per* (13.72). The *per* is our indication that to call gods "recognizable" is against expectation, a contradiction in terms, as it were. We shall later understand why this is true when we consider the relations between gods and men as a problem in phenomenology, i.e., to what extent are gods, as deathless and changeless entities, knowable to men, who exist only in time and space?

Here let us observe only that the hero constantly needs assurance in the form of a mirror to reflect his own excellence. That mirror can be a vicious deception, as when Apollo, the double of Patroklos' double Achilles, strips Patroklos for Hektor to kill, and when Athene appears to Hektor as Deïphobos so that he will stop his flight and do battle with Achilles. Generally, though, the hero demands his companion-in-arms or his enemy or his god to reflect back to him his potential as a warrior, as an active force in the world. Note, however, and this I think is the most telling argument in favor of my general thesis on the operation of the Achilles complex in the *Iliad* (by which I mean the importance of narcissistic orientation of desire) that the male mirrors are almost always men and the female mirrors are almost always goddesses. Certainly the maternal trio of Thetis, Hera, and Athene give Achilles all the self-assurance he needs to be the best warrior before Troy. We have already suggested and will continue to make further suggestions as to why this assurance is insufficient after the death of Patroklos. Now let us only allow that the three figures combine to form the perfect mother—so perfect, of course, that she is not desirable in any mortal manifestation of herself—with the result that women do not provide the heroes of the *Iliad* with sufficient raison d'être.

While the goddesses sustain men in battle, only other men, libidinally and aggressively invested self-images, can comprise the actual framework of their self-consciousness. In this different sense, then—different from that used above to distinguish the three modes of Athene's phenomenal presence to Achilles—gods and goddesses can function only symbolically, not imagistically, certainly not in reality. Hence the assurance they give men of their existence and excellence is more fragile than the assurances of other men, loved and hated.

This distinction, making men more important than gods to other men in their self-determinations, congrues with the conventional humanist perception that Homer validates the pathos of the human condition against the frivolity of the gods. In developmental terms, we recognize that the mother, originally all-important, cannot maintain for the child a barrier against those experiences which will compromise his original conception of himself. With Hegel (against Plato) we see that things can exist only in tension with their opposites, which must be concrete similars and not removed abstracts: Homer presents Thetis, Athene, and Hera as a complex of "mothering" like a Platonic idea, which, though real, fades in the brilliant light of actual experience: men in war.

II.9

NARCISSISM IN HOMER AND
HOMOSEXUALITY IN GREEK HISTORY

 In our general argument
that women do not mat-
ter in and of themselves
in the *Iliad*, but serve
only as excuses for men
to align themselves with
or against each other
and that it is in these
companionships and en-
mities that men define
themselves, we have always insisted upon the generative paradox
that women are so infinitely available and supportive (both in that
situation which first is actually, and then that which emotionally recalls, the pre-oedipal experience of the male child whose father is
absent) that women do not themselves become men's objects of desire;
rather men look to other men, as we have seen, in their recollection
and desire for the image of themselves which their mothers first projected to them.

One might at this point be tempted to indulge in comparative family
psychology. There is the serious study by Slater of family life in fifth-
century Athens to which we have made reference. There the constellation is different from the pattern we discern in the *Iliad*, because
misogyny—the active fear and loathing of women—is the animating
force. Even more remote is the modern Greek material, the vast body
of Kleftic poetry, for instance, where the mother raises her son to fight
the Turks and then when the son lies dying from wounds inflicted by

the Turks, he begs his companions not to tell his mother of his death.[1] We note that the Homeric Achilles himself fantasizes the news of his death being delivered to his father, whereas Cavafy writes his poem about the death of Achilles from Thetis' point of view.[2]

The distinctions we attempt to make here are extremely difficult, both theoretically and practically. There is a certain matri-centricity in Greek literature from fifth-century tragedy on down through Hellenistic pastoral and epyllion. We can even trace it back to the Odyssey. The large differences between the Iliad and the Odyssey are for us just as embarrassing as they are for other critics interested in other aspects of the poems. If we try even here, however, to accommodate ourselves to a historical framework or perspective, we would have to say that there was not some sudden and decisive change in child-rearing patterns between the composition of the Iliad and that of the Odyssey which could account for such differences in the men's attitudes toward women as expressed in the two poems; rather that there is a fundamental difference in the two traditions themselves, which we designate as epic and romance. In the former women are neither feared nor desired; in the latter both. There are, of course, degrees of romantic inclination: the Hellenistic critics thought the Odyssey should end with Odysseus in bed with Penelope,[3] and one critic even compares Odysseus to Smikrines, the miser in Menander's Epitrepontes, because he values his property more than his wife.[4]

As with all great issues, the attitude toward women as expressed in Greek literature is not one- or two-dimensional. F. Zeitlin has shown us how complicated is Aeschylus' treatment of misogyny in the Oresteia.[5] It works simultaneously on the psychosexual, familial, social, political, philosophical, and religious levels. It seems to have both its origin in and an influence over class structure. Certainly its presentation in Greek tragedy is dependent upon the urban and domestic, if not bourgeois, background of that genre. Men seem to be fighting there with women for the freedom for which they fought with men in epic. In later comedy (the late fourth-century comedy of Menander) men have stopped fighting altogether, and are content with only the woman of their choice and an adequate income. There is a notorious narrowing of vision traceable from the sixth century through the fourth century in the major Greek city-states, particularly Athens, and we are simply giving a sexual and familial interpretation to it. Whether this change in sexual orientation and expectations is originary to the other changes or a relatively unimportant side effect can be argued endlessly, and no agreement is possible among readers of different perspectives. I think, though, that we should all admit that there is something economical and therefore attractive about the critical model which can balance metaphysical and phenomenological biases.

We keep insisting that our attention is focused on the response of the modern reader to the *Iliad*, rather than upon its historical genesis. It is for this reason that we emphasize constantly our identity with Achilles, that like him we have all, ever so briefly, experienced a period of omnipotence, our own "heroic age," and that this period is dominated by the mother, but because of her benevolent presence, she herself is not desired, but rather our attention is focused upon the constitution of our own self-image, which originates in her conception of ourselves: she causes us to be born again in our own minds. As she conceives this image of us to project to us, she integrates all the expectations derived from her own domestic, social, political, and religious experience. It is she who makes us children of our own time. In the same way Thetis makes of Achilles a hero, projecting to him her own and his society's expectations of him. At the same time he makes of himself what we know him to be, an extreme and transcendent expression of that society's ideals.

Metaphysically speaking then (and speaking in the historical mode) Achilles is always already there in his mother's and his society's expectations of him, but phenomenologically speaking (and here we speak for all men in every period) Achilles makes himself in his own image, becoming what he will. The man who steps outside Hegel's "free nation" is the same as Achilles and each one of us. His consciousness of death makes the expectations of his society seem petty and insignificant to him. If he is to continue to live in society (in the world) he must suspend his disbelief and accept the limitations imposed socially (and existentially) upon him. Achilles refuses to do this. His is the "everlasting No," the refusal to be. This must seem to us—if the *Iliad* makes sense to us—the only reasonable answer for Achilles to make, for he is a man whose only desire is for a reflection of his own perfection, and that is the *one* thing which no society, no world-in-which-one-is-able-to-be, can provide. There must be some substitution for that desire, some compromised demand for what the world can offer, and that is, of course, something different from the self, something that can complete the self,and for the man this must be the woman. The Achilles complex must yield to the Oedipus complex for both the individual and society to survive.

For the *Iliad*, then, and the stage in our own development that it stimulates us to reexperience, there is neither misogyny nor anaclisis, in the sense of dependence upon the mothering figure and therefore desire for the female, but pure narcissism. Narcissism, we insist, is not homosexuality. Homosexuality is a perversion in the sense that it is an extension into adult life of a preoccupation with the self and its images which is phase-appropriate only to the first two or three years of life, and to the recapitulation of this preoccupation in adolescence. Homosexuality is always accompanied by misogyny.

There have been three recent serious attempts to deal with homosexuality in Greece in its historical perspective. Dover has argued that the undeniable prevalence of pederasty among upper classes from the sixth through the fourth centuries in those city-states where we have good evidence is almost a historical accident, due to the constant warfare that was the experience of these men and shaped their social and sexual expectations. He finds no evidence for homosexuality of any type in Homer, but sees it strongly expressed in the lyric poets as the manly way of life, and going through several stages of decadence until it reaches the preciosity of Plato. Obviously we cannot accept this, though it depicts a situation we know from modern life: in armies, prisons, and boarding schools men take other men as their sexual partners when no women are available. This sometimes seems to set their sexual orientation so that even when women are available they come to prefer other men. In such circumstances the pattern is usually one we could call pederastic: the older, stronger men take as their sexual partners the younger, more effeminate men and force them to accept the passive role in sexual intercourse and generally to serve them in other aspects of social life. The eponymous example of this kind of social structure is the institution of "fagging" at English public schools, where juniors perform onerous tasks for seniors. Never is the younger boy's role an honorable one, and the only thing that makes it tolerable for him is the expectation that in future years he will have a younger boy "fagging" for him. In prison, expectedly, the whole situation takes on more sinister aspects. Sadomasochism is blatant and the territorial imperative so consistently associated with sexual prerogatives in the various animal communities is transparent: "This boy is mine; anyone else had better not touch him."

Our evidence for pederasty in ancient Greece is best for Athens in the fifth century. Dover convincingly shows its great prominence early on, but suggests it might, by the end of the century, almost have become a pretense, an affectation of old aristocratic customs.[6] Our evidence from Aristophanes and the courts and vase-painting is certainly that the passive role was never accepted willingly. Young boys were bribed with gifts originally and they were expected to refuse the older man's advances for some time if, indeed, they ever did, in some cases, yield. To continue to yield after a certain age was as much considered a form of degeneracy as any form of homosexuality is considered degeneracy today. Aristophanes, of course, has terms for these types. (Is it evidence for cultural continuity that modern Greeks more meticulously distinguish the active from the passive role in their denominations of homosexuals than is the rule in Western European countries?)[7]

Dover, then, documents the continuation into a later historical period of a sexual practice that might have been specific in time, place, circumstance, and class if it had not been socially validated. Again we find phylogenetic analogies for ontogenetic patterns. Though he originally intended to collaborate with Devereux in this study, his frame of reference is not Freudian, and I do not think that he even unconsciously suggests Freud's distinction between narcissism and homosexuality or, indeed, Freud's whole notion of phase-appropriate behavior becoming perverse when extended beyond that phase. He is content simply to record the evidence without providing it with a conceptual model.

All of this does come back into conceptual play, however, in Devereux's own study, wherein he argues that the particular features of Greek homosexuality show it to have been a pseudo-homosexuality. The fascination of male with male was not according to the modern pattern, whereby men choose men because they do not like women and are attracted by the male characteristics (which, perhaps, they feel to be lacking in themselves) in other men. Instead, in the ancient Greek pattern, men chose sexually ambiguous younger boys, often simply because this was the social custom, and their real fascination was with youth and (true "fascination") with the penis, i.e., the most visible manifestation of sexual excitement, whether their own or their partner's.[8] Devereux goes on to associate this fascination with youth with creativity, suggesting that the "Greek miracle" was due in large part to Greek males retaining sexual aims and objects we associate with adolescence.

This is interesting indeed, if we can accept the notion of an adolescent recapitulation of primary narcissism, i.e., that we retrace the same ontogenetic progress we made during the pre-oedipal period in the period after latency, once more attempting to define ourselves in terms of the mirrors which our society (first our mother, then our peers) presents to us. The latter, of course, corresponds to what Freud considered "the homosexual stage" in human male development. Freud's narcissistic infant, Freud's "homosexual" adolescent, Devereux' mature Greek male and, indeed, all creative men (he cites Mozart, in particular) share a tendency to retain themselves as their own objects of desire, to obtain sexual satisfaction not from the pleasure they can give to a partner, but only from the pleasure they feel themselves. Devereux mentions Mozart's playful personification of his own penis, and Simone de Beauvoir has remarked on men's tendency to regard their penises as somehow apart from themselves, leading a separate existence. She finds in this an explanation for the male preeminence in philosophy: that through the mediation of his external genitals he can relate to the world and experience himself *pour soi*, whereas the female is confined *en soi* anatomically.[9]

For Slater Greek homosexuality is a pathology based on misogyny. Greek heroism is the male attempt to placate the insatiable female, the mature Greek male's nightmare fantasy of the mature female, based upon his experience of his mother, who both resented him (because he was male and therefore like his father, her husband, who neglected her socially and sexually) and stimulated him, the child, sexually, encouraging him to take his absent father's place, which, of course, he was ill-equipped to do.[10] I do not think this general picture can be denied as a reflection (only perhaps slightly distorted) of Athenian family life in the fifth century. I have tried to argue, though, that it does not depict the world of the *Iliad*. Again, it seems to me that the Greeks developed the different literary genres as their social and political circumstances changed, not to mention their patterns of thought. Slater discusses the urban, middle-class experience of the Athenian fifth century. Aeschylus and Sophocles and Euripides are notoriously already there in Homer, but their derived material is completely transformed in the transition from one period to another, one genre to another, one social structure to another. Achilles and Patroklos are not *erastēs* and *erōmenos*: they are ego and ideal ego, or subject and object-as-self-consciousness, or self and self-object, or self and libidinally invested self-image.

Conceptually, the most difficult thing for us to deal with is the "force-field" created by presence, absence, and desire. Because Achilles does not experience himself as an integrated being, his desire is for such an image of himself. Because he does experience an ever-present and all-sufficient mother, he does not desire the mother or any image of her. His concerns are so purely ontogenetic that the structures of homosexuality (choice of true object apart from the self) and misogyny (refusal of the cross-sex object because of the threat associated therewith) are not part of his experience. He is pre-oedipal, pre-social, pre-philosophical, and pre-religious. It is because he refuses to enter any of these structures, share any of these experiences, accept any of these consolations for the loss of his "archaic grandiose self-image" that he ceases to be; rather, chooses not to be.

I hope what our reading of the *Iliad* has done is to show that later Greek homosexuality—socially, intellectually, and even politically (e.g., Harmodius and Aristogeiton) the single most important and distinctive feature of Greek life—is not a historical accident, as Dover would have it, or a pure pathology, as Slater construes it (though it does take on certain frightening aspects in the late fifth century), nor even with Devereux can we define it as pseudo-homosexuality, a kind of national fixation in the sexually indiscriminate period of adolescence. I hope that what we have shown, with our Freudian and Hegelian models for human development (ontogenetic and phylogenetic), is that the tendency for Greek men to define themselves in terms of each other rather than in terms of their need for and desire of women is always already there. Homer's *Iliad*, with its concentration on the relation between Achilles and Patroklos, stands to the later institutionalization of homosexuality in sixth-, fifth-, and fourth-century Athens as does Freud's period of primary narcissism stand to the later homosexual object-choice. There is almost deterministic potential in both cases.

To put this conceptual model in the most cruelly revealing light possible, I say that Alcibiades (the "historical" figure of Thucydides combined with the Platonic character) is not only an imitation of Achilles, but a "natural" and expected development of Achilles. Alcibiades looks back to Achilles and assimilates himself to that model, but Achilles is constantly coming into being until he fulfills himself in Alcibiades. Beyond that, of course, we get into the "tragic destiny of Greece," her determination to overreach and destroy herself in a historical version of the "suicide of Achilles." (Could not the Aristophanic Aeschylus' advice about what to do with Alcibiades—"If you raise a lion in the state, it is best to humor him"[11]—have been given with advantage to Agamemnon about Achilles?)

We can ask ourselves to what extent the goddess-mothers of the *Iliad* predict the female monsters of tragedy. Do we already see Klytaimnestra and Medea in Hera, and is Athene always the same? Sexual differentiation is, after all, only minimally physical and metaphysical: "the female principle." To a much larger extent it is phenomenological: how do men at a given time, in a given place, producing a given type of literature, declare their difference from and dependence upon women? Is the hermaphroditism of Athene some kind of summary of the Greek male's ideal of himself, incorporating all that is best in both sexes and needing nothing outside of or beyond himself? One is reminded of those clever youths in Shakespeare's comedies, so quick of wit and "fascinating" in appearance, and usually boy actors playing young women who are disguised as young men trying to win back the affection of young men who have fallen in love with other young women. To try to say anything significant about the relations between Rosalind-Ganymede and Orlando in terms of homosexuality is too simplistic by far. One might as well try to discuss the theory of relativity in terms of Euclidean geometry.

If Homeric narcissism becomes classical homosexuality, what becomes classical misogyny? Is there any indication in the *Iliad* of the
tendency that culminates with the seclusion and derogation of women
in fifth-century Athens? Perhaps we must distinguish between mortal
women and goddesses in the *Iliad*, but, then, is there really any difference between Thetis' telling Achilles that to lie with a woman in
love, along with good eating and sleeping habits, will prove beneficial
to him, and the inclination of Zeus to have sexual intercourse with
Hera? Are we not speaking in both cases of men's physical require-
ments; in Freudian terms, the necessity for the release of tension? This
is a dangerous topic to pursue. We are forced to consider historically,
which means conceptually, in Hegel's terms, when men began to have
sexual intercourse with women that could be considered, in Freudian
terms, anything more than masturbation *per vaginam*.

With the help of literary documents we can characterize the affect
of sexual relations in any given period. We move from the pure "physical fitness" of Homeric epic, to the fear and loathing of Attic tragedy,
through the romantic anesthesia of late classical comedy and Hellenistic pastoral, to the full mystification of Marianism and the courtly
love tradition, into the Renaissance, where, for the first time, perhaps
in Shakespeare, we begin, with conflicts like that between Beatrice
and Benedick, to see men and women as each both subject and object,
each incorporating features previously restricted to the other. Surely,
in the eighteenth century, we have women moving freely in the male
world, mastering male arts, and manifesting male attributes, and
thereby, as previously in Shakespearean comedy, becoming worthy
of male affection. The inescapable identity of assimilation and desire,
is, after all, the contradiction of the compromise forced upon men by
their movement from the Achilles to the Oedipus complexes, their
surrender of narcissism to anaclisis. I would go so far as to say that
in every great comedy of erotic attraction (which means every great
comedy that is not only satire) there is a reigning hermaphroditic deity,
some kind of barometer of desire, whether the sexual ambivalence
built into Shakespeare's plays by the convention of the boy actors, or
the triumphant notion of Chérubin in Beaumarchais' *Figaro*. Who
can tell male from female characters in Oscar Wilde's *Earnest*? They
all speak the same language of wit and desire.

If we agree that there has been a gradual revelation of the sameness of the sexes in art and literature and life—a negation of the negative notion that the sexes are clearly and definitively distinguishable—then what, again, is happening in Homer? Does he not use Hera in the *Iliad* as Hesiod uses Pandora in the *Theogony* and *The Works and Days*? Surely Hera is in the seduction scene a seeming delight, but throughout the rest of the poem a real evil. Is there any passage in the *Iliad* where we are given any indication of there being any true intimacy and interdependence between Hera and Zeus? On the contrary, already in Homer Hera is almost completely the negative aspect of whatever it is that is female: hostile, scheming, frustrated, resentful, bitter, vindictive. She is not so far from Semonides' bitch or fox or sow. The distance is probably generic and class. The *Iliad* is epic, and therefore, by definition, aristocratic. Semonides is, as is also Hesiod, bourgeois.

One is tempted to correlate class distinction with sexual proximity. It seems that at almost any time when men have leisure to move freely in the world and define themselves in the terms of other men they meet, there is a contrasting generosity in their treatment of women, which is at worst a benign neglect, as we have seen in the *Iliad*. It is only when men find themselves confined in the same prisons they have built for their women—the conscientious domesticity which so sets the scene for murder and corruption in fifth-century tragedy— that women become the objects of fear and loathing. I think this kind of observation is well advanced in the criticism of comedy. George Meredith pointed out that only societies that value women—such as the eighteenth century in France—can produce great comedy.[12] I have argued in several places that this kind of comedy is of a particular sort, the post-oedipal comedy which is post-Menandrean.[13] When Menander consolidated, in the late fourth century, the comic stereotypes and formulaic plots of his predecessors he presented to us for the first time that comedy which has since dominated our stages: boy meets girl, boy loses girl, boy wins girl. Northrop Frye had already described this as a comic oedipal situation, where the young man had to overcome the barriers between him and his desired object, whether these be miserly father, older and richer lover (for the girl), or some other paternal figure.[14] Pre-Menandrean comedy was not like this at all, however. Rather, in Aristophanes, and even in some of the miserable remains of the so-called Middle Comedy (and their Roman adaptations), we see a comedy of a different kind, where the object of the young man's desire (and in Aristophanes it is usually a rejuvenated old man) is not one young girl with whom he will spend his life in monogamous bliss, but a whole, polymorphously perverse world of sensual gratification, sometimes even expressed in terms of reunion with his mirror-image, a long-lost twin. This we rightly refer to, following Whitman, as "heroic comedy."[15]

If the sexual argument is so clear in the historical development of comedy, where we have a gradual narrowing of libidinal interest until it focuses on the erotic complement (the anaclitic object) rather than upon the idealized image of the self (the narcissistic object), what can be said of epic? Hera is already there, ready to eat Priam raw; Hekabe is already there, ready to eat Achilles' liver. How can we say that misogyny is not already there in the *Iliad*, especially when, already in the *Odyssey*, we find ourselves surrounded by female figures who are simultaneously alluring and destructive: Calypso, Circe, the Sirens, Penelope herself? Male poets project their fears and the fears of their audience as their female characters. If one loves what one lacks, then one hates what one has. Misogyny seems to be a function of a socially and politically imposed dependence of men upon women—not true in the *Iliad*, except, perhaps for Hektor, who shows some slight impatience with Andromache. Compare Telemachos' impatience with Penelope, using the slightly altered formula that Hektor uses to dismiss Andromache: *mythos d'andressi melēsei* (*Od.* 1.358) "it's man's place to talk"; *polemos d'andressi melēsei* (*Il.* 6.492) "it's man's place to do battle." It is just barely conceivable that the same poet in the same generation could present two such different world views, so convinced am I of the determining force of story pattern.

It is not altogether unlike the difference between Shakespeare's middle tragedies and later romances, or, for that matter, between Euripides' middle tragedies and late romances. Men's minds can rearrange the very furniture of their sexual fantasies dependent upon the patterns inherent in the material at hand. It is a measure of his greatness that Shakespeare could create both a Lady Macbeth and a Hermione, but he did, and within a decade. The patterns (Aristotle's *mythos* in its triple sense of story, plot, and truth) in the poet's chosen material—though of course, the fact that he chose the material is significant—cause the poet to think about all aspects of the world as it is, particularly about sexual relations as they can be, in ways that perhaps he never before considered. So much the more exciting, then, to think of Homer working in his tradition of oral-verse composition, with its inheritable repertoire of myths, formulas, and themes.

I am not content simply to see in the three great goddesses who mother Achilles—Hera, Athene, and Thetis—a conventional decomposition of the complete maternal type: hostile but helpful (she has her own selfish goals to reach by proxy of her son in the male world where she cannot move freely), the mother as pure image of the self, a sort of conflation of narcissistic and anaclitic objects and, of course, the all-good mother who gives so liberally that she disappears, literally, into the sea, and imagistically into the background of her son's perspective, whereas the foreground is all mirror. Rather, I think there is some kind of assimilation going on here and Athene now in the *Iliad*, as so clearly later in, at least, Athenian conceptual life, becomes the standard hypostasis of the male's desire for the female. She is androgynous, combining women's handiwork and nurturing breasts with men's war work. She is virgin, which means she has never been forced to assume the passive role in sexual intercourse, something for which we know the Greeks could never forgive a man[16] and so we suggest this as one of their bases for despising women.

Elizabethan analogies again spring to mind: the absolute adoration of the Virgin Queen "married to her people": the fierce competition of bright young noblemen to serve this female deity. It seems that in these extraordinarily creative periods men, having once dealt definitively with their ambivalence toward women by apotheosizing their most admired (masculine) qualities in queen or goddess, could then get on seriously with their own most serious business, which is defining themselves in terms of each other. I think I am suggesting a new dimension to narcissism, though it is clearly predicted in the preoccupations of Freud's sometime collaborators Fliess and Jung in their preoccupation with bisexuality, i.e., both sexes combined in each individual. I think that already in the *Iliad,* and certainly later in the Athenian fifth century, Greek heroism is a fantasy of sexual completeness, a refusal to acknowledge an other who is different and desirable because of a lack in the subject. At this point we turn once again to Plato and the sexual dialectics of the *Symposium* and *Phaidros.*

II.10
PLATONIC LOVE

 We continue to use the image of the mirror (the mirror image) in our speculation on the reflective qualities of the relationship between Achilles and Patroklos, which is but the most distinct manifestation of the basic theme of the *Iliad*, adumbrated at all levels of its action and narrative, that men define themselves in terms of other men rather than in terms of their desire for women. When we first suggested that in this respect the *Iliad* is a prediction, a prefiguration of the peculiarly strong later Greek obsession with male beauty and homosexual alliances, the suggestion might have seemed sensational or simplistic. In the context of our Hegelian and Freudian models, however, I hope all of this makes more sense now. We do not here—nor do we ever in literature and life— deal with simple, spontaneous identifications; we must always consider traditions, tendencies, and influences. Again we turn to Hegel for a description of one moment in the progressive revelation to itself of self-consciousness, which in turn is one moment in the self-revelation of Absolute Spirit:

A self-consciousness has before it a self-consciousness. Only so and only then is it self-consciousness in actual fact; for here first of all it comes to have the unity of itself in its otherness. Ego which is the object of its notion, is in point of fact not "object" . . . when a self-consciousness is the object, the object is as much ego as object.[1]

In this way we see Achilles in his relations with Patroklos, Achilles somehow in the world, but seeing Patroklos outside the world, and through identification with him, rather than with the world, he moves outside the world; it is in Patroklos that Achilles sees himself and identifies himself over against and apart from the world. Patroklos himself—or rather his *psychē* after death—defines this function:

> No longer shall you and I, alive, sit apart from our other
> beloved companions and make our plans, since the bitter destiny
> that was given me when I was born has opened its jaws to take me.
> And you, Achilleus like the gods, have your own destiny.   (23.77–80)

The Hegelian distinction between absorption in the world and gradual self-conscious separation of the subject from the world, until the world is absorbed in the self, is equally apparent in Freud's description of primary narcissism. If the child refuses the mother as object (the first in a series of others as objects, the world itself being the full expression of that Otherness), but insists instead on the separation of himself from the mother as Other and the gradual definition of himself in these terms of identity, then, again, we feel that we are watching the action of the *Iliad* from a superior perspective, on an illuminated stage:

> We say that a human being has originally two sexual objects—himself and the woman who nurses him—and in doing so we are postulating a primary narcissism in everyone, which may in some cases manifest itself in a dominating fashion in his object-choice.[2]

We have even referred briefly to the erotic basis on which Plato built his entire metaphysical system, the *erastēs-erōmenos* relationship, and cited a passage from the *Phaidros* to show how essential the visual (specular, reflective, imaginary) element is to his conception:

> So as he continues in this converse and society, and comes close to his lover in the gymnasium and elsewhere, that flowing stream which Zeus as the lover of Ganymede called the "flood of passion," pours in upon the lover. And part of it is absorbed within him, but when he can contain no more the rest flows away outside him, and as a breath of wind or an echo, rebounding from a smooth, hard surface, goes back to its place of origin, even so the stream of beauty turns back and reenters the eyes of the fair beloved . . . So he loves, yet knows not what he loves; he does not understand, he cannot tell what has come upon him; like one who has caught a disease of the eye from another,

he cannot account for it, not realizing that his love is as it were a mirror in which he beholds himself.[3]

Plato's insistence on nonconsummation, if this sort of alliance is to facilitate philosophical progress, must remind us of Freud's theory, most fully developed in *Civilization and its Discontents*, but discernible in all his metapsychological work, that the sublimation ("displacement upwards") of individual sexual desires (especially those incestuous oedipal desires) is the motivating force for social progress. We are faced here with agreement and contradiction. The two great philosophers of Eros agree that men's deathless works are built with the energy "normally" expended in the consummation of desire, but the kinds of works with which they are concerned and the kinds of desire which must be sublimated are not the same. Freud speaks of society, and essentially heterosexual, oedipal love: because the father denies to the son the erotic possession of the mother, the son individually and the society generally (as so many sons suffering delayed gratification) seek other outlets for their energy: commerce, statecraft, art. If we can agree that there is a Freudian connection between the sublimation of oedipal desire and the progress of civilization, then perhaps we can also agree that there is a Platonic connection between the sublimation of narcissistic (pre-oedipal) desire and philosophical progress.

This distinction is attractive and helpful: philosophy is a search for the self and we are not surprised to find its impetus in narcissism. We are especially glad to find further support for our distinction between narcissism and homosexuality, though in conventional psychoanalytic terminology the distinction might appear rather as between latent and manifest homosexuality. So, too, we are pleased with the recognition that Freudian psychology is a "social science," for this is what we would expect of a structure that is based on the erotic tensions in the nuclear family, a microcosm of the larger social world. We cannot, however, be satisfied with this distinction, however neat. Freud is preeminently the philosopher of the self, and Plato predicates all good on the good of the state: "Now, by far the most important kind of wisdom . . . is that which governs the ordering of society, and which goes by the name of justice and moderation."[4]

Here, again, Hegel resolves all seeming contradiction. In his description of the "free nation" and the "unhappy consciousness" which breaks away from it, we recognized fifth-century Athens, perhaps Socrates himself. Certainly Socrates, the great critic of his society who insisted on his society's right to condemn him, is a Hegelian hero. No more can the man without a social structure, in which he simultaneously defines himself and from which he distinguishes himself, be completely a man, than can the man who does not risk his life in establishing himself as different from other men, which latter consideration has proved to us that Achilles is a Hegelian hero.

I think we can bring this discussion to a swift, however inadequate, conclusion, by simply hypothesizing in both the Platonic and the Freudian systems the refusal to sublimate. If we collapse the three great Freudian principles of infantile sexuality, oedipal conflict, and the death drive into one conception of the absolute locus of man's desire, it would have to be expressed as restitution of symbiosis with the mother. If we ask of Plato's potential philosophers what would become of them if they refused to sublimate their desire for the younger, more beautiful images of themselves, which they see in their *erōmenoi*—i.e., if the Platonic hero were not Socrates but Alcibiades, who always insists on the consummation of his desires—then we would have to imagine an infinite anticipation of orgasm as the *erastēs* gazes into the eyes of the *erōmenos* and sees there the *glēnē*, the specular, effeminized image of himself. In other words, we have come to another great paradox: it is Plato who gives us the definitive statement on narcissism, though it is Freud who first elaborated its ontogenetic importance. Platonic love is *le stade du miroir* constantly recapitulated at ever higher levels of self-consciousness, whereas Freudian psychology, though capable of postulating primary narcissism and considering its influence on later sexual orientation, was distracted from a full and sufficient consideration of its ontological importance by the persistent fascination with oedipal attraction.

Auerbach distinguishes foreground and background in the two great traditions, Greek and Hebrew; we can certainly see in Homer and Plato a preoccupation with the individual as he creates himself in his own image, "rebounding from a smooth, hard surface," whereas with Freud, man constantly slips back into the darkness of the womb. German philosophers of the classical tradition are notorious for claiming their direct and exclusive descent from the Greeks and their clarion calls of absolute and definitive originality might perhaps remind us of the boasts exchanged by Homeric heroes. I refuse to consider the misogyny of Schopenhauer and Nietzsche; indeed the misogyny of Plato is a complex phenomenon. I am convinced, however, that the Freudian perception of narcissism, however it was suppressed and bypassed in his evolving theories of human desire and motivation, could be used effectively in considering the continuity of the Western philosophical tradition. Though Freud originally conceived of the reality principle as the child's barrier against continued immediate gratification, it soon became, for him and the child, the loss of the mother. This is simply not true in the Greek and German philosophical traditions: there reality is always the contradiction of the flotsam and jetsam of everyday life and is a celebration of the self in opposition to such changing, momentary manifestations as are consistently associated with nature in general and women in particular. I see Achilles as a premonition of all this, the first philosopher, refusing gifts, words, and women, which is all his society can pay him against the necessity of death. This refusal is narcissistic: because he never experienced oedipal conflict, his mother was never constituted for him as essential object of desire, and his father never became the pattern for future deprivation. Like Sartre he could say, "I never developed a superego."

II.11
"HE WHOM THE GODS LOVE
DIES YOUNG"

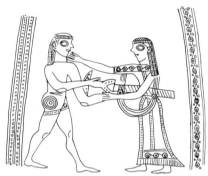 So completely does the childlike
Achilles reject all suggestion of
compromise socially and politically imposed that he rejects the
process of aging itself, what we
would define as the "normal"
acceptance of limitations by the
maturing male. What is the general view expressed in the *Iliad*
on youth, age, and death? Can
we distinguish it simultaneously from later Greek thinking on the
subject and, if our ontogenetic model is accepted, oedipal and post-
oedipal thinking? What are the permutations through which the concept of dying young has passed before it finds expression in Menander's
trimeter, ὅν οἱ θεοί φιλοῦσιν ἀποθνῄισκει νέος, which I have
translated as the heading for this section of the discussion.[1]

The hallmark of the heroic society is the code demanding death in
battle when the warrior is at his best. This concept we call, in the
Iliad, aristeia. In fact we speak of *aristeia* without death—the *aristeia*
of Diomedes in Books V-VI; the *aristeia* of Agamemnon in Book XIII—
but I think we all appreciate that the greatest *aristeia* in the *Iliad*—
exclusive of Achilles' own, to which the implied end is death—is the
aristeia of Patroklos in Book XVI, where he kills so many of the enemy
and is so close to breaking through the gates of the citadel, but is
finally killed by "a god and a man." In much Norse, Germanic, Celtic,
and Anglo-Saxon heroic poetry the pattern is just as clear: the warrior's

life is an ideal that is only fully realized in a glorious death. This teleology, this conceptual insistence on climax with no falling off afterward, is the strongest expression of the whole absolutist tendency of the type, and I, of course, associate all of this with the absolute, uncompromisable demands of early childhood.

Our response to heroic poetry can be condescending. We can dismiss this central aspect of its world view as primitive and barbaric: to fight for no good reason (a woman) is foolish enough, but actually to pursue death, seemingly for its own sake, is simply absurd. If this is our view of their view of the world, then we feel positive identification with Achilles in Book IX when he says it is not worth it, and our reading of the poem is reassuringly humanistic. Achilles knows it is a silly thing to fight and die, but because his friends need him, he sends his best friend in his place, and then, to avenge that friend's death, he must fight again and die. We then speak of Achilles' tragic dilemma, his knowing better (self-consciousness, even *anagnorisis*), but doing the same, because of the bonds of friendship that are the heroic code.[2]

We have discovered, however, that there is a vicious economy on the battlefield—warriors live by other warriors' deaths—and if we compare Sarpedon's speech on winning glory and living well in Lykia (12.310–28) to Achilles' complaint that there is no correlation between fighting well and being well rewarded, since death is the final reward for every warrior (9.308–429), then we realize that this is not a tragic situation (at least if we want to use that term in any specific sense) and the humanistic reading is inadequate. Tragedy implies guilt; guilt implies responsibility; responsibility implies social integration. We are getting farther and farther away from the world of the *Iliad*, where men fight to define themselves in terms of themselves.

Even if we had not constructed our Freudian model for the reading of the *Iliad*—which insists on the mirror and refuses the compromise of individual freedom which guilt implies: phylogenetically and ontogenetically the *Iliad* is guiltless because it is pre-oedipal—we would have to account somehow for the death wish which holds in tense opposition the search for glory. Here our Hegelian model is essential, because it shows us that the life-and-death struggle is essential to self-definition. In the *Iliad* this struggle is given double validation: not only

is it glorious to die young, but old age is useless and ugly. We shall
have no difficulty in associating both these premises with our overall
theory of Greek narcissism, and its preparation in Homer for the *erastēs-erōmenos* relationship in later Greek poetry, philosophy, and life.
The very nature of this relationship is the celebration of youth, the
mature man's worship in his adolescent partner of his own idealized
image of himself. Obviously, he can accept no change in that image,
no aging. Again, it is no accident that Plato took as the model for his
theory of ideas—those ageless, changeless patterns—the particular
demands of the *erastēs* upon the *erōmenos*.

On the one hand we hear the poet's comment on the pathos of the
warrior dying young:

Ὣς ἄρα μιν εἰπόντα τέλος θανάτοιο κάλυψε·
ψυχὴ δ' ἐκ ῥεθέων πταμένη Ἄϊδόσδε βεβήκει,
ὃν πότμον γοόωσα, λιποῦσ' ἀνδροτῆτα καὶ ἥβην.   (16.855–57)

He spoke, and as he spoke the end of death closed in upon him,
and the soul fluttering free of his limbs went down into Death's house
mourning her destiny, leaving youth and manhood behind her.

This is, however, the climax (though not, perhaps, the absolutely
required climax) of the paradigmatic *aristeia*, Patroklos'. (The formula
is repeated at Hektor's death—22.361–63.) Also, on the other hand,
we have Priam's testimony to the beauty of the young man's death,
although it comes in the context of his appeal to the young Hektor
not to die:

"πρὸς δ' ἐμὲ τὸν δύστηνον ἔτι φρονέοντ' ἐλέησον,
δύσμορον, ὅν ῥα πατὴρ Κρονίδης ἐπὶ γήραος οὐδῷ
αἴσῃ ἐν ἀργαλέῃ φθίσει, κακὰ πόλλ' ἐπιδόντα,
υἷάς τ' ὀλλυμένους ἑλκηθείσας τε θύατρας,
καὶ θαλάμους κεραϊζομένους, καὶ νήπια τέκνα
βαλλόμενα προτὶ γαίῃ ἐν αἰνῇ δηϊοτῆτι,
ἑλκομένας τε νυοὺς ὀλοῆς ὑπὸ χερσὶν Ἀχαιῶν.
αὐτὸν δ' ἂν πύματόν με κύνες πρώτῃσι θύρῃσιν
ὠμησταὶ ἐρύουσιν, ἐπεί κέ τις ὀξέϊ χαλκῷ
τύψας ἠὲ βαλὼν ῥεθέων ἐκ θυμὸν ἕληται,
υἷς τρέφον ἐν μεγάροισι τραπεζῆας θυραωρούς,
οἵ κ' ἐμὸν αἷμα πιόντες ἀλύσσοντες περὶ θυμῷ
κείσοντ' ἐν προθύροισι. νέῳ δέ τε πάντ' ἐπέοικεν
ἀρηϊκταμένῳ, δεδαϊγμένῳ ὀξέϊ χαλκῷ,

κεῖσθαι· πάντα δὲ καλὰ θανόντι περ, ὅττι φανήῃ·
ἀλλ' ὅτε δὴ πολιόν τε κάρη πολιόν τε γένειον
αἰδῶ τ' αἰσχύνωσι κύνες κταμένοιο γέροντος,
τοῦτο δὴ οἴκτιστον πέλεται δειλοῖσι βροτοῖσιν." (22.59–76)

. . . . "Oh, take
pity on me, the unfortunate still alive, still sentient
but ill-starred, whom the father, Kronos' son, on the threshold of old age
will blast with hard fate, after I have looked upon evils
and seen my sons destroyed and my daughters dragged away captive
and the chambers of marriage wrecked and the innocent children taken
and dashed to the ground in the hatefulness of war, and the wives
of my sons dragged off by the accursed hands of the Achaians.
And myself last of all, my dogs in front of my doorway
will rip me raw, after some man with stroke of the sharp bronze
spear, or with spearcast, has torn the life out of my body;
those dogs I raised in my halls to be at my table, to guard my
gates, who will lap my blood in the savagery of their anger
and then lie down in the courts. For a young man all is decorous
when he is cut down in battle and torn with the sharp bronze and lies there
dead, and though dead still all that shows about him is beautiful;
but when an old man is dead and down, and the dogs mutilate
the grey head and the grey beard and the parts that are secret,
this, for all sad mortality, is the sight most pitiful."

Once we can recover from the full impact of this speech, with its consistent and therefore overwhelming interpretation of human life as a constant struggle in which the rewards are fewer and fewer as we age and change for the worse—and death is the final insult—we begin to realize how central its conceptual framework is to the whole poem. Several important statements are made here, and though the general tenor of the argument is negative—all is deprivation, despair, and desecration in old age—there is the surprisingly positive comparison: in youth even death is beautiful. We shall find, in fact, that these two points of view are complementary: age and youth have qualities that are defined by death. For the moment, though, let us pursue the notion that death is beautiful for the young, and try to reconcile it with the notion that the young man who dies in youth resents his fate: his soul begrudges the strength and youth it leaves behind. We have already noted Hegel's description of the hero as individual alienated from his society—"who feels the strength and splendour of his life broken and mourns the early death he sees before him"—and recognized in him Achilles. We now see precisely the passages in the *Iliad* from which this description derives.

First, let there be no question that youth and all that is best in man's life are synonymous: the zeugmas are explicit, such as *androtēta kai hēbēn* (16.857, 22.363) "manhood and youth"; *kai d'ekhei hēbēs anthos, ho te kratos esti megiston* (13.484) "Likewise the flower of youth is his, where man's strength is highest"; *eith' hos hebōoimi, biē de moi empedos eiē* (7.157, 11.670, 23.629) "If only I were young now, as then, and the strength still steady within me." The most persistent image for youth, especially when death contradicts it, is that of a flower or tree: youth in bloom. Simoeisios is *thaleros* (4.474) and Hektor calls himself the *thaleros posis* of Andromache (8.190) "blooming bridegroom." Hermes appears as Priam's guide like a beautiful young man, *prōton hypēnētēi, tou per khariestatē hēbē* (24.348) "with beard new grown, which is the most graceful time of young manhood." Most secure in our memories are the young men who die like bent poppies or felled trees: Gorgythion—

μήκων δ᾽ ὡς ἑτέρωσε κάρη βάλεν, ἥ τ᾽ ἐνὶ κήπῳ,
καρπῷ βριθομένη νοτίῃσί τε εἰαρινῇσιν,
ὣς ἑτέρωσ᾽ ἤμυσε κάρη πήληκι βαρυνθέν. (8.306–8)

He bent drooping his head to one side, as a garden poppy
bends beneath the weight of its yield and the rains of springtime;
so his head bent slack to one side beneath the helm's weight.

Krethon and Orsilochos—

τὼ μὲν ἄρ᾽ ἡβήσαντε . . . (5.550)

. . . .

τοίω τὼ χείρεσσιν ὑπ᾽ Αἰνείαο δαμέντε
καππεσέτην, ἐλάτῃσιν ἐοικότες ὑψηλῇσι. (5.559–60)

These two as they were grown to young manhood . . .

. . . .

such were these two who beaten under the hands of Aineias
crashed now to the ground as if they were two tall pine trees.

Simoeisios, the son of Anthemion (whose name itself suggests youth and perfection):

. . . ὁ δ᾽ ἐν κονίῃσι χαμαὶ πέσεν αἴγειρος ὥς,
ἥ ῥά τ᾽ ἐν εἰαμενῇ ἕλεος μεγάλοιο πεφύκει

λείη, ἀτάρ τέ οἱ ὄζοι ἐπ᾿ ἀκροτάτῃ πεφύασι·
τὴν μέν θ᾿ ἁρματοπηγὸς ἀνὴρ αἴθωνι σιδήρῳ
ἐξέταμ᾿, ὄφρα ἴτυν κάμψῃ περικαλλέϊ δίφρῳ·
ἡ μέν τ᾿ ἀζομένη κεῖται ποταμοῖο παρ᾿ ὄχθας.   (4.482–87)

He dropped then to the ground in the dust, like some black poplar,
which in the land low-lying about a great marsh grows
smooth trimmed yet with branches growing at the uttermost tree-top:
one whom a man, a maker of chariots, fells with the shining
iron, to bend it into a wheel for a fine-wrought chariot,
and the tree lies hardening by the banks of a river.

He was born beside the river, took his name from it, and dies like a
poplar growing by the river, in his prime, ripe, like the tree, for cutting.

Two young men are likened to an *ernos* ("sapling"), Euphorbos, the
son of Panthoös, when he is killed by Menelaos—

αἵματί οἱ δεύοντο κόμαι Χαρίτεσσιν ὁμοῖαι
πλοχμοί θ᾿, οἳ χρυσῷ τε καὶ ἀργύρῳ ἐσφήκωντο.
οἷον δὲ τρέφει ἔρνος ἀνὴρ ἐριθηλὲς ἐλαίης
χώρῳ ἐν οἰοπόλῳ, ὅθ᾿ ἅλις ἀναβέβροχεν ὕδωρ,
καλὸν τηλεθάον· τὸ δέ τε πνοιαὶ δονέουσι
παντοίων ἀνέμων, καί τε βρύει ἄνθεϊ λευκῷ·
ἐλθὼν δ᾿ ἐξαπίνης ἄνεμος σὺν λαίλαπι πολλῇ
βόθρου τ᾿ ἐξέστρεψε καὶ ἐξετάνυσσ᾿ ἐπὶ γαίῃ·
τοῖον Πάνθου υἱὸν ἐϋμμελίην Εὔφορβον
᾿Ατρεΐδης Μενέλαος ἐπεὶ κτάνε, τεύχε᾿ ἐσύλα.   (17.51–60)

and his hair, lovely as the Graces, was splattered with blood, those
braided locks caught waspwise in gold and silver. *As some*
slip of an olive tree strong-growing that a man raises
in a lonely place, and drenched it with generous water, so that
it blossoms into beauty, and the blasts of winds from all quarters
tremble it, and it bursts into pale blossoming. But then
a wind suddenly in a great tempest descending upon it
wrenches it out of its stand and lays it at length on the ground; such
was Euphorbos of the strong ash spear, the son of Panthoös,
whom Menelaos Atreides killed, and was stripping his armour.

and, of course, Achilles, twice, by Thetis—

"ὤ μοι ἐγὼ δειλή, ὤ μοι δυσαριστοτόκεια,
ἥ τ᾿ ἐπεὶ ἄρ τέκον υἱὸν ἀμύμονά τε κρατερόν τε,
ἔξοχον ἡρώων· ὁ δ᾿ ἀνέδραμεν ἔρνεϊ ἶσος·
τὸν μὲν ἐγὼ θρέψασα, φυτὸν ὣς γουνῷ ἀλωῆς,

νηυσὶν ἐπιπροέηκα κορωνίσιν Ἴλιον εἴσω
Τρωσὶ μαχησόμενον·   (18.54–59)

"Ah me, my sorrow, the bitterness in this best of child-bearing
since I gave birth to a son who was without fault and powerful,
conspicuous among heroes; *and he shot up like a young tree*
and I nurtured him, like a tree grown in the pride of the orchard.
I sent him away with the curved ships into the land of Ilion
to fight with the Trojans:"

"Ἥφαιστ', ἦ ἄρα δή τις, ὅσαι θεαί εἰσ' ἐν Ὀλύμπῳ,
τοσσάδ' ἐνὶ φρεσὶν ᾗσιν ἀνέσχετο κήδεα λυγρά,
ὅσσ' ἐμοὶ ἐκ πασέων Κρονίδης Ζεὺς ἄλγε' ἔδωκεν;
ἐκ μέν μ' ἀλλάων ἁλιάων ἀνδρὶ δάμασσεν,
Αἰακίδῃ Πηλῆϊ, καὶ ἔτλην ἀνέρος εὐνὴν
πολλὰ μάλ' οὐκ ἐθέλουσα. ὁ μὲν δὴ γήραϊ λυγρῷ
κεῖται ἐνὶ μεγάροις ἀρημένος, ἄλλα δέ μοι νῦν·
υἱὸν ἐπεί μοι δῶκε γενέσθαι τε τραφέμεν τε,
ἔξοχον ἡρώων· ὁ δ' ἀνέδραμεν ἔρνεϊ ἶσος·
τὸν μὲν ἐγὼ θρέψασα φυτὸν ὣς γουνῷ ἀλωῆς,
νηυσὶν ἐπιπροέηκα κορωνίσιν Ἴλιον εἴσω
Τρωσὶ μαχησόμενον·"   (18.429–40)

"Hephaistos, is there among all the goddesses on Olympos
one who in her heart has endured so many grim sorrows
as the griefs Zeus, son of Kronos, has given me beyond others?
Of all the other sisters of the sea he gave me to a mortal,
to Peleus, Aiakos' son, and I had to endure mortal marriage
though much against my will. And now, he, broken by mournful
old age, lies away in his halls. Yet I have other troubles.
For since he has given me a son to bear and to raise up
conspicuous among heroes, *and he shot up like a young tree,*
I nurtured him, like a tree grown in the pride of the orchard.
I sent him away in the curved ships to the land of Ilion
to fight with the Trojans."

Just as it has been shown that any hero who is called *isos daimoni*
("like a god")[3] or *phaidimos* ("radiant")[4] will soon be killed, so it is
clear that, in the context of all the young men dying like trees (and,
of course, in the context of Thetis' straightforward prediction and
lament), calling Achilles *isos ernei* "like a young tree" is equivalent to
describing his death. Trees are grown to be cut in their prime and
warriors fight to be killed in their prime, to escape the unseemliness
and uselessness of old age itself; note Thetis' juxtaposition of her de-

serted and decrepit husband Peleus, "overwhelmed by cruel old age," and her blooming young son Achilles. Again we suggest that the place-name Phthia, as well as being thematically associated with the contrast between "vegetal death" and immortality in cult (as Nagy has suggested) is also associated with Peleus' destructive old age.[5]

Before we can examine the attitude toward age more closely, I shall push my argument on youth and death to its limit: the beautiful young man killed in his prime has his youth and beauty hypostatized. He will always be remembered as he was when he was best (*aristeia*) and thus immortalized; he becomes in this way a god, or a statue of a god; a moment of masculine perfection becomes the full notion of masculine perfection. If we have ever wondered why the Athenian cemeteries were so full of *kouroi* or why these statues lined the sacred way at Delphi, and flanked the temple of Poseidon at Sounion, let us now allow that Homer predicts all this. It is Greek narcissism triumphant, and though it changes its manifestations from century to century, from Achilles to Alexander, it is still Greek narcissism, and its extreme though varied statement must be taken seriously into account in any consideration of the extreme and varied statements of Greek creative genius.

The concept of ripeness for cutting—Achilles cuts his hair *tēlethoōsan* (23.142)—persists into related contexts and is at the heart of the central image in the poem for the human condition: men live and die like the leaves on a tree, i.e., in their season. Again, we cannot deny the pathos. When Priam laments that Achilles has killed so many of his sons *tēlethaontas* (22.423) and Hekabe calls Hektor her *philon thalos* (22.87), our immediate reaction is pity for the untimeliness of these deaths. But if we stop there we ignore the larger "philosophical" framework of the poem. The whole conception of the hero is based upon the tension he maintains between obscure mortality and brilliant divinity: his paradox is that he must be brilliant in a short space:

"Man, supposing you and I, escaping this battle,
would be able to live on forever, ageless, immortal,
so neither would I myself go on fighting in the foremost
nor would I urge you into the fighting where men win glory.
But now, seeing that the spirits of death stand close about us
in their thousands, no man can turn aside nor escape them,
let us go on and win glory for ourselves, or yield it to others." (12.322–28)

Achilles comforts Priam with the same general argument—the difference between gods and men—that Sarpedon uses to encourage Glaukos:

. . . . "There is not
any advantage to be won from grim lamentation.
Such is the way the gods spun life for unfortunate mortals,
that we live in unhappiness, but the gods themselves have no
    sorrows."   (24.524–26)

There is limitlessness and lack of variety in the gods' existence, whereas men change, age, and strive, experiencing good fortune and adversity, the blessings and evils Zeus bestows from his two urns, and it is this contrast which defines life for men, makes features knowable to them.

It is fitting that Zeus himself should give the definitive statement to the human condition, and that it should come at the climax of the poem, after the death of Patroklos, which determines all future action within the poem (the death of Hektor) and beyond it (the death of Achilles). The god is touched by the immortal horses, given formerly to Peleus, and now weeping at the death of Patroklos. They are like a grave monument, motionless, their beauty unfading, since they are ageless and changeless, so that living they can symbolize the achievement Patroklos could make only in death, the glory which comes only to young men in battle:

. . . "Poor wretches,
why then did we ever give you to the lord Peleus,
a mortal man, and you yourselves are immortal and ageless?
Only so that among unhappy men you also might be grieved?
Since among all creatures that breathe on earth and crawl on it
there is not anywhere a thing more dismal than man is."   (17.443–47)

I think that only Cavafy, of all the poets and critics inspired by this passage, has captured its essence, and I do not hesitate to suggest that this is because of his sexual orientation. In *Ta Aloga tou Akhilleos* he wonders at the pity expended by Zeus upon the dead youth, and if we want a conventional contrast to his peculiarly Greek response, then we need only read something like Frost's "Out, Out—".

If once we are allowed to hypothesize the stage of narcissism, perhaps dramatizing our hypothesis with the term "Achilles complex"— we have already mentioned Cavafy's poem on the news of Achilles' death brought not, as he fantasized it, to his aged father back in Phthia, but rather to his goddess-mother—then we can conceive of homosexuality as fixation in or regression to that stage, as we have begun to do historically (phylogenetically) in the evolution of Greek homosexuality from Homer to Plato. Cavafy puts all this in perspective from his perspective as the last decadent witness to that long-dead civilization, viewing it from its actual detritus in Alexandria, finding his pleasure with young boys, and his most percipient critic in E. M. Forster.[6] Many poets can evoke nostalgia and meditate upon the fading flower, but who but Cavafy in his "Iliadic" poems—and Shakespeare in his sonnets to the "Fair Youth"—so completely captures in lyric the obsession of the heroic poet with masculine youth in bloom and the rightness (ripeness) for death?

We first hear of men as leaves in the "Catalogue":

ἔσταν δ' ἐν λειμῶνι Σκαμανδρίῳ ἀνθεμόεντι
μυρίοι, ὅσσα τε φύλλα καὶ ἄνθεα γίγνεται ὥρῃ.   (2.467–68)

They took position in the blossoming meadow of Skamandros,
thousands of them, *as leaves and flowers appear in their season.*

And Iris, appearing as Polites, speaks to Priam:

"λίην γὰρ φύλλοισιν ἐοικότες ἢ ψαμάθοισιν
ἔρχονται πεδίοιο μαχησόμενοι προτὶ ἄστυ."   (2.800–1)

"These look terribly like leaves, or the sands of the sea-shore,
as they advance across the plain to fight by the city."

Apollo points up to Poseidon the absurdity of gods fighting with each other for the sake of men, and uses the same image:

"ἐννοσίγαι', οὐκ ἄν με σαόφρονα μυθήσαιο
ἔμμεναι, εἰ δὴ σοί γε βροτῶν ἕνεκα πτολεμίξω
δειλῶν, οἳ φύλλοισιν ἐοικότες ἄλλοτε μέν τε
ζαφλεγέες τελέθουσιν, ἀρούρης καρπὸν ἔδοντες,
ἄλλοτε δὲ φθινύθουσιν ἀκήριοι" . . .   (21.462–66)

"Shaker of the earth, you would have me be as one without prudence
if I am to fight even you for the sake of insignificant
mortals, *who are as leaves are,* and now flourish and grow warm
with life, and feed on what the ground gives, but then again
fade away and are dead". . .

The definitive statement of this analogy, however, comes, appropriately, from a man, a hero speaking to a hero about heroic lineage. Glaukos speaks to Diomedes:

"Τυδεΐδη μεγάθυμε, τίη γενεὴν ἐρεείνεις;
οἵη περ φύλλων γενεή, τοίη δὲ καὶ ἀνδρῶν.
φύλλα τὰ μέν τ' ἄνεμος χαμάδις χέει, ἄλλα δέ θ' ὕλη
τηλεθόωσα φύει, ἔαρος δ' ἐπιγίγνεται ὥρη·
ὡς ἀνδρῶν γενεὴ ἡ μὲν φύει ἡ δ' ἀπολήγει."   (6.145–49)

"High-hearted son of Tydeus, why ask of my generation?
As is the generation of leaves, so is that of humanity.
The wind scatters the leaves on the ground, but the live timber
burgeons with leaves again in the season of spring returning.
So one generation of men will grow old while another
dies."

We have been warned not to confuse the thought of this passage with that of its echo in Bacchylides, where the point is not so much the succession of generations, as it is here, but rather the inconsequentiality of dead men, dry and brittle, like dead leaves upon the ground.[7] This is salutary advice, but I think that after we have considered the Iliadic perception of the aging process we will have to admit that all of this is already there in Homer, that youth is all, so we celebrate each new generation of young men and forget about the old men, rustling brittly about our feet, almost as inconsequential in their age and verbiage as they will be in death itself.

If one thinks about the age groups of the *Iliad*, one begins again to see patterns established that become clearer and clearer in the classical and post-classical periods. Menandrean comedy is notoriously lacking in middle-aged men: there is a great gap between the callow youths and their decrepit old fathers. The line of Menander quoted above comes from his *Dis Exapaton*, which Plautus translated as his *Bacchides*, and there the context changes its whole affect: it is said by a clever slave Chrysalus to his young master's old father Nicobulus, whom he has just tricked out of a large sum of money:

Oh fool, fool! Don't you see you're up for sale?
You stand upon the very block, as the crier cries.
NIC. Tell me, who sells me? CH. He whom the gods love
Dies young, while he's well, has sense and senses.

If any god loved this one here, more than ten years past,
More than twenty, he should have died.
Now he walks a weight upon the world, with neither sense
Nor sense, no more than a gangrenous growth.   (814–21)

One has to allow for some Plautine expansion here, but essentially
what we have is a late fourth-century recapitulation of the very sen-
timents expressed by Priam in his great speech, with an echo between
dum valet, sentit, sapit (817) "while he has sense and senses" and
dustēnon eti phroneont' (22.59) "the unfortunate still alive, still sentient." In the *Iliad* we see many young men die and a few others live
long enough for us to appreciate their vitality and individual characteristics. Diomedes, in his outspoken resistance to Agamemnon's various suggestions, and in his prowess in battle, is the hot-blooded youth
of noble parentage and great natural abilities. He differs from Achilles
(taking Achilles' place in the narrative during the wrath) primarily in
refusing to overstep certain boundaries: he knows not to fight with the
gods, for instance. There is not the contradiction in his nature between
immortal excellence and the certainty of death. He is the perfect hero
in the sense of an aristocrat who excels as a warrior and demands his
due, but, of course, technically he is no hero at all, since both his
parents are mortal.

When Diomedes speaks up in assembly to dispute Agamemnon's
intention of returning to Greece without taking Troy, Nestor defines
the difference between youth and age, even in the style of his own
speech with its rambling structure:

"Son of Tydeus, beyond others you are strong in battle,
and in counsel also are noblest among all men of your own age.
Not one man of all the Achaians will belittle your words nor
speak against them. Yet you have not made complete your argument,
since you are a young man still and could even be my own son
and my youngest born of all; yet still you argue in wisdom
with the Argive kings, since all you have spoken was spoken fairly.
But let me speak, since I can call myself older than you are,
and go through the whole matter, since there is none who can dishonour
the thing I say, not even powerful Agamemnon."   (9.53–62)

This is a constant theme in the *Iliad*, with Nestor its most frequent
enunciator: young men fight and old men counsel, or young men are
deeds and old men are words, a prefiguration of the fifth-century
preoccupation with the difference between *logos* and *ergon*.

Old men are circumspect, as Menelaos observes:

"Always it is, that the hearts in the younger men are frivolous,
but when an elder man is among them, he looks behind him
and in front, so that all comes out far better for both sides."   (3.108–10)

This is wonderfully recapitulated in Book XXIII when Menelaos disputes the second prize for the chariot race with Nestor's young son Antilochos, and Antilochos characterizes himself and all youth deprecatingly, so as to still the older man's objections, after having addressed the great Achilles with all the candor and self-confidence which Diomedes has shown before Agamemnon:

"Enough now. For I, my lord Menelaos, am younger
by far than you, and you are the greater and go before me.
You know how greedy transgressions flower in a young man, seeing
that his mind is the more active but his judgement is lightweight. Therefore
I would have your heart be patient with me."   (23.587–91)

We know, of course, because he tells us, that Achilles is the best fighter at Troy, though there are many his age and older who are better in counsel (18.105ff.). Menoitios had told Patroklos that he must restrain Achilles and, being older, give him good counsel (11.785–89). It is clear that there is a continuum then between youth and age, and another between deeds and words, and quite precisely the two run parallel. Certainly the greatest of the fighters at Troy is very young and cares not at all for words, whereas the wordiest men are the oldest men, Nestor and Phoinix, who, even though they might still go into battle, are useless there. Between these extremes are the middle-aged warriors like Agamemnon, Menelaos, and Odysseus, who combine counsel with fighting, sometimes good at both, sometimes at neither. Idomeneus seems to be somewhere between middle-aged competence in battle and the threshold of military uselessness in old age (13.361, 23.476).

Lest there be any question which contribution to the war effort—young men's deeds or old men's words—weighs heaviest in the scale of military success, there are frequent exchanges that define good counsel and its recognition as the compensation given some old men for their loss of martial prowess, and the most memorable statement

of this definition comes in one of those passages where similar sound-
ing words are forced into conjunction, i.e., where the poet creates an
etymos logos that the philologist might not acknowledge. Agamemnon
speaks to Nestor and Nestor responds:

"ὦ γέρον, εἴθ', ὡς θυμὸς ἐνὶ στήθεσσι φίλοισιν,
ὥς τοι γούναθ' ἕποιτο, βίη δέ τοι ἔμπεδος εἴη·
ἀλλά σε γῆρας τείρει ὁμοίϊον· ὡς ὄφελέν τις
ἀνδρῶν ἄλλος ἔχειν, σὺ δὲ κουροτέροισι μετεῖναι."
    Τὸν δ' ἠμείβετ' ἔπειτα Γερήνιος ἱππότα Νέστωρ·
"'Ατρεΐδη, μάλα μέν τοι ἐγὼν ἐθέλοιμι καὶ αὐτὸς
ὣς ἔμεν ὡς ὅτε δῖον 'Ερευθαλίωνα κατέκταν.
ἀλλ' οὔ πως ἅμα πάντα θεοὶ δόσαν ἀνθρώποισιν·
εἰ τότε κοῦρος ἔα, νῦν αὖτέ με γῆρας ὀπάζει.
ἀλλὰ καὶ ὣς ἱππεῦσι μετέσσομαι ἠδὲ κελεύσω
βουλῇ καὶ μύθοισι· τὸ γὰρ γέρας ἐστὶ γερόντων.
αἰχμὰς δ' αἰχμάσσουσι νεώτεροι, οἵ περ ἐμεῖο
ὁπλότεροι γεγάασι πεποίθασίν τε βίηφιν."   (4.313–25)

"Aged sir, if only, as the spirit is in your bosom,
so might your knees be also and the strength stay steady within you;
but *age* weakens you which comes to all; if only some other
of the fighters had your age and you were one of the young men!"
Nestor the *Gerenian* horseman spoke and answered him:
"Son of Atreus, so would I also wish to be that
man I was, when I cut down brilliant Ereuthalion.
But the gods give to mortals not everything at the same time;
if I was a young man then, now in turn *old age* is upon me.
Yet even so I shall be among the riders, and command them
with word and counsel; such is the *privilege* of the *old men*.
The young spearmen shall do the spear-fighting, those who are born
of a generation later than mine, who trust in their own strength."

The *geras* for *gēras*, then, is the respect shown for their words; their
existence is in a different realm from that of the young men. Though
they might still risk their lives in battle, as indeed Nestor does—whose
locative epithet is *Gerēnios*: cf. Peleus growing old in Phthia—they do
not go in the forefront, committing themselves self-consciously to the
action of definition as Hegel insists the truly free man must. Rather
they hang back in abstraction, the unreal experience of words.
    Diomedes saves Nestor from difficulties in battle and almost scolds
him with his helplessness, and for once, Nestor is silent, without reply

or reminiscence:

"ὦ γέρον, ἦ μάλα δή σε νέοι τείρουσι μαχηταί,
σὴ δὲ βίη λέλυται, χαλεπὸν δέ σε γῆρας ὀπάζει,
ἠπεδανὸς δέ νύ τοι θεράπων, βραδέες δέ τοι ἵπποι."   (8.102–4)

. . . "Old sir,
in very truth these young fighters are too much for you,
and all your strength is gone, and hard *old age* is upon you,
your henchman is a man of no worth, and your horses are heavy."

Phoinix wants to scrape off his old age (*gēras apoxusas*—9.446), so that once more he would be a young man blossoming (*neon hēbōonta*) and go in the forefront of the battle. So closely are words and age associated that even Odysseus, one of the middle-aged heroes, claims the superiority of counsel over Achilles, though admitting, as all men and gods must, Achilles' superiority in fighting (19.216ff.). *Gerontes* is used of leaders in counsel, when they gather to advise Agamemnon, though Diomedes, at least, is still very young (2.404).

All of this is explained to some extent by the shield, where we see men in council inside the city in a time of peace, and men in battle outside the city in a time of war. Though the counsel of age must restrain the impulsiveness of youth even in war—generally the distinction is sharp and old men do not talk in battle, but only before and after battle about battle; the battleground is the arena for youth—there is a suggestion that the words of age are appropriate only to peace, when men are not defining themselves actively and aggressively in terms of each other, but only moving in the shadow world of words. Iris, appearing as Polites, says to Priam:

"Old sir, dear to you forever are words beyond number
as once, when there was peace; but stintless war has arisen.
In my time I have gone into many battles among men,
yet never have I seen a host like this, not one so numerous."   (2.796–99)

We might recall here that in the lamentation over the dead Patroklos the old men are said to weep with Achilles, each for his own grief, just as do the women:

Ὣς ἔφατο κλαίουσ', ἐπὶ δὲ στενάχοντο γυναῖκες,
Πάτροκλον πρόφασιν, σφῶν δ' αὐτῶν κήδε' ἑκάστη.   (19.301–2)

So she spoke, lamenting, *and the women sorrowed around her*
grieving openly for Patroklos, but for her own sorrows
each.

Ὣς ἔφατο κλαίων, ἐπὶ δὲ στενάχοντο γέροντες,
μνησάμενοι τὰ ἕκαστος ἐνὶ μεγάροισιν ἔλειπον·   (19.338–39)

So he spoke mourning, *and the elders lamented around him*
remembering each those he had left behind in his own halls.

Old men and women talk and weep; children do, too, of course, and
we recall Achilles' image of Patroklos as a little girl weeping and pulling
at her mother's skirt. Only young men fight, and therefore, in this
world of war, only young men are men and have full, true being.

The old men stay inside the walls with the women in time of war,
and young men go outside to fight and define themselves in combat
with other men. In epic true being is outside, in the action of battle;
in tragedy it is inside, domestic. Agamemnon and Herakles come home
from war to face the frustrations and resentment of their wives, and
there they meet death. In New Comedy men have entirely lost sight
of the world outside, and direct all their energies toward the home and
family. Do we not see here again, in the evolution of the literary
genres, phylogenetic and ontogenetic parallels? Surely we must admit
that the focus of Greek life moves from the wide, new world of col-
onization in the seventh century to the city in the sixth and fifth
centuries, and finally to the family in the fourth. At the same time
men's attitude towards women changes from the benign neglect of
epic to the misogyny of tragedy to the romanticism of New Comedy:
when men no longer have an active political role to play they idealize
(*faute de mieux*) their domestic lives. Suddenly we are in a position
to see the origins of misogyny, both socially and individually. Mature
men always blame women for the restrictions they feel upon their
movement, actually and self-conceptually, just as the male child feels
restriction from the overly attentive but never fully pleased mother.
Only when men are reconciled to such restriction is some kind of
equilibrium established and then it is in the self-consciously compromised world of romance, where the maternal figure is deified and the
aim of desire is re-incorporation and undifferentiated bliss.

Clearly these cycles are historically determined, specific in space and time, but just as clearly their original pattern (whether we see that pattern as causative or analytical, or, better, admit that there is no difference) is infantile experience. Civilization—which so far has meant the ways men see themselves in relation to women (their mothers) and gods (their idealized images of themselves)—is a vast pathetic fallacy, not unlike the creation myths where the tensions of the nuclear family are projected upon the cosmos, so that mother aids son in usurping the father's position.

The great contradiction between words and deeds comes on the battlefield when part of the ritual of single combat is the insult spoken before and after the actual duel. At crucial encounters, though, this formula is rejected. Patroklos responds to Meriones, who has said that though Patroklos is generally the better fighter, he might nevertheless be killed by Meriones' spear and "give to him glory."

"Μηριόνη, τί σὺ ταῦτα καὶ ἐσθλὸς ἐὼν ἀγορεύεις;
ὦ πέπον, οὔ τοι Τρῶες ὀνειδείοις ἐπέεσσι
νεκροῦ χωρήσουσι· πάρος τινὰ γαῖα καθέξει.
ἐν γὰρ χερσὶ τέλος πολέμου, ἐπέων δ' ἐνὶ βουλῇ·
τῶ οὔ τι χρὴ μῦθον ὀφέλλειν, ἀλλὰ μάχεσθαι."   (16.627–31)

"Meriones, when you are a brave fighter, why say such things?—
See, dear friend, the Trojans will not give back from the body
for hard words spoken. Sooner the ground will cover them. Warfare's
finality lies in the work of hands, that of words in counsel.
It is not for us now to pile up talk, but to fight in battle."

When Aeneas meets Achilles on the battlefield he prefaces and concludes his genealogy with these observations on the difference between words and deeds:

"Son of Peleus, never hope by words to frighten me
as if I were a baby (*nēputíon hōs*)". . .

(Note that so many insults begin with the epithet *nēpie*, which seems to suggest that, as here, the object of derision cannot distinguish between word and deed.)[8]

. . . "I myself understand well enough
how to speak in vituperation and how to make insults.
You and I know each other's birth, we both know our parents
since we have heard the lines of their fame from mortal men;"

. . . .
. . . "I believe we will not in mere words like children
(*ou gar phēm' epeessi ge nēputioisin*)
meet, and separate and go home again out of the fighting."
. . . .
"But come, let us no longer stand here talking of these things
like children (*nēputioi hōs*), here in the space between the advancing
    armies.
For there are harsh things enough that could be spoken against us
both, a ship of a hundred locks should not carry the burden.
The tongue of man is a twisty thing, there are plenty of words there
of every kind, the range of words is wide, and their variance.
The sort of thing you say is the thing that will be said to you.
But what have you and I to do with the need for squabbling
and hurling insults at each other, as if we were two wives
who when they have fallen upon a heart-perishing quarrel
go out in the street and say abusive things to each other,
much true, and much that is not, and it is their rage that drives them.
You will not by talking turn me back from the strain of my warcraft,
not till you have fought to my face with the bronze. Come on then
and let us try each other's strength with the bronze of our
    spearheads."   (20.200–58)

Hektor says the same thing to Achilles two hundred lines later.

"Son of Peleus, never hope by words to frighten me
as if I were a baby (*nēputíon hōs*). I myself understand well enough
how to speak in vituperation and how to make insults."   (20.431–33)

We have a triple identification with words then: old men who cannot
fight use them; women who cannot fight use them; and children who
cannot tell the difference between words and things use them. This
all prepares us for Hektor's great moment of decision. We have already
called attention to Hektor's vision of himself going armless before
Achilles to ask for mercy:

"I might go up to him, and he take no pity upon me
nor respect my position, but kill me naked so, as if I were
a woman, once I stripped my armour from me. There is no
way any more from a tree or a rock to talk to him gently
whispering like a young man and a young girl, in the way
a young man and a young maiden whisper together."   (22.123–28)

Again, when the two have faced each other and Achilles has refused
Hektor's request for an oath that the victor will return the victim's

body, and Achilles has cast the first spear, Hektor speaks:

"You missed; and it was not, o Achilleus like the immortals,
from Zeus that you knew my destiny; but you thought so; or rather
you are someone clever in speech and spoke to swindle me,
to make me afraid of you and forget my valour and my
　　strength."　　　　　　　　　　　　　　　　　　　　　　(22.279–82)

We must deal at some length hereafter with the whole problem of
a man's being what another man or a god tells him he is. Here, though,
we insist only that the *Iliad* clearly distinguishes along these lines: old
men and women and children use words and find their limited existence inside the city in time of peace; young men all need war, so they
can define themselves in their confrontations with other young men.
When we come finally to realize why it is Achilles chooses death rather
than life without killing Hektor, part of our realization must be that
old men, like women in the *Iliad*, though seemingly respected and
admired, are, in fact, despised, and the failure to reach old age is no
great threat to the young warrior, but almost a comfort, for what are
old men but words, like Tithonos, who was granted immortality by
Eos, but forgot to ask for eternal youth?

Οἱ δ' ἀμφὶ Πρίαμον καὶ Πάνθοον ἠδὲ Θυμοίτην
Λάμπον τε Κλυτίον θ' Ἱκετάονά τ', ὄζον Ἄρηος,
Οὐκαλέγων τε καὶ Ἀντήνωρ, πεπνυμένω ἄμφω,
ἥατο δημογέροντες ἐπὶ Σκαιῇσι πύλῃσι,
γήραϊ δὴ πολέμοιο πεπαυμένοι, ἀλλ' ἀγορηταὶ
ἐσθλοί, τεττίγεσσιν ἐοικότες, οἵ τε καθ' ὕλην
δενδρέῳ ἐφεζόμενοι ὄπα λειριόεσσαν ἱεῖσι·
τοῖοι ἄρα Τρώων ἡγήτορες ἦντ' ἐπὶ πύργῳ.　　　　(3.146–53)

Now those who sat with Priam: Panthoös and Thymoites,
Lampos and Klytios, Hiketaon, scion of Ares,
with Antenor and Oukalegon, both men of good counsel:
these were seated by the Skaian gates, elders of the people.
Now through old age these fought no longer, yet were they excellent
speakers still, and clear, as cicadas who through the forest
settle on trees, to issue their delicate voice of singing.
Such were they who sat on the tower, chief men of the Trojans.

This passage must have manifold resonance throughout the epic
tradition. While there is no early reference to Tithonos' metamor-
phosis into a cicada—it comes first in scholiastic comment on *Iliad*

9.5—he is mentioned in the *Iliad* as Priam's brother: 3.147 *Lampon te Klytion th' Hiketaona t', ozon Areos* = 20.238, which is preceded by *Tithōnon teketo Priamon te*. Tithonos' gradual attenuation into merely a singing voice is at least as early in the tradition as the Homeric Hymn to Aphrodite:

Τοῦ δ' ἦ τοι φωνὴ ῥεῖ ἄσπετος, οὐδέ τι κῖκυς
ἔσθ' οἵη πάρος ἔσκεν ἐνὶ γναμπτοῖσι μέλεσσιν.   (237–38)

His voice continues to flow ceaselessly, but there is no force
left in his limbs, not as there once was.

(The last three words of 237 and all of 238 are repeated from *Odyssey* 11.393–94, where the description is of Agamemnon's ghost coming to drink blood at the pit Odysseus has dug in the underworld.) We know that the *Aithiopis* was focused on the *aristeia* of Tithonos' son Memnon:

Memnon, the son of Eos, in his armour made by Hephaistos, arrives to help the Trojans. Thetis warns her son about Memnon. Antilochos is killed by Memnon when they meet; then Achilles kills Memnon. Having begged immortality for her son from Zeus, Eos bestows it upon him. Routing the Trojans, Achilles storms their citadel and is killed by Paris and Apollo. There is a great battle for the body, which Ajax captures and takes back to the ships. Odysseus is driven back by the Trojans. Then they bury Antilochos and lay out the body of Achilles. Thetis comes with the Muses and her sisters and mourns her son. (Proclus, II)

The parallels between this plot and that of the *Iliad* have been much discussed:[9] that Achilles should kill Memnon (in revenge for his having killed Achilles' dear friend Antilochos, the son of Nestor, who became Achilles' *therapōn* after Patroklos' death) and then himself be killed as a consequence, seems a recapitulation of the sequence: death of Patroklos, death of Hektor, predicted death of Achilles. The similarities that the common bond of Tithonos suggests, however, are these: Memnon is like Achilles in having a divine mother and a mortal father; they both wear armor made by Hephaistos (certainly in the *Iliad* an indication of the glory the mother can bestow upon her son); in both the age and weakness of the mortal father is stressed, perhaps Peleus' by association with the place name Phthia, certainly Tithonos' by his goddess-wife's failure to ask for him eternal youth (a boon which Zeus had given his ancestor Ganymede) as well as immortality.

It is wrong to think of the *Aithiopis* as an imitation of the *Iliad*, or even, as some do, vice versa, that is, that an earlier version of the *Aithiopis*—Proclus' summary is of Arktinos' poem, which was post-Homeric in date—influenced the composition of the *Iliad*. Rather we should think of a common tradition producing both poems, a tradition insistent upon a particular relationship: the mother is a goddess; the father is weak and aged; the son is a hero and loves a male companion. The thematic concerns inevitable upon this situation are an association between youth and beauty and fighting strength, on the one hand; age, ugliness, and weakness, on the other. Imaged with the former range of qualities is the son, under the benevolent protection of his mother, and this son defines himself in terms of his male companion. The father is identified with the other negative qualities, and the strongest statement of his weakness is that he is only words, not action. The son seems almost to pursue death in glorious action simply to escape the fate of the father, as though his attenuation into a speaking shadow were the negative paradeigma held up to him, the very figure of death: Tithonos is aligned formulaically with Agamemnon's ghost in the later tradition. The later tradition also identifies Tithonos and his brothers as cicadas, and we already have Priam, on the Trojan side, as that figure of weak old age which Nestor, Phoinix, and Peleus provide on the Greek side.

II.12
THE PHENOMENOLOGY OF WAR

Why should Hegel have said that a man must risk his life to gain recognition as an independent self-consciousness, and did he say this because of his reading of Homer, and, if so, what is there in Homer which encourages such a reading?

The relation of both self-consciousnesses is in this way [a two-fold action aimed at the destruction of the other's life and at the risk of its own life] so constituted that they prove themselves and each other through a life-and-death struggle. They must enter into this struggle, for they must bring their certainty of themselves, the certainty of being for themselves, to the level of objective truth, and make this a fact both in the case of the other and in their own case as well. And it is solely by risking life that freedom is obtained; only thus is it tried and proved that the essential nature of self-consciousness is not bare existence, is not the merely immediate form in which it at first makes its appearance, is not merely its absorption in the expanse of life. Rather it is thereby guaranteed that there is nothing present but what might be taken as a vanishing moment—that self-consciousness is merely pure self-existence, being-for-self. The individual, who has not staked his life, may, no doubt, be recognized as a Person; but he has not attained the truth of this recognition as an independent self-consciousness.[1]

The crucial passages in the *Iliad* that involve death, appearance, and "reality" present themselves to our attention because their sense turns on the very word from which Hegel takes his central concern. Iris, coming to Achilles from Hera, gives him instructions:

"εὖ νυ καὶ ἡμεῖς ἴδμεν ὅ τοι κλυτὰ τεύχε' ἔχονται·
ἀλλ' αὔτως ἐπὶ τάφρον ἰὼν Τρώεσσι φάνηθι," (18.197–98)

"Yes, we also know well how they hold your glorious armour.
But go to the ditch, and *show* yourself as you are to the Trojans."

These instructions recall those which Nestor had given Patroklos:

"καί τοι τεύχεα καλὰ δότω πόλεμόνδε φέρεσθαι,
αἴ κέ σε τῷ εἴσκοντες ἀπόσχωνται πολέμοιο
Τρῶες, ἀναπνεύσωσι δ' ἀρήϊοι υἷες 'Αχαιῶν
τειρόμενοι· ὀλίγη δέ τ' ἀνάπνευσις πολέμοιο."   (11.798–801)

"And let him give you his splendid armour to wear to the fighting
if perhaps the Trojans might think you are he, and give way
from their attack, and the fighting sons of the Achaians get wind
again after hard work. There is little breathing space in the fighting."

The connection between the armor and the "identity" of Achilles is
therefore made and, of course, when Patroklos presents his plan to
Achilles (16.40ff.) Achilles' first concern is that Patroklos—wearing his
(Achilles') armor and believed to be Achilles—not usurp his (Achilles')
own true place, and take his glory:

"τύνη δ' ὤμοιιν μὲν ἐμὰ κλυτὰ τεύχεα δῦθι,
ἄρχε δὲ Μυρμιδόνεσσι φιλοπτολέμοισι μάχεσθαι,
. . . .
ἀλλὰ καὶ ὧς, Πάτροκλε, νεῶν ἀπὸ λοιγὸν ἀμύνων
ἔμπεσ' ἐπικρατέως, μὴ δὴ πυρὸς αἰθομένοιο
νῆας ἐνιπρήσωσι, φίλον δ' ἀπὸ νόστον ἕλωνται.
πείθεο δ' ὧς τοι ἐγὼ μύθου τέλος ἐν φρεσὶ θείω,
ὡς ἄν μοι τιμὴν μεγάλην καὶ κῦδος ἄρηαι
πρὸς πάντων Δαναῶν, ἀτὰρ οἱ περικαλλέα κούρην
ἂψ ἀπονάσσωσιν, ποτὶ δ' ἀγλαὰ δῶρα πόρωσιν.
ἐκ νηῶν ἐλάσας ἰέναι πάλιν· εἰ δέ κεν αὖ τοι
δώῃ κῦδος ἀρέσθαι ἐρίγδουπος πόσις "Ηρης,
μὴ σύ γ' ἄνευθεν ἐμεῖο λιλαίεσθαι πολεμίζειν
Τρωσὶ φιλοπτολέμοισιν· ἀτιμότερον δέ με θήσεις·"   (16.64–90)

"So do you draw my glorious armour about your shoulders;
lead the Myrmidons whose delight is battle into the fighting."
. . . .
"But even so, Patroklos, beat the bane aside from our ships; fall
upon them with all your strength; let them not with fire's blazing
inflame our ships, and take away our desired homecoming.
But obey to the end this word I put upon your attention
so that you can win, for me, great honour and glory

in the sight of all the Danaans, so they will bring back to me
the lovely girl, and give me shining gifts in addition.
When you have driven them from the ships, come back; although later
the thunderous lord of Hera might grant you the winning of glory
you must not set your mind on fighting the Trojans, whose delight
is in battle, without me. So you will diminish my honour."

He goes on to show concern for Patroklos' safety: "lest some god come
against you," etc., and finally to make an almost complete identification between himself and Patroklos, with their mutual apotheosis
in battle, all other men, both comrades and enemies, having been
killed:

"αἲ γάρ, Ζεῦ τε πάτερ καὶ Ἀθηναίη καὶ Ἄπολλον,
μήτε τις οὖν Τρώων θάνατον φύγοι, ὅσσοι ἔασι,
μήτε τις Ἀργείων, νῶϊν δ' ἐκδῦμεν ὄλεθρον,
ὄφρ' οἶοι Τροίης ἱερὰ κρήδεμνα λύωμεν." (16.97–100)

"Father Zeus, Athene and Apollo, if only
not one of all the Trojans could escape destruction, not one
of the Argives, but you and I could emerge from the slaughter
so that we two alone could break Troy's hallowed coronal."

Since, in one construction, the whole poem focuses on Achilles'
distinction between the superficial attraction of material *geras* (tripods,
cattle, women, etc.) and the actuality of death, we must be sensitive
to the change from *geras* in 16.54ff.: "What really annoys me is that
Agamemnon took my *geras* from me"; to *timē* in 16.90: "Don't you
fight on without me; so you will make me dishonoured" (*atimoteron
de me thēseis*). He is, of course, simply putting to Patroklos Zeus' plan,
though he insists his mother has not told him anything specific about
this (16.50ff.). *Timē* obviously suggests here, as elsewhere (e.g., 1.353,
2.197, 17.251), the immortal honor that a man wins with the help of
a god. We see then this heroic concept entering in to balance Achilles'
anguish at the loss of his *geras* (perishable and insignificant) and his
anguish at the prospect of death (he will himself perish and lose significance). His *timē* becomes the only reality, and it rests with Patroklos. Patroklos has the armor, and therefore the appearance of
Achilles.

After Patroklos falls and is stripped *gymnos* of Achilles' armor by

Hektor, Achilles knows he cannot go into battle himself *gymnos*, but must wait his mother's delivery of new armor from Hephaistos. In the meantime Iris, sent by Hera, instructs him, as we have seen above: "appear (*phanēthi*) to the Trojans" (18.198). One wants specifically to know here, as generally throughout the *Iliad*—and we shall give below some examples of the wide range which *phainō* covers—what is the illusion and what the reality. Although Achilles does not have his armor (he gave it to a friend but it is now worn by an enemy) and cannot go into battle, nevertheless his mere appearance will turn the tide of battle, just as previously, when his friend wore his armor, his friend's mere appearance would turn the tide of battle. (The same formulaic sequence is used by Nestor—11.799–801, Patroklos—16.41–43, and Iris—18.199–201).

Our concern for this subtlety grows when we see the same collocation of themes in the scene of Hektor's death:

τοῦ δὲ καὶ ἄλλο τόσον μὲν ἔχε χρόα χάλκεα τεύχεα,
καλά, τὰ Πατρόκλοιο βίην ἐνάριξε κατακτάς·
φαίνετο δ' ᾗ κληῗδες ἀπ' ὤμων αὐχέν' ἔχουσι,
λαυκανίην, ἵνα τε ψυχῆς ὤκιστος ὄλεθρος·   (22.322–25)

. . . but all the rest of the skin was held in the armour,
brazen and splendid, he stripped when he cut down the strength of
    Patroklos,
yet *showed* where the collar-bones hold the neck from the shoulders
the throat, where death of the soul comes most swiftly;

We might recall what Bowra said about heroes never wounding but always killing their opponents.[2] If we think of the death of Patroklos we might extend this axiom to include the manner of killing: it will be superlative; Patroklos was killed with a spear thrust *neiaton es keneōna* (16.821) and this is described elsewhere as the most painful death for men (*malista . . . alegeinos* (13.568–69)). Beyond this, though, there is the question of appearance and reality. The reality of Hektor's weakness, his naked flesh, is revealed where he is most vulnerable. He had, of course, considered previously whether he might not lay down his arms and approach Achilles *gymnos*, like a woman (22.124–25). Not only does the armor, which is not his, but in which he appears, fail to protect him, but it exposes him to the deadliest blow. We are then forced to speculate generally on the phenomenology of war in the

Iliad. Our attention has been called to it by the central theme of the exchanged armor and identity, but we know it to be always important. Not only is it crucial how men appear to each other, but, of course, how gods appear to men. We have already suggested that men are effective to the extent that they are aware of a god's presence. Hera's speech to Poseidon and Athene about the necessity of their revealing themselves to Achilles when he faces Aeneas (the son of a goddess) is definitive in this respect and its conclusion is ambiguous, as we have seen: *khalepoi de theoi phainesthai enargeis* (20.131) "it is difficult for gods *to be shown* in their true shapes." The consideration might be the same as that explained to Priam by Hermes; he will accompany the old man only so far:

"ἀλλ᾽ ἤτοι μὲν ἐγὼ πάλιν εἴσομαι, οὐδ᾽ Ἀχιλῆος
ὀφθαλμοὺς εἴσειμι· νεμεσσητὸν δέ κεν εἴη
ἀθάνατον θεὸν ὧδε βροτοὺς ἀγαπαζέμεν ἄντην·"   (24.462–64)

"But now I am going back again, and I will not go in
before the eyes of Achilleus, for it would make others angry
for an immortal god so to face mortal men with favour."

There is, of course, a contradiction here, since, as Willcock has shown, a god's favor and a man's worth are synonymous. Certainly there can be no question of *nemesis* against the god who openly shows his favor to a particular man; it must mean that the man himself suffers when other men see that a god is helping him, and, indeed, we shall see below some passages where just such taunts are made. The contradiction, however, persists. Is a man always as he is, or can a god make him better, and, in the latter case, must not the man be aware of the god's effort on his behalf so that the effort will not be wasted, and, furthermore, how does all this congrue with a man's consciousness of himself, his "memory of his war-strength"?

The first thing to appreciate is that gods change the appearance of things. In their most effective and bewildering interventions there is always the confusion of appearance. Aphrodite carries off Paris to save him from Menelaos:

. . . . . . τὸν δ᾽ ἐξήρπαξ᾽ Ἀφροδίτη
ῥεῖα μάλ᾽ ὥς τε θεός, ἐκάλυψε δ᾽ ἄρ᾽ ἠέρι πολλῇ,   (3.380–81)

. . . But Aphrodite caught up Paris
easily, since she was divine, and wrapped him in a thick mist.

Apollo carries off Hektor:

. . . . . τὸν δ' ἐξήρπαξεν Ἀπόλλων
ῥεῖα μάλ' ὥς τε θεός, ἐκάλυψε δ' ἄρ' ἠέρι πολλῇ.   (20.443–44)

. . . but Phoibos Apollo caught up Hektor
easily, since he was a god, and wrapped him in a thick mist.

Nestor says that Poseidon saved the sons of Aktor:

"καί νύ κεν Ἀκτορίωνε Μολίονε παῖδ' ἀλάπαξα,
εἰ μή σφωε πατὴρ εὐρὺ κρείων ἐνοσίχθων
ἐκ πολέμου ἐσάωσε, καλύψας ἠέρι πολλῇ."   (11.750–52)

"And now I would have killed the young Moliones, scions
of Aktor, had not their father who shakes the earth in his wide strength
caught them out of the battle, shrouding them in a thick mist."

Apollo saves Agenor:

ἀλλά μιν ἐξήρπαξε, κάλυψε δ' ἄρ' ἠέρι πολλῇ   (21.597)

but caught [Agenor] away closing him in a dense mist.

In each of these cases the god conceals the man and removes him.
To those men in battle about him—especially to the enemy who pursues him—the illusion is that he has vanished, not "into thin air," but
into a thick mist with which the god has enveloped him. Now we have
already seen that not only is the same verb *mignumi* used of both
sexual intercourse and martial engagement in the first ranks of men,
but also, occasionally, it is used of assimilation with the crowd, to
escape such an engagement. Thus we contrast the use of the formula
promachoisin emichthē (5.134, 8.99, 13.642, 15.457) "he was mixed
with the front fighters," with *mikto d'homilōi* (11.354, 16.813) "he
mixed in the crowd," and variations such as Diomedes' cry to Odysseus
when Nestor needs help: *pēi pheugeis, meta nōta balōn, kakos hōs, en
homilōi* (8.94) "where are you going, turning your back, like a coward,
in the crowd?" Men in battle do emerge from the throng to fight among
the foremost and they also shrink back to mix with the many. It is the
Hegelian alternative, and Homer does present it to us as "phenome-

nal": a man is seen confronting another man, to prove his own existence as not only *an sich* or *für sich*, but both simultaneously, in reference to the other man.

It is this, of course, which redeems Homeric battle scenes from the charge of chaotic carnage that is often made against them. These are not the mass movements of troops which one maniacal commander controls, adjusting the reality of men's lives to his pathologically grandiose image of himself (the "Napoleon complex"), but rather each man's single attempt to define himself in terms of another single man whom he faces in a life-and-death struggle. The phenomenology of war in the *Iliad* is interpsychic in that one man needs another, libidinally or aggressively, and suddenly he is not there (but, of course, originally intra-psychic in that each man calls upon a friend or confronts an enemy to restore his elusive and often lost image of himself), and the poet tells us what the confused spectator believes, that some god has saved him because all that appears in his place is a bit of mist. The saved man is completely confused, having literally lost his place in the world.

In many other places in the narrative men do not actually disappear, but the gods come to them wrapping themselves in mist, such as Apollo to Patroklos (16.788) and to Agenor (21.549), or the gods send confusion upon the men in battle by setting a mist upon it, and the phenomenology of war becomes little more than the aesthetics of metaphor: Zeus sends a mist over the Trojans' helmets (17.269) and Hera confuses the Trojans (21.6). There can be no question that the great visual appeal of the *Iliad* is closely bound up with its philosophical and psychological center. There is the constant contrast between the obscure (mist, dark seas, clouds, Tartaros) and the brilliance of particular moments in the activities and experience of gods and men.

We have been made aware by Snell of the relation between sense perception and cognition in the various "see" verbs. We know that the poet insists on the visual brilliance of the heroes and their most impressive feats, and indeed everything associated with them and the gods. Their shields and eyes are *phaeinos*; they themselves are *phaidimos*. As with Zeus' own thunderbolt, these moments are illumined and hence men's perceptions of themselves are altered. Again we see the tripartite nature of the Homeric world: there are men and heroes and gods; death, purely self-evident existence (passivity) and glorious action; Tartaros, earth, and the brilliant heavens; dark, mist, and light.

In one of those passages (where we have learned to read closely for the poet's own attempt at resolution or definition of complex association), Ajax prays to Zeus for illumination:

"Ζεῦ πάτερ, ἀλλὰ σὺ ῥῦσαι ὑπ' ἠέρος υἷας Ἀχαιῶν,
ποίησον δ' αἴθρην, δὸς δ' ὀφθαλμοῖσιν ἰδέσθαι·
ἐν δὲ φάει καὶ ὄλεσσον, ἐπεί νύ τοι εὔαδεν οὕτως."
Ὣς φάτο, τὸν δὲ πατὴρ ὀλοφύρατο δάκρυ χέοντα·
αὐτίκα δ' ἠέρα μὲν σκέδασεν καὶ ἀπῶσεν ὀμίχλην,
ἠέλιος δ' ἐπέλαμψε, μάχη δ' ἐπὶ πᾶσα φαάνθη· (17.645–50)

"Father Zeus, draw free from the mist the sons of the Achaians, make bright the air, and give sight back to our eyes; in *shining daylight* destroy us, if to destroy us be now your pleasure."
He spoke thus, and as he wept the father took pity upon him, and forthwith scattered the mist and pushed the darkness back from them, and the sun blazed out, and all the battle *was plain* before them.

On several occasions Zeus simply flashes his favor upon a man or an entire army (*phainōn*: 2.353, 4.381, 9.236). And, of course, Athene appears to Achilles and only to Achilles:

στῆ δ' ὄπιθεν, ξανθῆς δὲ κόμης ἕλε Πηλεΐωνα
οἴῳ φαινομένη· τῶν δ' ἄλλων οὔ τις ὁρᾶτο· (1.197–98)

The goddess standing behind Peleus' son caught him by the fair hair, *appearing* to him only, for no man of the others saw her.

There are all the times that dawn *appears* (9.618, 9.682, 11.685, 24.13, 24.600), and there is a particular formula for its appearance *phanē rhododaktylos Eōs* (1.477, 23.109, 24.788) "rosy-fingered Dawn *appeared*," which is altered to fit the circumstances of a hero's sudden recognition that his death is upon him: "then *was revealed* to you the end of your life."

ἔνθα κέ τοι, Μενέλαε, φάνη βιότοιο τελευτὴ (7.104)

ἔνθ' ἄρα τοι, Πάτροκλε, φάνη βιότοιο τελευτή· (16.787)

We recall the suggestion that the use of the epithet *phaidimos* is a prophecy of doom, and expand on that by saying that a man's death comes to him as a revelation. Not only is the glorious man, the man round whom the glory of the gods shines, envied and the object of the anger of other men and gods—the *Iliad* itself gives us the examples of Bellerophontes and Oedipus, not to mention Patroklos and Achilles— but his being conspicuous is both the sign to other men that he is favored and the revelation to himself that such moments cannot often be repeated, so that an early death is both inevitable and desirable. In Priam's phrase—

". . . πάντα δὲ καλὰ θανόντι περ, ὅττι φανήῃ·" (22.73)

". . . and though dead still all that *shows* about him is beautiful. . . ."

We know that this beauty is ephemeral and that it is hypostatized in early death. Priam himself makes the connection, because we have previously heard Hektor described:

Ἕκτωρ δ᾽ ἐν πρώτοισι φέρ᾽ ἀσπίδα πάντοσ᾽ ἐΐσην.
οἷος δ᾽ ἐκ νεφέων ἀναφαίνεται οὔλιος ἀστὴρ
παμφαίνων, τοτὲ δ᾽ αὖτις ἔδυ νέφεα σκιόεντα,
ὣς Ἕκτωρ ὁτὲ μέν τε μετὰ πρώτοισι φάνεσκεν,
ἄλλοτε δ᾽ ἐν πυμάτοισι κελεύων· πᾶς δ᾽ ἄρα χαλκῷ
λάμφ᾽ ὥς τε στεροπὴ πατρὸς Διὸς αἰγιόχοιο. (11.61–66)

And Hektor carried the perfect circle of his shield in the foremost,
as among the darkened clouds the bale star *shows forth*
in all shining, then merges again in the clouds and the darkness.
So Hektor would at one time *be shining* among the foremost,
and then once more urging on the last, and complete in bronze armour,
glittered like the thunder-flash of Zeus of the aegis, our father.

Priam then sees Achilles in the forefront of the battle and it is this that stimulates his meditation on youth and beauty and death:

Τὸν δ᾽ ὁ γέρων Πρίαμος πρῶτος ἴδεν ὀφθαλμοῖσι,
παμφαίνονθ᾽ ὥς τ᾽ ἀστέρ᾽ ἐπεσσύμενον πεδίοιο,
ὅς ῥά τ᾽ ὀπώρης εἶσιν, ἀρίζηλοι δέ οἱ αὐγαὶ
φαίνονται πολλοῖσι μετ᾽ ἀστράσι νυκτὸς ἀμολγῷ· (22.25–28)

The aged Priam was the first of all whose eyes saw him
as he swept across the flat land *in full shining*, like that star
which comes on in the autumn and whose conspicuous brightness
far outshines the stars that are numbered in the night's darkening.

We know what happens to this concept in lyric and tragedy. In Pindar's *First Olympian* Pelops prays to Poseidon not to allow him to waste his life in obscurity, but to gain glory even at the risk of death, and throughout the plays of Aeschylus, Sophocles, and Euripides it is the conspicuous man who is in danger of attracting the *phthonos* of the gods: *presbuteroisin Erinyes aien hepontai* (*Iliad* 15.204) "The Furies always follow the leaders." We distinguish the *Iliad* from these later considerations of the alternative modes of man's existence by its insistence on seeming, and being through seeming. It presents us with the mirror stage where there is not yet a true locus of being, but only a reflection in the Other and an insistence that that Other, whether the self-image as libidinally or aggressively invested, be not the self, because then there is no psychic space for the self. The phenomenology of war in the *Iliad* is the phenomenology of the self, which paradoxically requires and denies doubles, whether they be dear companions, deadly enemies, or the gods themselves. As Nagy has shown, Patroklos would take the place of Achilles and Achilles would take the place of Apollo. In both instances the self would become the idealized image of the self as reflected by the mother, but always this illusion of omnipotence is unrealizable and death lies on the other side of the mirror. It is, however, the death of Narcissus, with the beauty and aspirations of youth hypostatized in the fragile monument of the flower always fresh in the reflecting pool.

We have attempted to explain how men in the *Iliad* appear to themselves and each other in terms of mirror imagery. This is obviously an inadequate model because it is only dyadic, and on most occasions when Homeric psychology reveals itself there are at least three elements involved. These are the occasions on the battlefield when men decide to fight or not to fight because they become convinced that one (or more) of the gods is with them or with their enemies. An extreme statement of this is, of course, when men decide whether to fight with the god or gods themselves, but here we are back to a one-against-one argument.

In the narrative of Book XIII we seem to have an attempt by the poet to examine all aspects of the man-god-man encounter. The battle is for the ships themselves and Poseidon introduces the theme of man's consciousness of the god's assistance early in the sequence, when Hektor has reached the gates of the ramparts the Greeks have built to protect their ships. Even the introduction to his speech defines the complexity (or redundancy) of god and man determining that the man should fight:

First he spoke to the Aiantes, who were burning for battle already:
"Aiantes, you two, remember the spirit of warcraft
and not that of shivering panic, must save the Achaian people.
Elsewhere in truth I do not fear the Trojans' invincible
hands, though in full force they have swarmed over our great wall;
since the strong-greaved Achaians will be able to hold the rest of them.
But I fear most terribly disaster to us in the one place
where that berserk flamelike leads them against us, Hektor,
who claims he must be son of Zeus of the high strength. May this
be the message some one of the gods gives your minds to carry,
that you stand fast strongly yourselves, urge the next to stand also.
Thus, hard though he sweeps on, you might stay him beside the fast-
     running
ships, even though the very Olympian wakes him to battle."   (13.46–58)

We have already discussed Hera's speech to Poseidon and Athene at 20.115ff.: she tells them they must assure Achilles that the strongest gods are with him in his confrontation with Aeneas, since Aeneas is the son of a goddess and enjoys the favor of Apollo:

"Come, then, we must even go down ourselves and turn him
back from here, or else one of us must stand by Achilleus
and put enormous strength upon him, and let him not come short
in courage, but let him know that they love him who are the highest
of the immortals, but those who before now fended the fury
of war, as now, from the Trojans are as wind and nothing.
For all of us have come down from Olympos to take our part
in this battle, so nothing may be done to him by the Trojans
on this day. Afterwards he shall suffer such things as Destiny
wove with the strand of his birth that day he was born to his mother.
But if Achilleus does not hear all this from gods' voices
he will be afraid, when a god puts out his strength against him
in the fighting. It is hard for gods *to be shown (phainesthai)* in their true
     shape."   (20.119–31)

Paris has another way of saying the same thing, explaining his seeming cowardice to Helen:

"Lady, censure my heart no more in bitter reprovals.
This time Menelaos with Athene's help has beaten me;
another time I shall beat him. We have gods on our side also."   (3.438–40)

The essential thing, then, seems to be that a man is aware of a god's presence in the battle, and, of course, if there is a conflict of divine wills, then it is important that the god favoring him is stronger than the god favoring his opponent, and that both men be aware of this differential. If we return our attention to Book XIII, however, we find that double motivation, mortal and divine, continues throughout the fight for the ships. Poseidon, disguised as Kalchas, speaks to the two Aiantes:

"Αἴαντε, σφὼ μέν τε σαώσετε λαὸν Ἀχαιῶν
ἀλκῆς μνησαμένω, μηδὲ κρυεροῖο φόβοιο." (13.47–48)

"Aiantes, you two, remembering the spirit of warcraft
and not that of shivering panic, must save the Achaian people."

But Oilean Ajax tells Telemonian Ajax:

"Αἶαν, ἐπεί τις νῶϊ θεῶν, οἳ Ὄλυμπον ἔχουσι,
μάντεϊ εἰδόμενος κέλεται παρὰ νηυσὶ μάχεσθαι,
οὐδ' ὅ γε Κάλχας ἐστί, θεοπρόπος οἰωνιστής·
ἴχνια γὰρ μετόπισθε ποδῶν ἠδὲ κνημάων
ῥεῖ' ἔγνων ἀπιόντος· ἀρίγνωτοι δὲ θεοί περ·
καὶ δ' ἐμοὶ αὐτῷ θυμὸς ἐνὶ στήθεσσι φίλοισι
μᾶλλον ἐφορμᾶται πολεμίζειν ἠδὲ μάχεσθαι,
μαιμώωσι δ' ἔνερθε πόδες καὶ χεῖρες ὕπερθε." (13.68–75)

"Aias, since some one of the gods, whose hold is Olympos,
has likened himself to the seer, and told us to fight by our vessels,
this is not Kalchas, the bird-interpreter of the gods, for I knew
easily as he went away the form of his feet, the legs' form
from behind him. Gods, though gods, are conspicuous. Therefore
as for me, the spirit inside my inward breast drives me
all the harder to carry on the war and the fighting,
and my feet underneath me are eager and my hands above them."

Telamonian Ajax responds:

"οὕτω νῦν καὶ ἐμοὶ περὶ δούρατι χεῖρες ἄαπτοι
μαιμῶσιν, καί μοι μένος ὦρορε, νέρθε δὲ ποσσὶν
ἔσσυμαι ἀμφοτέροισι· μενοινώω δὲ καὶ οἶος
Ἕκτορι Πριαμίδῃ ἄμοτον μεμαῶτι μάχεσθαι." (13.76–80)

"So for me also now the invincible hands on my spearshaft
are furious, my strength is rising, and both feet beneath me
are sweeping me onward, so that I long even for single combat
with Hektor, Priam's son, the forever avid of battle."

Slightly later Poseidon approaches other Greeks to threaten and scold them:

"εἰ δ᾽ ὑμεῖς πολέμοιο μεθήσετε λευγαλέοιο,
νῦν δὴ εἴδεται ἦμαρ ὑπὸ Τρώεσσι δαμῆναι." (13.97–98)

"but if you yourselves are to go slack from the sorrowful fighting
now is seen your day to be beaten down by the Trojans."

"ὑμεῖς δ᾽ οὐκέτι καλὰ μεθίετε θούριδος ἀλκῆς
πάντες ἄριστοι ἐόντες ἀνὰ στρατόν". . . (13.116–17)

"But you can no longer in honour give way from your fighting valour
being all the best men along the host". . .

And again, in the same speech, the emphasis is upon consciousness:

"ὦ πέπονες, τάχα δή τι κακὸν ποιήσετε μεῖζον
τῇδε μεθημοσύνῃ· ἀλλ᾽ ἐν φρεσὶ θέσθε ἕκαστος
αἰδῶ καὶ νέμεσιν· δὴ γὰρ μέγα νεῖκος ὄρωρεν." (13.120–22)

"O friends, soon you will bring to pass some still greater evil
with this hanging back. Let every one of you plant in his heart's depth
discipline and shamefastness. A big battle rises against you."

Menelaos, in the speech discussed above, where he analyzes the workings of koros upon the hearts of men, returns to the same theme, though he insists that the gods can inhibit rather than encourage a man in his fighting:

"ἀλλά ποθι σχήσεσθε καὶ ἐσσύμενοί περ Ἄρηος." (13.630)

"But you will be held somewhere, though you be so headlong for battle."

And finally we hear from Paris, in response to Hektor's encouragement:

"ἡμεῖς δ᾽ ἐμμεμαῶτες ἅμ᾽ ἑψόμεθ᾽, οὐδέ τί φημι
ἀλκῆς δευήσεσθαι, ὅση δύναμίς γε πάρεστι.
πὰρ δύναμιν δ᾽ οὐκ ἔστι καὶ ἐσσύμενον πολεμίζειν." (13.785–87)

"and we shall follow you eagerly; I think that we shall not
come short in warcraft, in so far as the strength stays with us.
But beyond his strength no man can fight, although he be eager."

This concept of limitation placed on a man's performance by his natural abilities is contradicted by Ajax at 17.629–32:

"ὦ πόποι, ἤδη μέν κε καὶ ὃς μάλα νήπιός ἐστι
γνοίη ὅτι Τρώεσσι πατὴρ Ζεὺς αὐτὸς ἀρήγει.

τῶν μὲν γὰρ πάντων βέλε’ ἅπτεται, ὅς τις ἀφήῃ,
ἢ κακὸς ἢ ἀγαθός· Ζεὺς δ’ ἔμπης πάντ’ ἰθύνει·”

"Shame on it! By now even one with a child's innocence
could see how father Zeus himself is helping the Trojans.
The weapons of each of these take hold, no matter who throws them,
good fighter or bad, since Zeus is straightening all of them equally."

Now it is true, here, that Ajax describes the phenomenon of the
men's weapons hitting their targets, rather than the men themselves
hitting each other, but elsewhere it is stated that Zeus can increase
a man's *aretē*. It is Aeneas speaking to Achilles and, having traced his
genealogy, and before saying that the time is right for deeds not words,
he insists:

“Ζεὺς δ’ ἀρετὴν ἄνδρεσσιν ὀφέλλει τε μινύθει τε,
ὅππως κεν ἐθέλῃσιν· ὁ γὰρ κάρτιστος ἀπάντων.”   (20.242–43)

"Zeus builds up and Zeus diminishes the strength in men,
the way he pleases, since his power is beyond all others."

From the context we may gather either or both of two things: that
aretē has varied in Aeneas' family, or that whatever his family, Zeus
can vary his (Aeneas') *aretē*. Hektor believes that in spite of the vast
difference between himself and Achilles, it is still possible that Zeus
may grant to him glory in their combat (22.130), which can perhaps
be taken as an indication that such a proposition is totally false, i.e.,
that a man's ability and the gods' determination of the outcome of his
combat can be at great variance. Indeed, on at least two occasions,
it is stated that men can succeed against the gods' wishes. The narrator
tells us that the Greeks might have seized glory and sacked Troy *kai
hyper Dios aisan* (17.321) "even against the fated ruling of Zeus," if
Apollo had not encouraged Aeneas; and Agamemnon is convinced
earlier in the same battle (over Patroklos' body) that if he could only
reach Ajax they might keep their spirit of battle *kai pros daimona per*
(17.104) "even against the god," though he knows that generally—

“ὁππότ’ ανηρ ἐθέλῃ πρὸς δαίμονα φωτὶ μάχεσθαι
ὅν κε θεὸς τιμᾷ, τάχα οἱ μέγα πῆμα κυλίσθη.”   (17.98–99)

"When a man, in the face of divinity, would fight with another
whom some god honours, the big disaster rolls sudden upon him."

The whole question of men fighting against gods is considered in the Diomedeia, where, in the midst of the different episodes of his *aristeia*, there is the long speech to Glaukos in which we hear that Lykourgos suffered because he fought with the gods (6.123ff.), which is exactly the lesson that Diomedes must learn:

νήπιος, οὐδὲ τὸ οἶδε κατὰ φρένα Τυδέος υἱός,
ὅττι μάλ᾽ οὐ δηναιὸς ὃς ἀθανάτοισι μάχηται,   (5.406–7)

. . . poor fool, the heart of Tydeus' son knows nothing
of how that man who fights the immortals lives for no long time.

Compare what Diomedes himself says to Glaukos of Lykourgos:

"τῷ μὲν ἔπειτ᾽ ὀδύσαντο θεοὶ ῥεῖα ζώοντες,
καί μιν τυφλὸν ἔθηκε Κρόνου πάϊς· οὐδ᾽ ἄρ᾽ ἔτι δὴν
ἦν, ἐπεὶ ἀθανάτοισιν ἀπήχθετο πᾶσι θεοῖσιν·"   (6.138–40)

"But the gods who live at their ease were angered with Lykourgos
and the son of Kronos struck him to blindness, nor did he live long
afterwards, since he was hated by all the immortals."

Of course, Diomedes can say this after his particular experience of having one god encourage him to fight against others: Athene has sent him against both Aphrodite (5.121ff.) and Ares (5.825ff.). The definitive moment of this notion might be Hektor's encouragement of his men and himself to stand up against Achilles, who has just compared himself to Ares and Athene (20.358–59).

"Do not be afraid of Peleion, o high-hearted Trojans.
I myself could fight in words against the immortals
but with the spear it were hard, since they are far stronger than we are.
Even Achilleus will not win achievement of everything
he says. Part he will accomplish, but part shall be baulked halfway done.
I am going to stand against him now, though his hands are like flame,
though his hands are like flame, and his heart like the shining of
     iron."   (20.366–72)

We have the association here between words and men, deeds and gods, whereas previously we have seen associated words, women, and weak old age on the one hand; deeds and strong young men on the other. Now we ask whether the gods, as complete fulfillment, are phenomenal (seeming) or real (being): the answer must be that they are neither, but rather something like Kant's *noumena*, i.e., human reason's projection of unknowable essence. It is indeed difficult for the gods to appear in their true form—they are constant and cannot be tied to ephemeral circumstances—and even if they did so appear, men could not recognize them, since men know only the ephemeral circumstance. The gods are what men think about themselves and their world, but these thoughts change. Achilles has been fighting with the gods and will continue to do so, becoming pure action, whereas the gods appear and recede, aiding one man now, and then another. Even Zeus pursues one course of action at this point, which contradicts that larger plan which he himself cannot control. Just as words are man's attempt to organize his reality, so are the gods his externalizations of his own motivations, his attempts to convince himself that the chaos of his existence does follow a plan. Here, as so often in the *Iliad*, we realize that Achilles is right for the world of the *Iliad* and Hektor is right only ideologically. Achilles looks for reality in the tension between himself and his similars—friends, enemies, gods— whereas Hektor insists on a larger reality beyond his control and comprehension.

How can we determine the point of view of the poem itself? Does Homer in any way contradict the surface action of his poem and the consistent attitude of his hero? I do not think he does. As one of his most perceptive critics has realized, the *Iliad* is a poem of force,[3] and the passive posture, the yielding and acceptance of fate that Hektor represents are a general proposition associated with all the concrete particulars that are negative (unreal) in the poem. It is as if Achilles were presented in his poem as the hard, real correction to Hektor's grace and theory. And where do we find in post-Homeric Greek history and literature Hektor's heirs? It is as if he never were, or, having been, were never taken as a model by subsequent poets and statesmen because of his weakness and ineffectuality.

The evidence on the gods seems totally ambiguous, and yet the constant factor is consciousness, whether a man's consciousness of his own power or of a god's presence, whether he "remembers his valor" or a god "appears to him." What we have then is truly a phenomenology rather than a metaphysics of war; it is not what a man is or what a god does, but rather what that man knows at a given moment of himself and his god. He can only think what the gods are (*noumena*), but he can test himself, as he seems, in combat with other men (*phenomena*); only then will the man know his own limits, i.e., the extent of the gods' favor towards him. Clearly the Homeric hero prefers death to ignorance in these respects, and in the case of Achilles we find that the supreme hero prefers death even in full knowledge of his limits and the extent of the gods' favor. It is here, of course, that he transcends Diomedes and all the rest of the men fighting at Troy. He has developed a positive image of himself in Patroklos and a negative image of himself in Hektor. The two cancel each other out and he dies, but by his own determination.

There is light and dark in Homer's *Iliad*, in Pindar's *First Olympian*, and in Sophocles' *Oedipus Tyrannos*. In each poem our concern is with a man who would know himself, and we try to appreciate and differentiate this self-knowledge as it moves more and more into world-knowledge (knowledge of the self-in-the-world), greater and greater compromises between *désir* and *demande*. We are most particularly impressed by the insubstantiality of the gods, their inability to feel desire and to adapt to demands made upon them: generally, to respond to experience. Zeus loves Sarpedon, but his grief for Sarpedon's death is not the same as Priam's grief for Hektor's death. Zeus' perspective is infinity and Priam's is his own mortality. The gods are, almost by definition, *noumena*, because they lack the definition men achieve in phenomenalizing themselves, making themselves into their own images. All men struggle against mysterious forces, but surely no one will doubt that the forces against which Achilles struggles are the originals of all these others. The plot, imagery, and vocabulary of the *Iliad* reveal to us the earliest stage in the development of the ego, the ontogeny of the self in the phenomenological struggle of the mirror stage.

If we then look back at Snell, who looks back at Hegel, who looks back at Homer, we realize that his heresy—believing that Homer presents man as having a fragmented image of himself—is not nearly so shocking as conventional critics would have it. In fact, it is inevitable. Homeric man lives in a fragmented world (which is his mirror), so of necessity he himself, in his consciousness of self, will be fragmented. We have already suggested that Fränkel's formulation of this fragmentation—*das Ich ist nicht abgekapselt*—is more acceptable to conventional critics because it is based on Heideggerian rather than Hegelian metaphysics. It makes of Homeric man a poetic creature, a negative capability, which is extremely attractive to these critics, whereas in Hegel's historical framework Homeric man seems simply to be primitive.

We cannot here pause to contemplate the primitive element in all poetry, though we have previously called attention to the notoriously childlike nature of all poets. We must, though, face the problem of nostalgia once more. We have suggested several models for it, but basically there is the same seeming contradiction in all nostalgic evocations—Gilgamesh, Genesis, The Winter's Tale—and this is the same contradiction Freud puts at the origin of the ego and the orientation of desire: narcissism and anaclisis. It is clear to me that those critics who read Homer's Iliad as a nostalgic evocation of social peace and well-being against the martial action on its surface are trying to find something that is indisputably there, but reversed. They are looking for the mother, and though maternal support is everywhere in evidence, it is not the primary issue of the poem. In Gilgamesh and The Winter's Tale it is quite clear that the nostalgia is narcissistic: the hero seeks the primitive image of himself which the woman (admittedly sexualized, nonmaternal woman) is responsible for destroying: the prostitute and the goddess Ishtar in Gilgamesh; Leontes' hallucination of an adulterous Hermione in The Winter's Tale. In the Greek material, too, there is abundant evidence for narcissistic nostalgia in post-Homeric literature, perhaps most obviously in Euripides' treatment of the Alkestis-Admetos story, where Apollo and Herakles are more important companions to the husband than is his wife. Even in the Garden of Eden itself (and certainly in Hesiod's two treatments of the Pandora myth) man loses his intimacy with his god (his idealized image of himself) because of the introduction of differentiation (otherness) in woman.

We find ourselves in the extraordinary position of equating the difference between narcissism and anaclisis with the difference between phenomenology and metaphysics. Hegel's evocation of Absolute Spirit at the end of the Phenomenology is his introduction (though it has always already been there) of the transcendent female element to resolve the seemingly endless succession of moments of male-against-male aggression and unconsummated desire. Metaphysical ultimates are always female because metaphysical systems are always made up by men trying to transcend themselves and the other men they refute philosophically. Whether the confrontation is between Achilles and Hektor, or Hegel and Kant, or Snell and Austin, we must always remember what Gouldner (and Slater and Girard) has told us about zero-sum conflicts: male phallic aggression (and its libidinal counterpart in the Hegelian other world of negation) can only be corrected and transcended by the celebration of the all-forgiving female. In this sense Diotima and Monica are the prefigurations of the Virgin at the center of the later Christian church, when men have given up the attempt to define themselves in terms of themselves and seek only solace and acceptance by the mother, which means loss of the self in the undifferentiatedness of symbiosis, a kind of death wish.

As critics we enjoy the superiority of irony and we should not relinquish it by confusing ourselves with our texts. We must not expect to find all that we know in Homer. It might be there implicitly, on the shield and in the marriage of Hektor and Andromache, but these moments are not the central focus of the *Iliad*, and even they seem to carry their own negation in the threat of the irreducible, original violence they contain. The *Iliad* is an examination of a man who cannot see beyond himself to a being different from himself: his friends and his enemies and his gods are all mirrors. It is a world of phenomenological struggle, and women hardly appear; they have not even the semblance of Being because they are not active in the struggle, but exist only as passive objects, their value created symbolically by the men who fight and die, and these battles and deaths are not for the women, but for the men themselves, to prove to themselves that they themselves are not merely passive objects.

III
RECAPITULATION

RECAPITULATION

My project began with the problem of the modern reader's response to the *Iliad*. I sought some explanation for the sense of recognition that binds us to Achilles. I found it in the principle that ontogeny recapitulates phylogeny, which I have attempted to reformulate in a Hegelian critical system: our self-conscious appreciation of Achilles' experience of seeking self-consciousness resolves that moment and the moment of our own infantile experience into the notion of self-consciousness itself. If we ask then how is our reading historical, we face the major objection, which can come both from the naive reader and from the critically sophisticated reader. The naive reader will object that we do not take into account the historical specificity of the *Iliad*, if not of Achilles himself. The sophisticated reader will object that we do not take into account post-Hegelian philosophy in our accommodation of Freudian and post-Freudian psychology to the *Iliad*.

I match my own naiveté with that of the first reader. I literally believe not only that ontogeny recapitulates phylogeny, but vice versa. I believe in the progress of the human spirit and that the *Iliad* represents its major landmark, one on which we must look back in awe but not with false nostalgia. For this very reason I find in Hegel an adequate critical model and in Heidegger a deceptive critical model. Heidegger's nostalgia is for Being, which in his historical reckoning was lost to man somewhere between Parmenides and Aristotle. I think he might have found its last traces in Greek tragedy. Certainly his insistence that *Dasein* can only be redeemed through *Angst* and *Schuld*, that death is the only reality which can render authentic (*eigentlich*) the individual's own (*eigen*) experience of life, is a tragic perspective. One might think that it is also the epic perspective, that the whole problem of Achilles is his failure to find *Schicksal* in the

Geschick of myth and history, but then one would be turning Heidegger on his feet. Heidegger wants man to define his individual destiny in terms of a collective destiny. This is precisely what Achilles refuses to do. He also refuses to live in the world of language, which is the only place where philosophy can happen. To deal critically with this figure who seeks himself in his difference from his similars, we need Freud, who stresses ontogeny. To deal with this figure who seeks himself in terms he cannot express, we need Hegel, who stresses phylogeny. We should not allow critical models, which collapse the individual into the society and the history of human thought into one semi-self-conscious moment, to distort our reading of the *Iliad*.

We have denied to Achilles a sense of guilt, certainly in the Heideggerian sense. He might recognize debt or obligation, but he certainly does not recognize stigma, and the two recognitions are confounded in *Schuld*. It is, in fact, Nietzsche who explains the relation between *Schuld* ("guilt") and *Schulden* ("debts"). In the fourth section of the second essay of his *Genealogy of Morals* he argues that the notion of responsibility was late in developing, that originally men imposed punishment upon one another not thinking that thereby they could change and govern one another's behavior, but rather in the belief that deeds were things that could be paid for, and, like things, of no intimate connection with the man who committed them. This we know also from Snell, Dodds, and Adkins writing on Homer. Clearly *Schuld* as a moral sense of failure develops only when man's failure to pay off his *Schulden* is felt internally, i.e., when the creditor is set up as a conscience, or, in Freudian terms, when the ego is indebted to the superego.

We have insisted that ontogenetically guilt is a function of the normal resolution of the Oedipus complex (which Achilles did not experience) and that phylogenetically guilt is a function of the false valuation of women which seems consequent upon the urbanization or domestication of men's lives. They value the things inside their houses rather than the action they might be involved in outside, in the world at large. Achilles' *oikos* does not mean the same to him that Odysseus' means to him, just as Briseis and Penelope are incomparable, and Klytemnestra, so prominent in the *Odyssey*, is inconceivable in the *Iliad*. In strictly reductionistic Freudian terms, castration anxiety is focused on the male antagonist in the *Iliad* and on the female antagonist in the *Odyssey*. In both cases fear and desire, aggressive and libidinal investment, are reverse and obverse of the same sexual coin.

The great advantage of a Hegelian critical perspective is that it negates nostalgia. It allows the critic to focus on an object—social, artistic, intellectual—which has historical *locus*, and admire it, without being absorbed by it. We compare here Lévi-Strauss assimilating to his Brazilian Indians, the conventional critic wanting to become Homer and write the *Iliad*, and Heidegger wanting to restore the bloom of Greek philosophy to flower. From all these perspectives authenticity is a lost reality that can only be approximated in the decadent critical present. This fosters an anti-criticism, which leaves the reader unable to appreciate the object of his attention.

We have already admitted that Hegel is not a completely acceptable critical model for the *Iliad*, that both he and Freud have to be allowed to correct each other. Certainly the self-revelation of Absolute Spirit at the end of the *Phenomenology*—though Hegel's title for his work (and the tense, active opposition that characterizes his work) is the very figure of being through seeming that we find in the mirror stage and in the *Iliad*—is an embarrassment to us, since we claim that this kind of embrace of and by the world is exactly what Achilles refuses. Hegel's task was to reestablish philosophy as a medium for man's knowing, and he went about it in a way reminiscent of the neo-Platonic Christianizing philosophers of the third century. Since God has become flesh, then the *logos* has been actualized, and every man in knowing himself knows the Absolute Self of Truth. In our terms, this is to argue that there is something behind the mirror, and our task has been to show that there is not even anything in front of the mirror, that the self as such does not exist, but is only perceived as a function of desire in the Other, originally the mother. Our vivid recollection of Hegel is of the earlier chapters of the *Phenomenology*, where the assimilating negation (*Aufhebung*) carries on its endless work of creating self-consciousness. We must only put "self" under erasure and then we begin to feel the full force of the *Iliad*, the inescapable recapitulation of the Achilles complex.

We cannot continue to talk about the *Iliad* the way conventional critics do, in disingenuous exaltation, cataloguing and explaining all its features according to the principle that everything which happens in the *Iliad* is the best thing that could happen in this best of all possible poems: Homer must hate war and love Hektor; men fight and kill each other, but because they face the common denominator of death they are united finally in love. This is the confusion of sentiment with aesthetic and intellectual judgments, which is allowed only in the field called literary criticism, where men regularly gain professional credit by forcing literary experience to fit patterns that lack any reference to human experience as explicated by science or philosophy. What really happens in the *Iliad* is what happens to every one of us. We recognize early on that the world will never return to us the image of ourselves that we would have projected on it; all our lives are spent in competition with others like ourselves whom we love or hate for being like ourselves; the only love we can know is not from the *semblables* but from those others unlike ourselves. But is this possible in a world where we condemn the people who are unlike us so effectively that they spend all their energy trying to assimilate to our desperate pattern?

I am trying to talk about sexual politics, and not doing it as well as others have before me. I am, however, insisting on the special place of the *Iliad* in the history of that argument, and this has not been done at all. No one has faced the great enigma of the poem: why do men fight for women when men despise women for not being men? The most important woman in the poem is the hero's mother, Thetis, and in her treatment of her son (in the absence of his father) we have the paradoxical answer to that enigma: the all-loving, all-giving mother creates in her son a Narcissus who will never seek the object which can only be validated by oedipal strife—the mother herself or her *semblable*—but only himself or his *semblable*.

We have thus formulated an Achilles complex, and somehow we must account for its absence from Freudian and post-Freudian metapsychology. Why is the closest parallel to be found in the conscientiously anti-Freudian French critic of literature Girard, with his theories of mimetic desire and the scapegoat as mirror image? Even Lacan, who has brilliantly advanced Freud's ontology of the ego, insists that the father is always already there, in the "imagination" of the child, and the phallos as indicator of the difference between desire and demand is all but identified with the mother's body. In the more clinically oriented American analysts we find clearer indications of dissatisfaction with a metapsychology that treats oedipal experience as almost the sole determinant of sexual orientation and self-definition. Kohut in his resistance to drive-theory and Kernberg in his development of object-relations theory can be read as slightly apostatic with reference to the Oedipus complex itself. Certainly the clinical evidence of Bettelheim and Mahler with disturbed children suggests that pre-oedipal experience should be seriously considered not only as preparation for oedipal experience but also, and perhaps more importantly, as predetermining the quality of oedipal experience. If the mother projects a purely positive image of her son to her son in the first months of life, will he ever confront the father for possession of the mother in the manner which has always, since Freud, been considered the action truly constitutive of the mature male psyche? Another way of posing this question, of course, is to ask what kind of mother can project such an image and is she a likely oedipal object?

Freud himself, as we have repeatedly pointed out, formulated the problem in its starkest and still most appalling outline: if the male child does not pre-oedipally make the oedipal choice—i.e., if he chooses for his first "object" not his mother, but continues to invest libidinally himself (or her projected image of himself)—then this can determine his later true object-choice to be homosexual. We are convinced that sexual orientation is the most important factor in human development, that the individual's entire world view is predicated on his seeking in the world a reflected image of himself or a completion of himself in a being unlike himself. We do not, however, believe that these are two clearly demarcated categories of human beings, the one pathological and the other normal. Nor, indeed, do we believe in simple polar opposites, an erotic (and therefore ontic) axis with "homosexuals" at one extreme and "heterosexuals" at the other and the mysterious (and probably pseudonymous) "bisexuals" in the center. Rather we insist on a vastly more intricate model, visually more conceivable as a laboratory model of the most complicated hydrocarbon molecule, to suggest all the possible sensual stimulations that affect a child's notion of what he needs and desires from his world and whether these qualities are likely to be most completely and satisfyingly combined in a creature like himself or different, a male or a female. We especially like the lack of center in a hydrocarbon molecule, because we want to use it as a model analogous to our model of the human psyche in its earliest stages of development, before we can speak of an existent ego.

The *Iliad* does not stand at the center of the Western humanistic tradition; the *Aeneid* does, and close beside it Sophocles' *Oedipus Rex* and Shakespeare's *Hamlet* (these latter two firmly established before Freud and Jones canonized them). Certainly in the *Aeneid* we see the emergence of the social hero: Aeneas is Achilles become Hektor, and we account for this transformation in the following way. One measure of the distance between Homer and Virgil is the distance between pre-oedipal and oedipal experience, and the startling manifestation of this in the *Aeneid* lies in the compromises demanded of the hero, the constant delays in gratification of desire until there is no desire, only violence. We might almost say that we have come full circle, beginning and ending with male phallic aggression, where the female does not matter—is Lavinia a woman or a territory?—but the difference in derivation of that violence should still be recognized. The *Iliad* touches us at a deeper level. What makes it alien is not just its distance in time and space and style (being older and perhaps more "Eastern" and certainly the product of a less familiar poetic tradition and idiom), but its distance in the experience of human development, both racial and individual.

Just as we only began to understand the technique of oral composition in this century with the research of Parry, so also, only in the decades since Freud have we begun to understand the determinative importance of infantile sexuality. The more we learn about our primitive selves (pre-selves and non-selves), the more we can appreciate this poem about a man who has yet to consolidate a self, but libidinally and aggressively invests images of himself as projected by his mother in her "foreknowledge" of his destiny. There is in the *Iliad* no Iokaste nor Dido nor Gertrude nor Ophelia, but only Thetis and the other maternal goddesses who variously advise and discourage Achilles in his search for a self, his love of Patroklos and hatred of Hektor. The female figures have no erotic value as such; they serve only to define men by their negative example and to give men an excuse to engage in the life-and-death struggle which is their only raison d'être.

Homeric men live and die in pairs: they need companions to function effectively in war, and for a man and his companion to die together in war is their complete obliteration, since neither will then have an avenger or a savior for his body. There is an erotic element to Homeric battle scenes and certainly an ontological dimension. Men emerge from the crowd to face each other singly (though their companions are close by) and at that point they must remember their battle spirit and prove to themselves that in mixing with their opponent in man-killing strife they can occupy his space and thereby prove their own existence. Action is all: not to be fighting is not to be living. The man must be outside on the battlefield with other men; he must be armed; he must be conspicuous; he must be conscious of a god's interest in him. He needs all these assurances that he is not a passive victim, a woman, a mere image in another man's eye, or worst of all, only words.

Young men in the *Iliad* despise old men almost as much as they despise women: old men are no longer action, but have become words. They stay inside the walls with the women, rather than going outside to fight. Young men seem almost actively to seek death in order to avoid the passivity of old age. There is such worship of the physical beauty of young men that there almost seems to be an aesthetic of death-in-youth, as if the body, though committed to the pyre, and then the ashes to the urn, would still be fixed, in its youth and beauty, for all time. No one would see it debased and disgraced by the wrinkles and misfortunes of time.

Obviously song has a great role to play in this. Though old men (and women and children and cowards) are ridiculed for using words instead of committing themselves to action, and though old men's stories of the past move in and out of focus, on and off the theme— how much of "ring composition" should be attributed to senility?— the singing of *klea andrōn* is obviously extremely important to the whole structure of Homeric society. I have no difficulty in associating all of this with narcissism as defined by Freud and his followers. To despise women and words—one thinks of Echo, despised by Narcis-

sus—congrues with the worship of young masculine beauty, and the
central image for this is the mirror, because the young man wants to
assure himself of his youth, and the aging man wants to restore his
youthful image of himself in a younger male. Are Shakespeare's *Sonnets* so different from Achilles' *klea andrōn*? The sung words thus
become deeds, just as generally we claim that poetry restores the
concrete experience that the abstraction of common language destroys.

At the conclusion of *The Elementary Structures of Kinship* Lévi-
Strauss presents his remarkable theory that women were the first signs,
used in exchange between men. But this brilliant observation frightens
him, because his critical model for human society is Saussurean lin-
guistics and the cardinal rule there is that the sign has no absolute
value but only exists in a system of differences: it signifies by not being
so many other things it could be and it is associated with a thing only
by convention. The sign as a symbol of absence, and therefore of
desire, is a post-structuralist proposition that is difficult to see prefigured in Lévi-Strauss. But even were it read there, and were Lacan
and Derrida invoked to gloss the text, I do not think Lévi-Strauss'
naiveté could be argued away. Lévi-Strauss has said women were the
original signs exchanged between men—exogamy the first currency—
but then he wants to valorize that currency, standardize and support
it with the gold of romanticism, oedipal romanticism:

But women could never become a sign, and only a sign, since, in a world of
men, she is nevertheless a person, and since, in so far as she is defined as a
sign, one is obliged to recognize her as a producer of signs. In the matrimonial
dialogue of men, a woman is never purely that of which one speaks, since
. . . each woman maintains a particular value, which depends upon her maintaining her part in a dual relationship, both before and after marriage. In
opposition to the word, which has totally become a sign, woman has remained
both a sign and a value at the same time. Thus is explained, no doubt, how
the relations between the sexes have been able to preserve that reflective
richness, that fervor and that mystery, which probably filled the whole universe
of human communications originally.[1]

This is, of course, pure Rousseau, pure nostalgia for an oedipal past.
It is not the world of the *Iliad*, which is harsher and truer. When
Freud used the term *Anlehnung* for the pre-oedipal relationship be-

tween mother and child he suggested (though he never developed and explained) that the later oedipal relationship is a compromise formation. If a man is originally convinced by a goddess-mother of his perfection, he will never seek completion of himself in an object chosen because it resembles her. This is Achilles' dilemma. It is not tragic; it is epic. It is not oedipal; it is pre-oedipal. What we should make of this from our superior critical position I cannot say. We recognize ourselves in Achilles and hope we can escape his determination to escape the compromises that women and words—the whole socially determined structure of value—represent to his conception of the world as self and action. We know that the romanticization of women is no answer. We think probably that the exploration of the similarities between the sexes has greater promise. Obviously, though, we shall all remain murderous and suicidal until we can choose true objects of desire outside of and different from ourselves, investing the world at large with that energy which internally directed destroys us. If this reading of the *Iliad* is true, then we need not wonder that it has not been fully revealed before, that, in fact, most previous readings have been seeming contradictions of it. We see ourselves clearly in the *Iliad*, but the world in which we live—first familial, then social, political, religious, and philosophical—convinces us that we should not be what we are, or at least originally were.

In reaching the conclusion of his study of kinship, Lévi-Strauss has occasion to refer to Freud's piece of mytho-poetics *Totem and Taboo*. Lévi-Strauss' argument is essentially that the taboo on incest is simply the negative statement of a positive social rule, exogamy: marry a woman outside the family so you will have more male relatives on whom you can depend in war and hunting. We have already seen how Lévi-Strauss must correct his own conclusion that women's value is only relative, that of exchange (*demande*), rather than absolute (*désir*), but now we must consider his case against Freud, for it puts clearly before us the contrast between two readings of the same material, and the contrast is the same whether that material is tribal structure or literary text.

Freud's argument is that men deny themselves their true objects of desire—mothers, daughters, and sisters—in retribution for a crime committed by their ancestors. In the primal horde the father claimed all women for himself, so the sons rose up and killed him; now all sons feel both guilt for this ancient crime and fear that their own fathers will castrate them if they carry through with their oedipal desires. Lévi-Strauss rejects this aitiology in terms that are Freud's own:

> . . . phenomena involving the most fundamental structure of the human mind could not have appeared once and for all. They are repeated in their entirety within each consciousness and the relevant explanation falls within an order which transcends both historical successions and contemporary correlations. Ontogenesis does not reproduce phylogenesis, or the contrary. Both hypotheses lead to the same contradictions. One can speak of explanations only when the past of the species constantly recurs in the indefinitely multiplied drama of each individual thought, because it is itself only the retrospective projection of a transition which has occurred, because it occurs constantly.[2]

Once we have admitted that Freud has created myth rather than written history, we are substantially in agreement with Lévi-Strauss. In passing we note only that Freud's "scientificism" led him always to seek an experiential origin for each human truth, whether universal or individual. In this we can see his tendency to be archaeological, to seek an original, tangible truth, rather than teleological, as Lévi-Strauss would like him, seeking meaning as a function of repetition. But what does Freud's myth explain? Why is it necessary? Lévi-Strauss expresses this truth as no more, and no less, than "the permanent expression of a desire for disorder, or rather counter-order. Festivals turn social life topsy-turvy, not because it was once like this but because it has never been, and never can be, any different."

Again we see Lévi-Strauss taking an individual negative and turning it into a social positive: men refuse to commit incest so that they can combine themselves socially, through intermarriage. He practices thereby his own archaeology, implying that man has always felt the power of social demands and that these, somehow, create individual desires. His reference to Saturnalian fetes is particularly instructive. In his order of things, individual sexuality becomes symbolic and social structures are the reality. One runs the risk of reducing this very sophisticated debate between two intricate minds, but one must finally ask which comes first *experientially*, infantile sexuality and ontogenesis, or social order? Surely each individual first knows his parents and only then the larger society of which he must become a part, and, to the extent that there is progress and change in the way man sees himself in and against that society, his ontogenesis does recapitulate phylogenesis: man is not originally a social animal, either ontogenetically or phylogenetically.

Achilles is not at all social, as we have seen, and rather than pursue Lévi-Strauss further among his "primitive" tribes—which offer so many situations analogous to Achilles' experience, not least of which is the intimate male companion so necessary to a young man's development, whose place is then taken after marriage by the invaluable brother-in-law—I shall conclude here with the suggestion that Nietzsche's "blond beast" is Achilles. Though it is Menelaos who is most consistently described as blond, Achilles' hair is *xanthē* at 1. 197; though several heroes are compared to lions, it is surely Achilles as the Homeric definition of hero—and not any actual or imagined lion, but perhaps also the figurative lion, Aristophanes' Alcibiades—on whom Nietzsche models his controversial figure:

Once they go outside, where the strange, the *stranger* is found, they are not much better than uncaged beasts of prey. There they savour a freedom from all social constraints, they compensate themselves with wildness for the tension engendered by protracted confinement and enclosure within the peace of society, they go *back* to the innocent conscience of the beast of prey, as triumphant monsters who perhaps emerge from a disgusting procession of murder, arson, rape, and torture, exhilarated and undisturbed of soul, as if it were no more than a student's prank, convinced they have provided the poets with a lot more material for song and praise. One cannot fail to see at the bottom of all these noble races the beast of prey, the splendid *blond beast* prowling about avidly in search of spoil and victory; this hidden core needs to erupt from time to time, the animal has to get out again and go back to the wilderness: the Roman, Arabian, Germanic, Japanese nobility, the Homeric heroes, the Scandinavian Vikings—they all shared this need.[3]

This evocation of a historically absolute and recapitulated past cannot be denied. We only insist that what Nietzsche saw in epic poetry we see as well in infantile development, so that our memory of such a wild and rapacious freedom is real in our own experience as well as vicarious in the history of our race. It is there, in the pre-social, pre-oedipal world of aggressive and libidinal investments of self-objects that we are all Achilles. To understand the *Iliad* we need to know not only the childhood of man, but our own childhood as well. What we find in the origins of both developmental systems—the social and the individual—is first void and then violence. Something comes into being out of nothing, so it is all an illusion, an image in a mirror without a real subject presenting himself. The great struggle is to maintain this image, so the violence is not only constitutive but constant. Achilles is the first and still the finest figure of this terrible tension. The criticism which is capable of reading his dilemma accurately in no way changes it, no more than psychoanalysis can "cure" a psychosis. Rather, by seeing ourselves in Achilles we raise the question of our own being to consciousness. We are no more centered in an actual core than he is; we too are functions of original void and the violence with which we struggle to fill it. The Achilles complex, with its speculation of the self, if uncorrected by oedipal displacement onto others of all our ontic energy, is a vector reversing to recover that void: the death drive.

NOTES

PREFACE

1. H.-G. Gadamer, *Truth and Method* (New York: Continuum, 1975), pp. 92–93: etymologies "are far less reliable because they are abstractions which are not performed by language, but by linguistic science, which can never be wholly verified by language itself: that is, by their actual usage. Hence, even when they are right, they are not proofs, but advance achievements of conceptual analysis, and only in this obtain a firm foundation."

2. There is now an exhaustive study of the history of this idea: S. J. Gould, *Ontogeny and Phylogeny* (Cambridge, Mass.: Harvard University Press, 1977). Gould not only shows how von Bauer's law—"the homogeneous, coarsely structured, general, and potential develops into the heterogeneous, finely built, special and determined" (p. 61), and thus higher forms repeat in embryo embryonic stages common to lower forms—could withstand the tests of Darwinian evolution and Mendelian genetics, whereas Haeckel's "law"—higher forms of life repeat in embryo adult stages of lower forms—had to be qualified out of existence, but he also shows how various forms of life adapt to changes in their environment by the process of "neoteny" ("retention of formerly juvenile characters by adult descendants produced by retardation of somatic development"): "Neoteny can now come to the rescue and provide an escape from specialization. Animals can slough off their highly specialized adult forms, return to the lability of youth, and prepare themselves for new evolutionary directions" (p. 283).

It is certainly seductive to use neoteny as a critical model for the "paedomorphic" qualities of fifth-century Athenians; Devereux has essentially already done this in speaking of their retention of adolescent traits into maturity. (See below, section II, chapter 9, note 8). Indeed it is seductive to use any model derived from what seems to be empirical evidence (e.g., salamanders) for what seems to be random speculation on huge psychological and cultural issues (e.g., Greek narcissism). This is the kind of "scientificism" which runs through psychoanalysis from its beginnings; one need only recall the attempt to read the death drive against the model of the second law of thermodynamics. What I find most appealing in Gould's study is its conceptual richness; he faces the problems of *dynamis* and *energeia* that have been with us since Aristotle (and he knows Aristotle). He shows that whole generations of philosophical and scientific thought cannot be discredited, that Haeckel and Lamarck, though they might have got it specifically wrong, were dealing conceptually with issues that will not go away. In this sense Gould establishes recapitulation in intellectual history in the very process of explaining its inadequacy to the biological record. In social and psychological histories it seems to me still secure: the child *must* learn to think the mind of the past, and adolescent sexual ambivalence *is* a recapitulation of primary narcissism. I must admit, though, that were I to renew completely my effort to read the *Iliad* against models of ontogenetic and phylogenetic development, I would try to think, with Gould, not of stages, but of processes. To some extent this is already implicit in my insistence that the battle of the mirror "stage" goes on and on, in the *Iliad* and in our own lives.

I.1   ON RE-READING SNELL'S HOMER

1. See the afterword to the second German edition of Marx, *Capital* (1873) and Engels, *Ludwig Feuerbach and the End of Classical German Philosophy* (1886).

2. Snell's insistence on self-consciousness as the determining distinction between Homeric man's mode of thinking and later modes is Hegelian: "Wenn in Folgenden etwa behauptet wird, die homerischen Menschen hätten keinen Geist, keine Seele und infolgedessen auch sehr viel anderes noch nicht gekannt, ist also nicht gemeint, die homerischen Menschen hätten sich noch nicht freuen oder nicht an etwas denken können und so fort, was absurd wäre; nur wird dergleichen eben nicht als Aktion des Geistes oder der Seele interpretiert: in *dem* Sinn gab es noch keinen Geist und keine Seele." *Entdeckung des Geistes* (Gottingen: Vanderhoeck und Ruprecht, 1975), p. 10. When his Anglo-American critics are unable to accept this distinction, the discussion quickly degenerates. See, for example, Snell's quotations from Lloyd-Jones in "Nachwort 1974," *ibid.*, pp. 286–87.

3. B. Snell, *The Discovery of Mind*, T. Rosenmeyer, tr. (Oxford: Oxford University Press, 1953), p. 198.

4. N. Austin, *Archery at the Dark of the Moon* (Berkeley: University of California Press, 1975), p. 84.

5. E.g., T. Buttrey, *Classical World* (1978–79), 72:177–78; cf. J. Clay, *Classical Journal* (1976–77), 72:359–62.

6. Snell, *Discovery of Mind*, pp. viii–ix.

7. Compare the discussions of E. R. Dodds, *The Greeks and the Irrational* (Berkeley: University of California Press, 1951), pp. 1–18, and H. Fränkel, *Early Greek Poetry and Philosophy*, M. Hadas and J. Willis, tr. (New York: Harcourt, Brace, Jovanovich, 1975), pp. 64–75.

8. I take the terms and their conceptual framework from J. Lacan, on whom, see section I, chapter 6; but M. M. Willcock has determined essentially the same "functions" for the gods in *Bulletin of the Institute for Classical Studies* (1970), 17:1–10.

9. M. Nilsson, "Götter and Psychologie bei Homer," *Archiv für Religionswissenschaft* (1924), 22:363–90; A. Lesky, *Göttliche und menschliche Motivation im homerischen Epos* (Heidelberg: C. Winter, 1961).

10. E. Auerbach, *Mimesis*, W. Trask, tr. (Princeton, N.J.: Princeton University Press, 1953).

11. Nor should we, for that matter, pretend to believe anything in poetry—pretend, that is, that anything actually happens in poetry. To believe in Athene is tantamount to believing that she exists in the poem, that the poem has evoked her presence, is a symbol of her existence that we must accept uncritically. Obviously we accept her only as allegory for certain mental processes. For a clearly stated distinction between symbol and allegory and the belief of "The New Criticism" that it is the essential distinction between poetry and prose, see F. Lentricchia, *After the New Criticism* (Chicago: University of Chicago Press, 1980), pp. 3–26. He assesses Coleridge's position, to which so many later assimilated theirs: "In so many words, symbol is ontologically full while allegory is thin at best, and at worst 'insubstantial' . . . only an illusion of being. As a special unarbitrary mode of language, symbol not only permits us a vision of ultimate being . . . but, because it 'partakes' of being . . . symbol permits *us*, as well to partake of being as it closes the distance between our consciousness and the ultimate origin of things" (p. 6).

12. Austin, *Archery*, pp. 91ff.

13. See F. Jameson's distinction between Lévi-Strauss' "culinary triangle" and Greimas' "semantic rectangle" in *The Prison-House of Language* (Princeton, N.J.: Princeton University Press, 1972), pp. 163ff.

14. Vico was no less a Homerist than Hegel and developed a similar conception of man-in-history. He combines the kind of perception which we associate with Snell on the difference between Homeric man and philosophical man with a recognition of the difference literacy makes: "for up to the time of Homer and indeed somewhat afterward, common script had not yet been invented . . . In that human indigence, the people, who were almost all body and almost no reflection, must have been all vivid sensation in perceiving particulars, strong imagination in apprehending and enlarging them, sharp wit in referring them to their imaginative genera, and robust memory in retaining them. It is true that these faculties appertain to the mind, but they have their roots in the body and draw their strength from it" (IX.819). *The New Science of G. Vico*, T. G. Bergin and M. H. Fisch, tr. (Ithaca, N.Y.: Cornell University Press, 1970), p. 260.

15. Snell, *Discovery of Mind*, pp. 228–29.

16. Fränkel, *Early Greek Poetry and Philosophy*, p. xi.

17. L. Tarán's commentary on the fragments of Parmenides—*Parmenides* (Princeton, N.J.: Princeton University Press, 1965)—illustrates the fundamental opposition between Cherniss' academic approach (the history of philosophy) and Fränkel's philosophical approach: what could Parmenides in his historical and linguistic context have meant to say, as opposed to how we read

him now, conscious of the explication of his thinking which the intervening tradition has provided.

18. Cf. F. Jameson, "Towards Dialectical Criticism," *Marxism and Form* (Princeton, N.J.: Princeton University Press, 1971), pp. 306–416.

19. C. Lévi-Strauss, *From Honey to Ashes*, J. and D. Weightman, tr. (New York: Harper and Row, 1973), p. 472.

20. Jameson, *Prison-House of Language*, p. 119.

21. H. Fränkel, *Dichtung und Philosophie des frühen Griechentums* (New York: American Philological Association, 1951), p. 113; *Early Greek Poetry*, p. 80.

22. Snell, *Entdeckung*, p. 28; Snell, *Discovery of Mind*, p. 20.

23. The term "decenteredness" suggests Derrida. We must be prepared for the suggestion that self-consciousness is a philosophical creation *ex nihilo*, that the ego is entirely the child's introjection of his parents' expectation of him, etc. This would seem almost to put the Homeric depiction in advance of all that has followed, and we are quite prepared to allow for this, if, at the same time, it is also allowed that Derrida's use of the term "decenteredness" does not require mutually exclusive definitions. Rather it should encourage us to see self-consciousness as a *function* of the individual's expectations of the world as *informed* by the world's expectations of him, or, that the ego is a *function* of the conflict between the child's desires for sensual gratification and the world's response, which is limited to his acceptably expressed demands. Derrida should be heard here; even when he speaks of language we can hear him considering the self, and even the Homeric hero: "This field is in fact that of freeplay, that is to say, a field of infinite substitutions in the closure of a finite ensemble. This field permits there infinite substitutions only because it is finite, that is to say, because instead of being an inexhaustible field, as in the classical hypothesis, instead of being too large, there is something missing from it: a center which arrests and founds the freeplay of substitutions. One could say—rigorously using that word whose scandalous signification is always obliterated in French—that this movement of the freeplay, permitted by the lack, the absence of a center or origin, is the movement of *supplementarity*. One cannot determine the center, the sign which *supplements* it, which takes its place in its absence—because this sign adds itself, occurs in addition, over and above, comes as a *supplement*." ("Structure, Sign, and Play in the Discourse of the Human Sciences," *The Structuralist Controversy*, R. Macksey and E. Donato, eds. (Baltimore, Md.: Johns Hopkins University Press, 1970), p. 260.

Derrida's concept of supplementarity as applied specifically to linguistic phenomena will be shown below to have relevance to recent analyses of formula systems: they develop out of an original absence, a desire to signify; thus to trace their "original form" is quixotic.

Derrida's deconstruction of Lévi-Strauss' technique of myth analysis consists in pointing to this center of free-play which Lévi-Strauss seems always to locate in his systems of myth: structure, no matter how relative and variable, still implies a center. Since Lévi-Strauss will not admit to point of view, to an organizing consciousness, a transcendental subject, the claim is implicit that his analysis, having assimilated itself with its material, is nature, or rather culture's ratification of the truth of nature. Homeric man hypostatizes no center for himself, but we must, if only because, as Derrida tells us, we cannot, in the Western tradition of metaphysical thought, fail to hypostatize a center. We shall always insist, however, that our definition of self-consciousness, our constitution of the ego, is shoring up phylogenetic fragments against our ontogenetic ruins. We know there is nothing there, but through a kind of psychic bricolage we constitute ourselves, and then we claim a center, a place to stand, so that we can view the world; or rather, having allowed the world to constitute us in its image, we return the favor.

I.2 HEGEL'S HOMER

1. G. Hegel, *The Phenomenology of Mind*, J. Baillie, tr. (New York: Harper, 1967), p. 150. Page reference to this edition will be given parenthetically in the text.

2. The terms "autoerotism" and "primary narcissism" are not consistently distinguished in Freud's work. The distinction is clearer if we use Mahler's term, "symbiosis," for the first six months of life, and Lacan's "mirror stage" for the following twelve months.

3. Plato, *Phaidros* 225 b-e, R. Hackworth, tr. *Plato: Collected Dialogues*, E. Hamilton and H. Cairns, eds. (New York: Pantheon Books, 1963), p. 501.

4. It might be instructive to rephrase this first in Platonic and then Freudian terms, so that we can appreciate Hegel's equation of desire for the object with expropriation (negation) of the object, and therefore of the aim of possessing the object with the aim of being the object. A Platonic paraphrase of Hegel's definition of desire would say simply that the *erastēs* desires the *erōmenos* insofar as the *erastēs* desires the quality of the *erōmenos*' beauty, so that recognizing the *erōmenos*' beauty to be his own (the *erastēs*' beauty), he frees beauty as such from the relationship, distills the notion of beauty from the erotic moment and celebrates it both in and of itself (Plato) and in its manifestation in himself (Hegel). Freud would say that the ego libidinally invests itself as object, creating an ideal ego in itself and projecting this image on to external objects, which are then again internalized as an ego ideal; the ego, then, introjects its objects, thereby establishing a pattern for future object-investment.

5. S. Freud, "On Narcissism: An Introduction," *The Standard Edition of the Complete Psychological Works of Sigmund Freud* (SE), J. Strachey ed. and tr., (London: Hogarth Press, 1953–74), 14:69–102.

6. We shall have to face the fact that Freud himself saw the ideal ego as the substitution in a later stage for the lost perfection of the infantile ego, i.e.,

that there is always already an ego and it libidinally invests a series of self-reflexive objects. (See Section I.6, especially note 1). When Freud says that "originally" the child has two objects of desire, himself and the woman who tends him, he means, of course, that the child originally is concerned only with his own well-being. We now realize, however, that the child's first perception of himself is of a closed system of satisfaction that includes the mother, and his first experience of desire is when he feels the lack of the mother, but, paradoxically, it seems this feeling of lack and therefore of desire is as much for his lost sense of completion and perfection as it is for her, herself, i.e., it is a narcissistic desire. Furthermore, the child's image of his lost object is constituted by the mother: it is her image of him as complete and perfect which he accepts as his pattern for desire. This image, then, in a "corrected" Freudian model, is the ideal ego.

7. It might be helpful to think of the gods as existing simply *an sich*, in and of themselves, whereas man, without fully tested self-consciousness, exists simply *für sich*, for himself without reference to others, especially to the gods, in their proximate representation of Absolute Spirit. To exist *an sich* and *für sich* man must become a hero, mediate between gods and men, establishing the meaning of his existence between the polarities of Absolute Spirit and pure self-relevance (which, of course, are not polarities at all, but functions of each other).

8. My reference here is to René Girard, *Desire, Deceit, and the Novel* (Baltimore, Md.: Johns Hopkins University Press, 1967) and *Violence and the Sacred* (Baltimore, Md.: Johns Hopkins University Press, 1976). Girard disingenuously disclaims Freudian influence on his formulation of the triangular pattern (*Desire*, p. 186n.). He shows more tolerance toward Freud in *Violence*, insisting that it is Freud's followers who have perverted their master's meaning in *Totem and Taboo* (Girard, pp. 193–218).

9. There is only one brief allusion in Dodds, *The Greeks and the Irrational*, to *Entdeckung*: "Homeric man has no unified concept of what we call soul or personality (a fact to whose implications Bruno Snell has lately called particular attention)" (p. 15).

10. *Ibid.*, pp. 17–18.

11. C. M. Bowra, *Heroic Poetry* (Oxford: Oxford University Press, 1948), p. 63.

12. A. Parry, "The Language of Achilles," *Transactions of the American Philological Association* (1956), 87:1–7; P. Friedrich and J. Redfield, "Speech as Personality Symbol: The Case of Achilles," *Language* (1978), 54:263–88. See section I, chapter 5.

13. See section I, chapter 3.

14. J. Redfield, *Nature and Culture in the Iliad: The Tragedy of Hector* (Chicago: University of Chicago Press, 1975); E. Havelock, *Preface to Plato* (Oxford: Oxford University Press, 1963) and *The Greek Concept of Justice* (Cambridge: Cambridge University Press, 1978).

I.3 STRUCTURALIST AND HUMANIST ATTEMPTS   257

15. F. Lentricchia, *After the New Criticism* (Chicago: University of Chicago Press, 1980), p. 164.

16. J. Derrida, "Differance," *Speech and Phenomena and Other Essays on Husserls' Theory of Signs*, D. B. Allison, tr. (Evanston, Ill.: Northwestern University Press, 1973), p. 159.

17. One might almost say that by definition metaphysical systems tend to establish unity or integration of philosophical man with Truth or Being. Indeed, so completely is the vulgar notion of philosophy identical with a superficial understanding of the metaphysical tradition that philosophy as such is thought to have this goal. Literature and its appreciation are similarly understood: the poem is thought to contain some great truth of nature and by entering into the system of the poem the reader is thought to be absorbed by the system of nature. All of this we call anaclitic, the establishment of a relationship of dependence with literature and life. We trace a different tradition and demand a different criticism; the *Iliad* is the beginning of that tradition and as yet there is no criticism suitable to it.

For my reading of Hegel as a realist, a philosopher who believes in Nature as independent of Man, I am indebted to A. Kojève. It is impossible to read his elucidation of the conclusion of the *Phenomenology* without thinking of Achilles as the negative paradigm, e.g.: "The *Selbst*—that is, Man properly so-called or the free Individual, *is* Time; and Time is History, and *only* History. Which, furthermore, is *das Wissende Werden*, 'the knowing becoming' of the Spirit—that is, in the final analysis, philosophical evolution.) And Man is essentially Negativity, for Time is *Becoming*—that is, the *annihilation* of Being or Space. Therefore Man is a Nothingness that nihilates and that preserves itself in (spatial) Being only by *negating* being, this Negation being Action. Now, if Man is Negativity—that is, Time—he is not external. He is born and he dies a Man. He is '*das Negative seiner Selbst*,' Hegel says. And we know what that means: Man overcomes himself as Action (or *Selbst*) by ceasing to *oppose* himself to the world, after creating in it the universal and homogeneous State; or to put it otherwise, on the cognitive level: Man overcomes himself as *Error* (or 'Subject' opposed to the object) after creating the Truth of 'Science'." *Introduction to the Reading of Hegel*, J. H. Nichols, tr. (Ithaca, N.Y.: Cornell University Press, 1969), pp. 159–60.

18. Marx, *Capital*, note on part I, chapter 1, section 3, A.2.a.

I.3 STRUCTURALIST AND HUMANIST ATTEMPTS TO READ HOMER

1. J. Redfield, *Nature and Culture in the Iliad: The Tragedy of Hector* (Chicago: University of Chicago Press, 1975), p. 22.

2. J.-J. Rousseau, *The Social Contract*, M. Cranston, tr. (London: Penguin Books, 1968), p. 64.

3. C. Lévi-Strauss, *Structural Anthropology*, C. Jacobson and B. Schoepf, tr. (New York: Basic Books, 1963), p. 367.

4. Redfield, pp. 102–4.

5. P. Ricoeur, *Archivio di Filosofia* (1963), 1(2):9 ff., quoted with approval by Lévi-Strauss in *The Raw and the Cooked*, J. and D. Weightman, tr. (New York: Harper and Row, 1969), pp. 10–11.

6. E. Havelock, *Preface to Plato* (Oxford: Oxford University Press, 1963), p. 89. We compare Vico: "By the very nature of poetry it is impossible for anyone to be at the same time a sublime poet and a sublime metaphysician, for metaphysics abstracts the mind from the senses, and the poetic faculty must submerge the whole mind in the senses; metaphysics soars up to universals, and the poetic faculty must plunge deep into particulars." (XI. 821)

". . . the heroic language was a language of similes, images and comparisons, born of the lack of genera and species, which are necessary for the proper definition of things, and hence born of a necessity of nature common to entire peoples." (XXII. 832)

7. Havelock, pp. 90 and 142.

8. C. Whitman, *Homer and the Heroic Tradition* (Cambridge, Mass.: Harvard University Press, 1958), p. 220.

9. *Ibid.*, pp. 183 and 187.

10. See F. Jameson, *Marxism and Form* (Princeton, N.J.: Princeton University Press, 1971), pp. 306–416.

11. Whitman, p. 209.

12. R. Sacks has helped me clarify my thinking on the "argument" of the shield and the place of Hektor in the argument of the poem. See section II, chapter 3 for a consideration of the shedding of kindred blood as "invaluable."

13. C. Lévi-Strauss, *The Raw and the Cooked*, pp. 11–12.

14. N. Austin, *Archery at the Dark of the Moon* (Berkeley: University of California Press, 1975), p. 116.

15. E.g., of the Lykaon episode (p. 86), and elsewhere (pp. 102–3).

I.4   ON RE-READING PARRY'S HOMER

1. N. Austin, *Archery at the Dark of the Moon* (Berkeley: University of California Press, 1975), pp. 11–80; N. Austin, *Arion* (1976) N. S. 3:220–41; M. Nagler, *Arion* (1976) N. S. 3:365–77.

2. M. Nagler, *Spontaneity and Tradition: A Study in the Oral Art of Homer* (Berkeley: University of California Press, 1974), p. 14.

3. *Ibid.*

4. B. Peabody, *The Winged Word* (Albany, N.Y.: State University of New York Press, 1975), p. 176.

5. See P. Pucci, *Hesiod and the Language of Poetry* (Baltimore, Md.: Johns Hopkins University Press, 1977), pp. 61–69, 71–73.

6. M. L. West, *Hesiod: Works and Days* (Oxford: Oxford University Press, 1973), commentary *ad loc.* and pp. 3–25.

7. Pucci, p. 133.

8. H. Bloom, *The Anxiety of Influence* (New York: Oxford University Press, 1973).

9. G. Nagy, *The Best of the Achaeans* (Baltimore: Johns Hopkins University Press, 1979) pp. 1–11.

10. *Ibid.*, p. 150.

11. R. Girard, *Violence and the Sacred* (Baltimore, Md.: Johns Hopkins University Press, 1976).

12. R. Girard, *Desire, Deceit, and the Novel* (Baltimore, Md.: Johns Hopkins University Press, 1967).

13. J. Russo and B. Simon, *Journal of the History of Ideas* (1968), 29:485–98.

I.5 ACHILLES' PLACE IN THE *ILIAD*, DEFINED LINGUISTICALLY AND PSYCHOANALYTICALLY

1. P. Friedrich and J. Redfield, "Speech as Personality Symbol: The Case of Achilles," *Language* (1978), 54:268, n.2.

2. A. Parry, "Language of Achilles," *Transactions of the American Philological Association* (1956), vol. 87.

3. D. Claus, *Transactions of the American Philological Association* (1975), 105:13–28.

4. Friedrich and Redfield, "Speech as Personality Symbol," p. 267.

5. My reference here is to Schlovsky and Todorov, whose work I know only through the summary in R. Scholes, *Structuralism in Literature* (New Haven, Conn.: Yale University Press, 1974), pp. 74–147. The key term is *ostraninie*, "defamiliarization," obviously to be compared with Heidegger's treatment of *alētheia*, "unforgetfulness."

6. H. Bloom, *The Anxiety of Influence* (New York: Oxford University Press, 1976).

7. B. Simon, *Mind and Madness in Ancient Greece* (Ithaca, N.Y.: Cornell University Press, 1978), p. 54.

8. *Ibid.*, p. 57.

9. *Ibid.*, pp. 83–86.

10. N. Holland, *Psychoanalysis and Shakespeare* (New York: McGraw-Hill, 1966) p. 42.

11. *Ibid.*, p. 130.

12. Hegel, *The Phenomenology of Mind*, J. Baillie, tr. (New York: Harper, 1967), pp. 735–36.

13. G. Devereux, *Helios* (1978–9) 6:3 and 8–9. See his fuller discussion in *Dreams in Greek Tragedy* (Berkeley: University of California Press, 1976), pp. xvii–xxxix.

14. Devereux, *Helios*, pp. 9–10.

15. C. Beye, *The Iliad, The Odyssey, and the Epic Tradition* (New York: Anchor Books, 1966), p. 85.

16. In the opening of Book XXIII, Achilles speaks first to the Myrmidons (6–11), then to the dead Patroklos (19–23), then to the kings (43–53) and finally to Patroklos' shade (94–98) about his debt to his dead friend. Elsewhere he tells Agamemnon that he wishes Briseis had been struck dead before his wrath over her being taken from him caused so many Greeks to die (19.56–62). He seems, then, to appreciate a cause-and-effect relationship between his refusal to fight and Patroklos' death, as he says at 18.98 ff.:

> I must die soon, then; since I was not to stand by my companion
> when he was killed. And now, far away from the land of his fathers,
> he has perished, and lacked my fighting strength to defend him.
> Now, since I am not going to the beloved land of my fathers,
> since I was no light of safety to Patroklos, nor to my other
> companions, who in their numbers went down before glorious Hektor,
> but sit here beside my ships a useless weight on the good land,
> I, who am such as no other of the bronze-armoured Achaians
> in battle, though there are others better in council—
> why, I wish that strife would vanish away from among gods and mortals.

Even if we think this is an admission of responsibility, it shows no conception of guilt. There is no ineradicable mark on his "soul," but only a debt to be paid, Hektor's death and other prizes and sacrifices. One might compare this debt of the living to the dead, to the debt of the killer to the family of the killed, i.e., blood price. Even so, the debt can be paid and the killer need not be punished. If one argues that such vengeance as Achilles pursues is more comparable to the conditions of bloodguilt, where no payment is possible since killer and killed are members of the same family, then one must admit that bloodguilt is a misnomer. While it is true that the killer of kin must be "absolved" by a king in another country, and even then cannot return to his home, still, that ablution seems to have been considered effective, so that there is a difference between the mental attitude of the Homeric killer and, for instance, Lady Macbeth, for whom ablution is impossible. This is, surely, yet another indication that the Homeric personality is unintegrated: there is not yet sufficient cohesion of self to create a soul which can bear the burden of guilt. See, further, A. W. H. Adkins, *Merit and Responsibility* (Oxford: Oxford University Press, 1960).

I.6 FREUD AND HIS FOLLOWERS

1. For Freud, at least in his final topography of the psyche (1923), the ego is definable in relation to the id, according to the integration of the uncon-

scious, pre-conscious, and conscious systems. The ego is grounded in the id, where unconscious desires arise, but emerges into the pre-conscious system, and is essentially constituted in the perceptive or conscious system. In fact, the distinction between an "idea" which is unconscious and an "idea" which is conscious is exactly its attachment to a word presentation—"feelings" enter the conscious system directly—which process takes place in the pre-conscious system. *The Ego and the Id*, in *The Standard Edition of the Complete Psychological Works of Sigmund Freud* (SE), J. Strachey ed. and tr. (London: Hogarth Press, 1953–74), 19:9–17. If we project this definition back upon the essay "On Narcissism" (1914), then Freud's reference to an "infantile ego" is something of a contradiction in terms, like "unconscious idea." In both cases there is potential, but no actuality. Hence, we must read passages like the following very carefully: "This ideal ego is now the target of the self-love which was enjoyed in childhood by the actual ego" (SE, 14:94).

At what point can we say that the child exists as ego distinguishing himself from object? In partially aligning the id with the pleasure principle of the unconscious and the ego with the reality principle of the conscious, Freud suggests that the ability to attach word-formations to "ideas," i.e., the acquisition of language, is the determination. The pre-verbal ego is not a contradiction in terms, but it is certainly only a developmental potential, a coming-into-being. For Lacan, we shall find, this difference between the pre-verbal ego and the ego is the difference between *désir* and *demande*, which is radical. Even when the child learns to speak he can never completely *express* his desires but can only use the language with which he is provided to make others partially *understand* those desires. (Cf. the distinction between the expressive and conative functions of language in Friedrich and Redfield, "Speech as Personality Symbol.")

For a technical statement of contemporary theory on the development of the ego, see O. Kernberg, *Object Relations Theory and Clinical Psychoanalysis* (New York: J. Aronson, 1976), pp. 59–80): "*Stage 4: Integration of Self-Representations and Object-Representations and Development of Higher Level Intrapsychic Object Relations-Derived Structures.* This stage begins in the latter part of the third year of life and lasts through the entire oedipal period. It is characterized by the integration of libidinally invested and aggressively invested self-representations into the definite self system and of libidinally invested and aggressively invested object-images into total object-representations. Ego, superego and id, as definite, overall intrapsychic structures are consolidated in this phase" (p. 67).

Perhaps the best image for this process, i.e, the image which most clearly recalls Homeric man as depicted by Fränkel—*das Ich ist nicht abgekapselt*—is that of "nucleation": "Glover's (E. Glover, *On the Early Development of Mind*—New York: International Universities Press, 1956) hypothesis of a multinuclear primitive ego structure, the partial autonomy of ego nuclei in the earliest phases, and the decisive influence of the original state of nucleation

of the ego on its later strength or weakness is another important source"
(Kernberg, p. 28).

2. Freud, "On Narcissism," *SE*, 14:69–102, 87–88.

3. Freud, *The Ego and the Id; SE*, 19:3–59.

4. Here I mean to suggest the twofold aitiology of the superego, ontogenetic
and phylogenetic: it is a formation resulting both from the individual experience of oedipal conflict and the resolution of that conflict, on the one hand
(castration anxiety causes the son to renounce his claim upon the mother and
delay his gratification of desire until he can obtain a similar but different
object, i.e., the latency stage), and, on the other hand, "the mind of the past":
that guilt and fear which is inherited from generation to generation of men
who "remember" their ancestors' murder of their father in the primal horde,
the psychoanalytic "myth" which Freud did not formulate until *Totem and
Taboo* (1912).

5. F. J. Sulloway, *Freud: Biologist of the Mind* (London: Burnett Books,
1979), pp. 395–96.

6. Sulloway, pp. 123ff., and index.

7. We thus find in Freud's text a prediction of the later position taken by
those who speak of object-relations as constitutive of the self; Kernberg, in
Object Relations Theory and Clinical Psychoanalysis, summarizes that position: "Introjection . . . is the reproduction and fixation of an interaction with
the environment by means of an organized cluster of memory traces implying
at least three components: (i) the image of an object, (ii) the image of the self
in interaction with the object, and (iii) the affective coloring of both the object-
image and the self-image under the influence of the drive representations
present at the time of the interaction (p. 29) . . . This active separation by
the ego of positive and negative introjections, which implies a complete division of the ego, and, as a consequence, of external reality as well, is, in
essence, the defensive mechanism of *splitting* (p. 36) . . . excessive, pathological early splitting threatens the integrity of the ego at that point and also
the future developmental capacity of the ego as a whole. It has to be stressed
that in the active keeping apart of introjections of opposite valence, what is
split is not only affect states of the ego, but also object-images and self-images.
Excessive, pathological splitting, therefore, interferes not only with the integration of affects but also with integration of the self and with the development
of the representational world. Because of the fundamental importance of early
introjections in the organization and integration of the ego as a whole, pathological splitting carries over into splitting of the ego as an organization" (p.
38). For normal consolidation of the ego Kernberg requires, among other
things, integration of good and bad self-images, so that the mature ego can
function as a compromise formation. Inordinate and prolonged splitting of
these contradictory self-images is pathological. For one moment Freud shows
awareness of this phenomenon: the ideal ego is all good, but the ego ideal and
later the superego warn the ego that it is not good enough. It might be helpful

to see Patroklos and Hektor as Achilles' good and bad self-images, pathologically split.

8. See the discussion of "Schema R" by A. Wilden, in J. Lacan, *The Language of the Self* (Baltimore, Md.: Johns Hopkins University Press, 1968), pp. 293–98.

9. Below I shall consider the reformulation of the oedipal experience in the developmental models of Kohut and Kernberg. It must be allowed, however, even in passing so quickly by these great revisionists, that their "psychologies of the self," unlike any ego psychology, are "narcissistically teleological": their interest is in the individual's development of a sense of self through his internalization of object relations. To the extent, then, that they concentrate on this constitution of the self-as-subject rather than the world-as-object, they displace oedipal conflict from its central position. Though they both use Freudian terminology which suggests that oedipal conflict is always already there, their clear message is that there is so much else there before—the struggle to define the self in terms of others—that it becomes secondary, developmentally and absolutely.

10. Girard's nonrecognition of Freud comes in a note on pages 186–87 of *Desire, Deceit, and the Novel* (Baltimore, Md.: Johns Hopkins University Press, 1967). His discussion of Hegel (pp. 110–11) is equally embarrassing.

11. *Beyond the Pleasure Principle*, SE, 18:3–64. In the second chapter, Freud says he used to watch his eighteen-month-old grandson, during the absence of his mother, cast a spool out of his crib saying *"Fort"* ("gone"), and reel it back on a string, saying *"Da"* ("there"). Freud concludes that the child is trying to manipulate his reality, symbolically. He makes the desired object (the spool, but also his mother) go away and return, and the repetition, though painful, is necessary to his development, and natural. Then there is an extraordinary footnote: "A further observation subsequently confirmed this interpretation fully. One day the child's mother had been away for several hours and on her return was met with the words "Baby o-o-o-o!" which was at first incomprehensible. It soon turned out, however, that during this long period of solitude the child had found a method of making himself disappear. He had discovered his reflection in a full-length mirror which did not quite reach to the ground, so that by crouching down he could make his mirror-image gone."

12. I take as their spokesman J. LaPlanche, *Life and Death in Psychoanalysis*, J. Mehlman, tr. (Baltimore, Md.: Johns Hopkins University Press, 1976).

13. See Sulloway *Freud: Biologist of the Mind*, pp. 374–75.

14. Freud, *Beyond the Pleasure Principle*, SE, 18:42.

15. If we combine Freud's mirror with Mahler's terminology, we say that the end of symbiosis and the beginning of individuation is a process characterized by the child being deprived of the mother as part of himself, and as he is left more and more to himself, his desire for his former sense of completeness causes him first to seek in his mother's presence some assurance,

and later, in her absence, to seek it elsewhere in his environment, in an actual mirror, or in play, as Winnicott has shown. D. Winnicott, *Playing and Reality* (London: Tavistock Publications, 1971).

16. P. Slater, *The Glory of Hera* (Boston: Beacon Press, 1968).

17. Footnote added in 1915 to *Three Essays on Sexuality*, "The Sexual Aberrations," *SE*, 7:125–243.

18. *Symposium*, 180.

19. G. Vlastos, *Platonic Studies* (Princeton, N.J.: Princeton University Press, 1973), pp. 3–42.

20. The fact that the psychosexual concerns of fifth-century Athenians were already implicitly there in the mythology of Bronze Age derivation, which was their constant inspiration for literary and artistic creativity, is the basis for Slater's sophisticated argument against historically inclined scholars of mythology: later generations select from their tradition what is pertinent to their immediate experience. It seems to me that for Slater and other students of mythology, as for Freud and his followers, the Hegelian perspective is prerequisite. There was no doubt in the minds of Aeschylus and Plato that the relationship between Achilles and Patroklos was homosexual; we call it narcissistic. If the notion is the self-conscious individual *an sich und für sich*, then narcissism is a moment negated by the moment of homosexuality, and the negation of this negation is the notion itself. Male narcissism is an unawareness of women's difference, whereas homosexuality is a turning by men to men as sexual objects, in flight from women, who are seen as threatening and corruptive. Even if we do not accept the psychoanalytic argument for a homosexual stage in *normal* development—see, for an application of this theory to Greek culture, G. Devereux, "Greek Pseudo-homosexuality," *Symbolae Osloenses* (1967), 42:69–92—we must accept the universality of narcissism and thereby our common experience with Achilles.

21. J. Lacan, *Ecrits: A Selection*, A. Sheridan, tr. (New York: Norton, 1977), pp. 4–5.

22. M. Mahler, *On Human Symbiosis and the Vicissitudes of Individuation* (New York: International Universities Press, 1968); B. Bettelheim, *The Empty Fortress* (New York: Free Press, 1967); D. Winnicott, *Playing and Reality*.

23. Winnicott, p. 45.

24. O. Kernberg, *Borderline Conditions and Pathological Narcissism* (New York: Jason Aronson, 1975), p. 17.

25. *Ibid.*, pp. 283–85.

26. *Ibid.*, pp. 315–16.

27. H. Kohut, *The Search for the Self*, edited with an introduction by P. Ornstein (New York: International Universities Press, 1978).

28. See, for instance, the preface to H. Kohut, *The Restoration of the Self* (New York: International Universities Press, 1977) and *The Psychology of the Self* (New York: International Universities Press, 1979).

29. H. Kohut, *The Analysis of the Self* (New York: International Universities Press, 1971), pp. 50–51.

30. *Ibid.*, pp. 120–36 and xv.

31. *Ibid.*, p. 181, n. 10.

32. *Ibid.*, p. 210.

I.7   THE ACHILLES COMPLEX

1. H. Fränkel, *Early Greek Poetry and Philosophy*, pp. 170–88: "emotion is made event; . . . . a spiritual thing is seen in concerete form." Fränkel also recognizes the importance of the visual element in lyric and associates it with a particular quality of love: "The Greeks in general regarded homosexual love as more dignified and uplifting than love between the sexes. The untamed craving of that urge which finds fulfillment and satisfaction in the union of man and woman was not so celebrated in poetry as was homosexual love which feeds unquenchably on the sight, on the physical proximity and spiritual presence of another, and together with him seeks, by common action and united striving, the path to parallel self-fulfillment" (pp. 175–76). Fränkel stresses the visual element in homosexuality; we see in the homosexuality of mature males a recapitulation of infantile narcissism, an attempt to mirror the self. Fränkel, in speaking of Sappho, thinks of Plato, and the importance of mirroring in the relation of the *erastēs* to the *erōmenos*. We, in speaking of Achilles and his relation to Patroklos, think also of Shakespeare's *Sonnets* and the "mirroring" in the relation of the Poet to the Fair Youth.

II.1   THE VALUE OF WOMEN

1. P. Pucci, *Hesiod and the Language of Poetry* (Baltimore Md.: Johns Hopkins University Press, 1977), pp. 82–115.

II.2   WHY MEN FIGHT

1. A. Gouldner, *Enter Plato* (New York: Basic Books, 1965).

2. I am familiar with the work of L. Muellner on *eukhomai*, at least the dissertation (Harvard, 1973), although not the monograph, *The Meaning of Homeric Eukhomai through its Formulas* (*Innsbrucker Beitr. zur Sprachwiss.* XIII, 1976). He insists on "contextual meaning" for the word, distinguishing between sacral and secular contexts, and claiming that this distinction predates Homer. I am afraid he might accuse me of the kind of conflation he finds Adkins guilty of: "He (A. W. Adkins, *Classical Quarterly*, N.S. 19:1) does not discuss formulas or etymology. He simply tries to prove his point by exegesis of texts and then justifies it with generalizations about the difference between

Homeric society and our own." I am concerned about formulas and convinced that their systems create meaning in a way different from that in which other types of prose and verse do. I am not, however, concerned here with historical etymologies, but rather with what is usually referred to as "false" or "folk" etymology. Muellner has shown that Homer can cause a character to use the verb with a certain reference, secure in the experience that his audience will be aware of the reference, i.e., "pray to the gods," but "boast in battle." I think I have shown that Homer causes his characters to reveal their conception of the sources of their self-images by using this verb in battle and council: "I claim to be best, but I know I am only as good as the god makes me at any particular point."

II.4 MEN IN PAIRS

1. See, for an attempt to explain all difficulties in terms of poetic efficacy, C. P. Segal, *Greek, Roman, and Byzantine Studies* (1968), 9:1–14; but, now, G. Nagy, *The Best of the Achaeans* (Baltimore, Md.: Johns Hopkins University Press, 1979), pp. 41–58, offers the "traditional" explanation.

2. Nagy, *passim*: see "Index of Key Words and Themes," *ad loc.*

3. C. Lévi-Strauss, *The Elementary Structures of Kinship*, J. H. Bell, J. R. von Sturmer, tr.; R. Needham, ed. (Boston: Beacon Press, 1969), pp. 483–85.

II.7 NAKED MEN AS WOMEN

1. Devereux, *Helios* (1978–79), 6(2):6.

2. Cf. his discussion of Deianeira's "hari-kari" in Sophocles' *Trachiniae*: "Les manifestations de l'inconscient dans Sophocles' *Trachiniae* 922 sqq.," *Psychanalyse et sociologie commes methodes d'étude des phenomenes histo-riques et culturals* (Paris:, 1971), pp. 121–52.

3. J. Lacan, "The Signification of the Phallus," *Ecrits: A Selection*, A. Sheridan, tr. (New York: Norton, 1977), pp. 281–91.

4. F. Jameson, *Yale French Studies* (1977), 55/56:338–95.

II.8 THE MOTHER-GODDESSES

1. M. Detienne, *Cunning Intelligence in Greek Culture and Society* (Atlantic Highlands, N.J.: Harvester Press, 1978), pp. 133–74.

2. G. Nagy, *The Best of the Achaeans* (Baltimore, Md.: Johns Hopkins University Press, 1979), pp. 317–47.

3. Dover calls this passage, "The most daring and spectacular 'homosexualization' of myth" in Greek literature, since Pindar himself mentions the analogy of Zeus and Ganymede (40–45) on which he bases his version of

Pelops' disappearance: K. J. Dover, *Greek Homosexuality* (Cambridge, Mass.: Harvard University Press, 1978), p. 198.

4. M. M. Willcock, *Bulletin of the Institute of Classical Studies* (1970), 17:1–10.

5. *Ibid.*, p. 7.

II.9 NARCISSISM IN HOMER AND HOMOSEXUALITY IN GREEK HISTORY

1. E.g., "Children of the Moria," cited in translation by M. Johnston in "Songs of the Robbers," *The Athenian* (March 1980), p. 31; cf. "Song of Kitsos," *ibid.*, p. 33.

2. C. P. Cavafy, "*Apistia.*" R. Scodel, *Harvard Studies in Classical Philology* (1977), 81:55–57, suggests that *Iliad* 24.58–63 (a speech of Hera) shows knowledge of the tradition that Apollo both sang at Thetis' wedding and killed her son; Hektor also predicts Apollo's complicity when prophesying to Achilles his death at the hands of Paris, 22.358–60. She suggests that the lament of Thetis in the *Aithiopis* (see section II, chapter 11) was Aeschylus' source for the passage which Plato quotes at *Rep.*383 a-b, and this in turn is Cavafy's text for his poem.

3. *Scholia ad Od.* 23.296.

4. *Scholia ad Od.* 7.225f.

5. F. Zeitlin, *Arethusa* (1978), 11:149–84.

6. K. J. Dover, *Greek Homosexuality* (Cambridge, Mass.: Harvard University Press, 1978), pp. 185–203.

7. In modern Greek *poustēs* is the passive homosexual and *kōlomparas* is the active. In Aristophanes the passive homosexual is called *europrōktos, gynē, katapugōn*, and various phrases referring to the size of the anus; the active homosexual is called *kusolakōn, psōlos*, and various figurative expressions. See J. Henderson, *The Maculate Muse* (New Haven, Conn.: Yale University Press, 1975), pp. 209–19.

8. G. Devereux, *Symbolae Osloenses* (1968), 42:69–92.

9. Simone de Beauvoir, *The Second Sex*, H. M. Parshley, tr. (New York: Bantam Books, 1961), pp. 43–47.

10. P. Slater, *The Glory of Hera* (Boston: Beacon Press, 1968), pp. 3–74.

11. Aristophanes, *Frogs* 1431–32.

12. G. Meredith, "Essay on Comedy," in *Comedy* (New York: Anchor Books, 1956).

13. W. T. MacCary and M. M. Willcock, *Platus: Casina* (Cambridge: Cambridge University Press, 1976), pp. 1–38; W. T. MacCary, "The Comedy of Errors: A Different Kind of Comedy," *New Literary History* (1977–78), 9:525–36; W. T. MacCary, "Philokleon Ithyphallos," *Transactions of the American Philological Association* (1979), 109:137–47.

14. Northrop Frye, *English Institute Essays* (New York: Columbia University Press, 1948), p. 50.

15. C. Whitman, *Aristophanes and the Comic Hero* (Cambridge, Mass.: Harvard University Press, 1964).

16. See Dover, *Greek Homosexuality*, on the prosecution of Timarkhos, pp. 19–110, esp. pp. 100ff.; and Henderson, *The Maculate Muse*, pp. 209ff.

II.10 PLATONIC LOVE

1. Hegel, *The Phenomenology of Mind*, J. Baillie, tr. (New York: Harper, 1967), pp. 226–27.

2. Freud, "On Narcissism," in *The Standard Edition of the Complete Works of Sigmund Freud*, J. Strachey, ed. and tr. (London: Hogarth Press, 1953–74), 14:38.

3. Plato, *Phaidros*, R. Hackworth, tr., *Plato: Collected Dialogues* E. Hamilton and H. Cairns, eds. (New York: Pantheon Books, 1963), 255 b-d.

4. Plato, *Symposium*, M. Joyce, tr., *Plato: Collected Dialogues* E. Hamilton and H. Cairns, eds. (New York: Pantheon Books, 1963), 209 a.

II.11 "HE WHOM THE GODS LOVE DIES YOUNG"

1. Menander, *Dis Exapatōn*, fr. 4(Sandbach) = Stobaeus, *Ecl.* IV.52.27. Cf. Aristotle, *Eudemos*, fr. 6(Ross) = Plutarch, *Moralia* 115: "The best thing for all men is not to be born, and the next best thing is, having been born, to die as soon as possible."

2. I am trying to sketch Whitman's reading, which I find extremely attractive: C. Whitman, *Homer and the Heroic Tradition* (Cambridge, Mass.: Harvard University Press, 1958).

3. G. Nagy, *The Best of the Achaeans* (Baltimore, Md.: Johns Hopkins University Press, 1979), pp. 134–44.

4. R. Sacks, "*Hypo Keuthesi Gaiēs*: Two Studies of the Art of the Phrase in Homer" (Ph.D. dissertation, Harvard University, 1978). Note the connection between *gēras* and *phthinō* in Priam's appeal to Hektor, 22.59–61:

. . . "Oh, take
pity on me, the unfortunate still alive, still sentient
but ill-starred, whom the father Kronos' son, on the threshold of old age
    (*gēraos*)
will blast (*phthisei*) with hard fate."

5. Nagy, *The Best of the Achaeans*, p. 185.

6. E. M. Forster, "The Poetry of C. P. Cavafy," in *Pharos and Phaleron* (London: Hogarth Press, 1923).

7. M. Lefkowitz, *Classical Journal* (1972), 68:31–38.

8. S. Edmunds, "Homeric *Nēpios*" (Ph.D. dissertation, Harvard University, 1976), argues that the epithet means "one who cannot make connections"; cf. *ēpios*, used of counsel. Abstract in *Harvard Studies in Classical Philology* (1977), 81:299f.
9. W. Schadewaldt, *Von Homers Welt und Werk* (Leipzig: Koehler und Amelang, 1944), pp. 155–202.

II.12 THE PHENOMENOLOGY OF WAR

1. Hegel, *The Phenomenology of Mind* J. Baillie, tr. (New York: Harper, 1967), pp. 232–33.
2. C. M. Bowra, *Heroic Poetry* (Oxford: Oxford University Press, 1948), p. 63.
3. S. Weil, *The Iliad: or, The Poem of Force*, M. McCarthy, tr. (Wallingford, Pa.: Pendle Hill, 1947); cf. R. Bespaloff, *On the Iliad*, M. McCarthy, tr. (Washington, D.C.: Pantheon Books, 1947).

III RECAPITULATION

1. C. Lévi-Strauss, *The Elementary Structures of Kinship*, J. H. Bell and J. R. von Sturmer, tr.; R. Needham, ed. (Boston: Beacon Press, 1969), p. 496.
2. *Ibid.*, p. 491.
3. F. Nietzsche, *On the Genealogy of Morals*, W. Kaufmann and R. J. Hollingdale, tr. (New York: Vintage Books, 1969), pp. 40–41.

INDEX

Achilles: absolutism of, 126; and
    Agamemnon, 94; and Athene, 6–7, 15,
    163–77; and Briseis, 94, 99, 105; and
    Gilgamesh, 104; and Hektor, 24, 106,
    232–33; identification of reader with,
    8, 41; lack of an integrated ego, 69;
    lack of self-consciousness, 10; his
    language, 27, 55–65; as narcissist, 87;
    and other heroes, 13, 38–39, 41; and
    Patroklos, 22, 24; his "suicide," 63, 86;
    and Thetis, 93–96, 104–5, 163–77
Achilles complex, 93–96, 127, 181
Adkins, A. W. H., 260n16
aēdōn, 52
aēr, 221–23
Aeschylus, 29, 83, 179
Agamemnon: and Achilles, 94; and
    Chryseis, 99; and Iphigeneia and
    Klytemnaistra, 117
age, uselessness of, xii, 196–216
aideomai, 155–56
aidoia, 153
aidōs, 26, 52
Ajax, 129
Alcibiades, 84, 185
Alexander, 157
alienation, 43
anaclisis, 20–21, 67–70, 234
anagnorisis, 197
Andromache, 94, 105–12, 169
androtēs, 200
Antilochos, 133, 200, 208, 215
aoidos, 52
Aphrodite, 94, 163–77
apoina, 119–22
Apollo, 29, 103
aporia, 9, 118, 133
Archilochos, 52
Ares, 168

aretē, 42, 231
aristeia, 131, 196, 203, 215, 231
Aristophanes, 185
Aristotle, 10–11, 32, 96, 189, 252n2
Arktinos, *Aithiopis*, 215–16
armor, 127, 167, 218
atē, 26
Athene, 6, 9, 15, 93, 163–77
Auerbach, E., 8–9, 194
Augustine, 84
Austin, N.: correction of Parry, 48;
    review of Nagler, 49; and Snell, 4–10;
    social reading of Homer, 35–48, 46;
    and structuralism, xi, 10–11

de Beauvoir, S., 183
Bellerophontes, 138–40
Benedict, R., 91
Bespaloff, R., 269n3
Bettelheim, B., 85–86
biē, xi, 114
bipolar opposition, 10, 39, 46
blood-guilt, 122–25
Bowra, M., 26, 220
Brecht, B., 44
Briseis, 88, 99, 105, 108

cannibalism, 161–62, 172, 188
castration, 75, 82, 110, 122–25, 152–62
Cavafy, C., 179, 204–5
Cherniss, H., 12, 253n17
Chryseis, 99–101

daimōn, 10, 72
decenteredness, 14–15, 254n23
demande et désir, see Lacan
Derrida, J., 30–31, 33, 51, 254n23
Detienne, M., 163–65
Devereux, G., 63, 86, 89, 152–62, 182